BERTIE MEE

BERTIE MEE

Arsenal's Officer and Gentleman

David Tossell

Foreword by Graham Taylor

MAINSTREAM
PUBLISHING
EDINBURGH AND LONDON

First published in Great Britain in 2005 by
MAINSTREAM PUBLISHING COMPANY
(EDINBURGH) LTD
7 Albany Street
Edinburgh EH1 3UG

ISBN 1 84018 945 2

A catalogue record for this book is available from the British Library

Typeset in Caslon and UniversBQ

Printed in Great Britain by
Antony Rowe Ltd, Chippenham, Wiltshire

ACKNOWLEDGEMENTS

SINCERE THANKS ARE DUE TO THOSE WITH WHOM I HAVE discussed Bertie Mee during interviews for this book or for my previous title, *Seventy-One Guns* – or, in many cases, both. The story of Bertie Mee's life could not have been told without these generous people: Alan Ball, Elli Baram, John Barnes, Geoff Barnett, Steve Burtenshaw, David Court, Ken Friar, John Goodbody, Ron Goodman, George Graham, Harry Hopker, Don Howe, David Jenkins, Eddie Kelly, Frank McLintock, Bob McNab, Sammy Nelson, Graham Perry, Eddie Plumley, Jeff Powell, John Radford, Jon Sammels, Dave Sexton, Peter Simpson, Alan Skirton, Peter Storey, Fred Street, Graham Taylor, Ian Ure, Bob Wilson and George Wright.

I am additionally indebted to Graham Taylor for contributing the foreword to this book; to Bob McNab and Bob Wilson, who have been valuable sources of advice and contacts throughout; and to Richard Whitehead of *The Times* for support, phone numbers and a shared affliction for football history. Thanks also to those Arsenal fans who contributed their own memories of Bertie Mee.

Others who have helped in many different ways include Michael Paige at BBC Research Central; Ian Booth at the British Film Institute; the staff at the Army Personnel Centre in Glasgow; Mal Butler at the *News of the World*; along with Jim Brown, Brian Dawes, Christopher Davies, Rob Jones, Gary Ralston and Yeovil Town Football Club. Thanks to Colorsport and Getty Images for the photographs from their archives, and to Stephan Ottewill for his photographic contribution.

The following acknowledgements are due to those publishers who kindly gave permission to quote from their books. Extracts from the *Arsenal Football Book* series, edited by Reg Hayter and published by Stanley Paul, are reprinted by permission of The Random House Group Ltd. Extracts from *Arsenal in the Blood* by David Lemmon are courtesy of Breedon Books. Gratitude and acknowledgements are extended to all those publishers and writers whose works have provided essential research material, much of which is listed in this book's bibliography.

Huge thanks once again to Bill Campbell, Graeme Blaikie, Emily Bland and the entire team at Mainstream Publishing, particularly my editor Deborah Warner, for their advice and support, and to my own diligent in-house sub-editor, Lucy Parks.

My greatest debt of gratitude is to Bertie Mee's daughters, Beverley and Allyson, who agreed to support and participate in this project and offered valuable access to family information, mementoes, photographs and, of course, their own memories. On behalf of Beverley and Allyson, deepest thanks go to the staff at the North London Hospice in Finchley for the care they gave to Bertie in his final days, and for the comfort and kindness they showed to the whole of his family. A percentage of royalties from this book is being donated to the hospice (Registered Charity No. 285300). For further information, see www.northlondonhospice.co.uk.

David Tossell

We would like to thank David Tossell for enabling Bertie's story to be told. We hope that readers will enjoy learning about many aspects of his wonderful life which were not publicly known. We are very pleased that a percentage of the proceeds from the book will be going to the North London Hospice, whose staff cared for Bertie and our family so well in the last few days of his life.

Doris Mee, Beverley Miserotti
and Allyson Mee

CONTENTS

FOREWORD BY GRAHAM TAYLOR

NOT LONG AFTER I TOOK OVER AS MANAGER OF WATFORD IN 1977,
I received a letter from Bertie Mee. He wished me all the best and said
that if there was anything I ever felt he could do to help, he would be
happy to do so. This was the year after he stood down at Arsenal and
I discussed the letter with Elton John, the Watford chairman at the
time. We met up with Bertie, chatted for two or three hours, and he
agreed to join the club as assistant manager. We could not believe our
luck – and neither could the Watford fans. On the day Bertie's
appointment was announced, I was walking about five yards behind
the chap who used to release the dogs out of the traps on the old
greyhound track at Vicarage Road. He turned round and said excitedly,
'What about Bertie Mee, eh? Next thing we'll be signing Sir Alf
Ramsey as a turnstile operator!'

Bertie was arguably the best signing I ever made. People are not
really aware of what an important role he played in the rise of Watford
in the '70s and '80s. What we accomplished – reaching the FA Cup
final and playing in Europe – was a fantastic achievement for a small
club. A lot of the credit is given to me and the players but, behind the
scenes, Bertie Mee made a great contribution.

Obviously, it is Arsenal with whom Bertie is most closely identified
and when he passed away late in 2001, I wrote to both Watford and
Arsenal. I suggested to Watford that Bertie should have some
recognition in the new stand they were planning at that time and I
pointed out to David Dein, the Arsenal vice-chairman, that I was not
aware of any memorial for Bertie at Highbury and that I thought

perhaps now, following his death, that could be rectified. When I go to Arsenal, I find it amazing that there is no recognition of him, other than in books. His is a great story. How can the physio of the club end up being manager and win them the Double for the first time in their history and not have some kind of memorial? I hope this can be put right, perhaps when the club moves to its new stadium.

It was going to watch Arsenal that helped Bertie and me to really get to know each other. Shortly after he joined Watford, I went to his house in Southgate and we drove to Arsenal in his car with his wife, Doris. When we got to the ground, it was incredible to see the respect everyone had for him. I was walking behind Bertie and Doris as we made our way through the crowds and up to the directors' lounge and everyone who saw him stopped and said, 'Hello, Mr Mee. Hello, Mrs Mee.' The following day, I said to Bertie that it had been very kind of him to take me and that I would like to take him to experience the football I had been watching. We went to Rochdale versus Huddersfield because there was an outside-right playing that we wanted to watch. There was no sitting in the directors' box for us there; we paid to go in and stood down the side on the halfway line, right up against the fence. It turned out the player wasn't what we wanted and with 20 minutes left Bertie and I looked at each other and said, 'Let's go.'

We went to the gates, but they were locked! There was Bertie Mee, winner of the Double, locked inside Spotland. Bertie said, 'I know what we will do.' He marched me all round the ground in front of the crowd, straight up the players' tunnel and out of the stadium.

'Well, Bertie,' I said. 'This is my football. It's a far cry from Highbury.'

By having more trips like that together, we were able to work out exactly what his job involved and how we would work together – and we became good friends. I took to Bertie right away. A manager has to have somebody he trusts and he can talk to and invariably it is someone who is older. Bertie took that role. I was just starting to make my way in management and I knew what I wanted, but I knew I couldn't do it on my own. I think we were quite similar. I liked his strength as an organiser. I like discipline. I like players to dress smartly. I left one player out of the side because he'd been late arriving to travel to a game and hadn't had time to shave. At lunchtime, I told him he was being left out on the basis that if he couldn't organise himself enough on match day to be up in time to shave, then how could he be trusted on the field? That is the kind of thing Bertie Mee would have done. I think we got on because we were so much on the same wavelength when it came to how we as managers felt we should run our club.

There was something about Bertie you just had to admire. Maybe it was because he was not a big man and had had to fight his corner, but he was very strong in his views and dominant in the way he used language – I have seen him put down people twice his size by the strength of his words. Sometimes, he could be totally wrong in what he was saying but he could get away with it because of his aggressiveness. If you were strong enough to say, 'Bertie, you are wrong, these are the facts,' and to explain your point to him, though, he was big enough to accept it and he wouldn't fall out with you.

The thing I loved about Bertie was that, because of his background in the army and health service, there was so much more to him than football. If somebody was to ask me where I put Bertie in my life, it would be at a very high point, and not just because of what went on out there on the pitch. Bertie introduced me to other things outside football. For example, I joined the Guild of Freemen of the City of London through his contacts. I saw a different world and he opened up other areas of interest to me. The people that surrounded Bertie were intellectual in the sense that you could have conversations about things other than football. I loved meeting these people. I was this young man who had come down from Lincolnshire and was being introduced to a different way of life. Football can make you one-dimensional and you can lose perspective, but Bertie was excellent in developing me as a person, not just as a manager. That helped me a lot throughout my career, and my life, and for that I will always be very grateful.

I have some wonderful memories of times spent with Bertie. Once, two days after Watford got promotion from the Third Division to the Second by beating Hull in the last game of the season, we were invited by one of our sponsors to York races. Bertie and Doris, my wife, Rita, and myself, along with a few others, were seated at a table where the tent came down quite low. Outside, it was raining heavily on the canvas. Bertie was drinking red wine and a gentleman came up to us and mentioned our success a couple of nights earlier. Dear Doris said, 'Yes, the cocks were really porping.'

Of course, we all started laughing and Bertie, instead of letting it go, jumped up and said, 'Oh, Doris!' Now, he was not a tall man, but his head was right by the roof and down the seam on the marquee a little puddle had developed. Bertie went to push the water away, but the seam split. So now he was covered in water and was suddenly drinking rosé. You didn't usually laugh at Bertie but we were all killing ourselves; poor Doris was dabbing at him with a handkerchief. The whole thing was like a farce. If Bertie's trousers had fallen down, the picture would have been complete.

Bertie was a fantastic fellow. He received the OBE around the time when we had introduced a ritual where the staff and our wives would get together the evening before FA Cup games. We had bought a loving cup and we would pass it around the table. Steve Harrison, who was then the coach, started up a chant every time it was Bertie's turn. 'Ber-tie Mee. O-B-E. Ber-tie Mee. O-B-E.' Steve would play the spoons and the rest of us banged our knives and forks on the table in time. Doris loved it because she was so proud of Bertie. That was a special time for a lot of us and I think it was special for Bertie as well. He'd had this wonderful career with Arsenal, and when it came to an end he wasn't certain about what would happen next. He'd had the courage to write to a young manager whom he didn't really know and he was involved in the game again.

I remained friends with Bertie and Doris after we both left Watford and I went to see them a few times after he moved into the retirement home where he devoted his final years to looking after her. I have such tremendous respect for him for that. To be the type of person he was, the way his mind needed to be active and to be challenged, and for him to cut himself off from all of that to look after Doris showed what a loving and caring man he was. That is why I was very proud to speak at his funeral and am honoured to write a foreword for someone I consider to be a real man in the truest sense of the word – a gentleman, but also capable of mixing it. He set his own standards, yet if he had to duck and dive to achieve something, he would do it – although he would hate for his name to be associated with that phrase; he would have called it 'negotiation'.

His is an incredible story and I, like many, thought he was an incredible person.

Graham Taylor, 2005

INTRODUCTION

IT WAS A MEMORABLE YEAR. THE BROAD SMILE WORN BY BRITAIN as it celebrated the crowning of a young queen reflected the country's gradual emergence from the austerity of the immediate post-war period. The ration books would soon be consigned to history. Everest was conquered by a British expedition. England's cricketers even contrived to win back The Ashes.

For football fans, 1953 lives on in grainy black-and-white images of the most romantic of FA Cup finals: billowing shorts and joyously waved handkerchiefs as Stanley Matthews skips past his opposing full-back and tees up Blackpool teammate Bill Perry, thus ending his elusive quest for a winner's medal. Deservedly chiselled into history as 'The Matthews Final', Blackpool's rally to beat Bolton Wanderers was, however, only the second half of what ranks as one of English football's most dramatic 24 hours.

On the eve of the final, with their team requiring victory over Burnley to beat Preston to the title, more than 51,000 Arsenal fans filed excitedly along Gillespie Road and Avenell Road before squeezing themselves into every available corner of Highbury's world-famous arena. The shock of Joe Mercer putting the ball past his own goalkeeper after three minutes was forgotten in a burst of goals by Alex Forbes, Doug Lishman and Jimmy Logie before the 20-minute mark. The club's seventh First Division title in 22 years seemed secure. But Burnley scored again after 74 minutes and Arsenal hung on through moments of high anxiety before emerging as champions by less than one-tenth of a goal in the goal-average column.

The emotion of the evening was compounded when Mercer, the smiling, bandy-legged skipper who had led Arsenal since 1946 in a gloriously unexpected Indian summer to his career, emerged onto the polished steps of Arsenal's ornate main entrance. 'This has been the most wonderful day of my life,' he declared as reporters, frantically scribbling, strained to hear his words over the din of cheering fans. 'Now I am sorry to tell you that you have seen me playing for the last time. I am retiring from football.' There wasn't a dry eye for miles.

Any suggestion that Highbury would be kept waiting for 17 years before witnessing similar scenes would have produced further tears – of mirth. But so it would be. By the time Arsenal won their next trophy, England had been humiliated by the Hungarians, placed their fortunes in the hands of Alf Ramsey and reclaimed their place at the pinnacle of the sport; the '60s had swung through London, from White Hart Lane to Carnaby Street, while Manchester and Liverpool had been divvying up most of football's major prizes, presenting gifts of The Rovers Return and The Beatles to British culture along the way.

London N5 remained a mostly unfashionable and ignored address until four months into the '70s. Then, on one rainy Highbury night, it was suddenly like 1953 all over again, although the tossing of trilbies and the triumphant clack-clack-clack of rattles was replaced by a stampede of Dr. Marten boots, impelled as much by sheer bloody relief as pure joy. And while the club's previous success had been at the expense of that most English of teams, Preston North End, it was the modern phenomenon of Continental competition, specifically the European Inter-Cities Fairs Cup, that put Arsenal back on the map on 28 April 1970.

Ironically, the man responsible for reviving the club's fortunes seemed more suited to the bygone era. As players grew their sideburns and widened their trouser bottoms, his thinning hair was neatly parted and drawn back across his head; club tie and neat suit always in evidence. The word 'dapper' made frequent appearances in articles about him. His insistence on discipline and 'standards' was also borrowed from the past, from his own career as a sergeant in the Royal Army Medical Corps.

In 1953, the year Arsenal embarked upon their period of slumber, this prematurely retired winger was not even working in football. Employing his medical training in a London rehabilitation centre, he skirted around the periphery of professional football by advising on the latest physiotherapy techniques. It proved enough to get his name known around the sport and, in May 1960, Arsenal offered him a job as team physiotherapist. It was to be the club's most significant decision until 20 June 1966. That was the day Bertie Mee was promoted to the position of manager of Arsenal Football Club. The good old days were on their way back.

1

HEADLINES AND HEARTACHE

I was never really good enough to make the grade as
a player.

– Bertie Mee

ACCORDING TO THE 1901 CENSUS FOR ENGLAND AND WALES, THE boundary of the parish of Bulwell, situated in Nottingham's manufacturing and mining country, was partly formed on its south and west sides by Highbury Road. Bertie Mee, destined to become one of the most significant figures in the history of Arsenal Football Club, was, you might say, to the manor born.

Occupying one of the 144 homes in the parish early in the twentieth century were Edwin and Gertrude Mee, along with their growing family. Their first-born, George, had arrived on 12 April 1900 and, by 1918, a second son, Ernest, and daughter, Mavis, were around to celebrate the first Christmas since the end of hostilities with Germany. The holiday was to bring an additional gift to the family – on 25 December, the fourth child was born and, with a minimum of fuss that would probably have pleased him in future years, was simply named Bertie.

The Mee family home was typical of its time: modest in the physical comforts it afforded, generous in the love that surrounded the children and rigid in the discipline imposed on the household by Edwin. It was his uncompromising guidance on life's values and his identification of right and wrong that were the most enduring legacy to his third son – although his job as a hospital attendant was perhaps also responsible for instilling the interest in medical matters that would guide Bertie's career decisions in later life. If there were any of the severe hardships that blighted so many families between the wars, then Bertie chose not to bequeath such stories to his own children in later years.

A healthy boy with the usual interests in outdoor activities, Bertie grew up to attend Highbury Boys' Secondary School, where one of the most remarkable features was 'The Knocker', a metal hook that held open the school doors. The traditional rite of passage for new boys was to be held down and struck three times on the head by this particular piece of hardware. And anyone who cried was subjected to a second assault. Bertie emerged unscathed from the ordeal, and from the three-mile round trip to the St Albans Road playing fields for games lessons, to excel at several sports, the physical spoils of which – cups, trophies and the like – now occupy loft space in his daughter Allyson's home.

The family genes may not have turned out men of great physical stature – Bertie was to reach only 5 ft 6 in. – but athletic ability was clearly in abundance. The eldest brother, George, had signed for Notts County when professional football resumed after the war, transferring to Blackpool in 1920. Standing 5 ft 5 in., and known by the fans as 'Shortie', George was noted for his turn of speed and accurate crossing from the wing. He played 216 games for Blackpool, including a run of 195 consecutive contests. In February 1926, he moved to Derby County where he made another 148 League appearances and, in 1930, helped the Rams to second place in the First Division. Burnley, Mansfield, Great Harwood, Accrington Stanley and Rochdale were all to benefit from his services in a career that lasted until he was almost 40 years old.

By the time George's playing days were winding down, Bertie's own prowess with a football had taken him into the professional game at Derby, one of his brother's former clubs. In nearly two seasons at the Baseball Ground, however, no first-team opportunities were forthcoming and it took a move to Mansfield Town early in 1939 to engineer his Football League debut.

On Saturday, 4 February, as Arsenal – on their way to a fifth

Championship in eight years – were beating Sunderland 2–0, their future manager took his first tentative steps as a fully fledged professional footballer in the number 11 shirt for Mansfield. Struggling in the lower half of the Division Three South table, the club had been elected to the Football League less than eight years earlier and their home ground at Field Mill could scarcely have been further removed from the newly rebuilt Highbury with its stunning art deco stands and vast terracing. When Mee and his teammates emerged from the dressing-room huts that stood adjacent to the new Bishop Street Stand, which boasted wooden bench seating for 1,100, they discovered that a decent crowd of 5,500 had been enticed to the game, many curious to see the slight-looking 20 year old on the Stags' left flank.

It was to be the only time in his professional playing career that Bertie Mee made the headlines. In amongst the theatre and cinema reviews and testimonies for the local 'Indian Eye Doctor', the *Mansfield Reporter* trumpeted, 'Mansfield draw with Queens Park Rangers; Bert Mee makes good start.' The newspaper's match report recorded:

> George Mee's brother, Bert, of that ilk, made a very good start in his first match with Mansfield Town against Queens Park Rangers on Saturday on the Field Mill enclosure by opening the scoring with a smartly got goal. After 12 minutes Turner got across a centre and Mee, running in, scored with a right-foot drive, a smart and quickly taken opening.

Further assessment appeared in the 'Comments' section that followed the report. The writer acknowledged that Mee 'had few real chances, the ball coming very awkwardly to him most times' and noted that he had shown 'sufficient to prove that he will add to the value of the left wing'. The newspaper's 'Football Snaps' column highlighted the better than average attendance and went on to write whimsically about the young Mee and his brother:

> It is probable that many were present to see Bert Mee, Wee George Mee's brother. George is well-remembered at Field Mill. At one time he was regarded as a great forward when he was with Derby County. His brother went to Derby as a boy

and although he has shown promising form he cannot get a place in the first team, and George Jobey has released him. He had few chances in Saturday's game. We cannot recall three really useful passes out to him on the wing. What saved his reputation was the scoring of a smart goal – a first-timer, early in the game which put heart into the side.

We imagine that on a firm fast ground Mee will probably be found to be useful. The conditions on Saturday were against a lightweight like Mee and we shall be pleased to see him on a fast ground for he showed that he has a nice turn of speed. If he has a few of his brother's tricks which he possessed when he was with Derby County, young Bert will be an asset to Mansfield. George was for years a fine forward, although he was never overpopular at Mansfield because he hung on to the ball too much for the liking of some supporters. He is still like *Charley's Aunt*, running, with Accrington. George is, or was, a good singer, and we can recall him singing at the Grand Theatre whilst he was at Mansfield and he has done a lot of warbling at Blackpool. He is a good old 'un yet is George Mee.

A week after his debut, Mee retained his place in a 2–0 defeat at Southend. The Stags' performance had the *Mansfield Reporter* claiming, 'Mansfield have not shown such ineptitude in forward play in any match this season.' The anonymous journalist added, 'Mee, from whom much was expected – perhaps too much – was no better than the others in the front line.' Another 2–0 away defeat, this time at Watford, followed. Discussing Mansfield's wingers, the local paper explained, 'Mee and Turner tried hard enough but they had few opportunities.'

By the time Mee made his fourth appearance, a 1–1 draw at home to Swindon, the novelty of Wee George's brother had clearly worn off. He had to work for his mentions in the newspaper, although he did set up the home team's goal after 25 minutes with an accurate cross from the left.

Defeat by two goals at Bristol City had the *Mansfield Reporter* noting that Mee was 'less serviceable than in any game in which he has played since he came to Mansfield'. The report continued, 'Mee was disappointing when he was plied with good passes.'

A midweek rout against Torquay saw Mansfield score four goals without reply and Mee had his best review since his debut. He was noted to have 'lifted the ball in the centre many times'. The report continued, 'Turner and Mee finessed very well and did their share to a real fine victory.'

Mansfield recorded another win in their next game, a 1–0 success against Aldershot, but could have won more easily had Mee not 'missed the easiest of chances'. The newspaper reported, 'With the exception of one brilliant shot in the second half, little was seen of Mee, who did not seem at all sure of himself.'

Mee, it was noted, 'at last got going' in a 1–1 home draw against Notts County and almost scored in the next game, another 1–1 result against Northampton, when his lobbed cross from the left was touched onto the woodwork by the visiting goalkeeper. After scoring for the reserves in a victory against Burton Town, Mee was then reported to have had 'a poor afternoon' in the 0–0 draw at Newport. This time he 'never really got going'.

The Easter weekend saw Bertie Mee's Football League career come to a stuttering halt. A Good Friday crowd of 7,000 turned out at Field Mill for a 0–0 draw against Reading. 'We do not wish to be too critical but Turner and Mee were a long way behind in skill and pace,' wrote the *Mansfield Reporter*.

The following day's game produced a 1–0 win against Clapton Orient, play having been preceded by an event that reflected the country's concerns about its apparently inevitable journey towards another war. According to the local paper, 'Councillor Walter Ward made an appeal through the microphone for all to do their duty by supporting the country in these troublous times by joining the national services.' Describing the football, the paper recorded that 'Mee, on the right, was not very helpful,' and added, 'Mee was very uncertain and contributed little to the success of the side.' Following Easter Monday's goalless draw at Reading, Mee was dropped. He completed his season by scoring in two successive reserve-team games.

Mansfield finished 16th in the Division Three South table and the local press pointed the finger at the forwards' lack of goals and the club's failure to find better players. 'Strong and virile forwards are needed but where are they to be found?' asked the newspaper's review of the season. Mee was not considered to be the answer. The club announced that only nine players would be retained for the following season, and the young winger was not among them. Instead, Mee's name appeared on the list of players earmarked for a free transfer.

And that – 13 first-team games, a single goal, a headline-grabbing debut, a series of less-than-flattering critiques and ultimate rejection – was the sum total of Bertie Mee's playing career in the Football League. The intervention of war put paid to any hopes he may have had of continuing as a professional footballer, but it is unlikely that playing the game would have provided him with much of a living after he had failed to maintain his place in a team in the depths of the League's lower ranks.

Bertie's next career move was decided for him in July 1939 when he received his call-up papers. His enrolment on 15 July in the Royal Army Medical Corps – in which he was to serve for six and a half years – would have a significant bearing on his future and, as it transpired, enable him to remain active in the sport that appeared to have discarded him.

2

ARMY GAMES

I was doing a job of work and the nationality of the
wounded men I treated didn't pose a problem.
– Bertie Mee, interviewed by granddaughter Jianna
for a school project in 1998

DURING THE SUMMER OF 1939, AS WAR IN EUROPE GREW EVER closer, footballers all over Britain were joining the Territorial Army, declaring themselves ready to fight if the need arose. Liverpool players signed up en masse and Bolton Wanderers and West Ham United quickly followed. The Hammers' call-up papers for the Essex Regiment arrived on 30 August, four days after the new season had kicked off. With German troops poised on the Polish border and British children preparing to leave the big cities for relatives, or strangers, in the countryside, the Football League announced that the programme of games scheduled for Saturday, 2 September would go ahead. But, as footballs were being kicked around English fields, German air raids bombarded Poland and, on Sunday, 3 September, British Prime Minister Neville Chamberlain announced that the country was at war. A ban on the assembly of crowds brought about the immediate suspension of the League programme, although football was soon to resume in the form of regional competitions with crowds as big as 15,000 allowed, as long as the matches were all-ticket.

Bertie Mee, listed as a 'professional footballer' on his enrolment papers and classified as an A1 physical specimen, had been attending a church service during his basic training in Aldershot at the time of Chamberlain's grim declaration. As the fighting began, he was dispatched to the army's School of Physiotherapy in Netley, Hampshire, where he spent the next three years.

Football continued to play a large role in his life, however. Wartime fixtures offered the public an escape from the hardships of conflict and professional matches were well attended, as well as being keenly contested. The vast number of footballers posted overseas meant that teams would field whichever 11 players happened to be in the vicinity on any given weekend. Mee took the opportunity to turn out for Southampton and would also play for his brother's former team, Blackpool. The games added a little to his two-shillings-per-day army pay packet, which was further fattened by a rise of threepence per day after his first year of service, shortly before his promotion to the rank of corporal.

Armed with his qualification from the Chartered Society of Physiotherapy, Mee left England in May 1942 on attachment to the Eighth Army. By that time, he was serving as an acting sergeant, the full rank being bestowed on him in September of that year. He served in Egypt, Lebanon and, from early 1943 until the end of the fighting, at the Number 3 British Convalescent Depot in Palestine, an area now recognised as Israel and Jordan.

It was there that he had his first real taste of organising footballers. One of his tasks was to arrange games throughout the region, including those of the Wanderers, a travelling all-star side that featured the best of the available players. The team would tour for spells of two or three months at a time, playing games to raise the spirits of the British troops. Mee himself played in some games, as did future England international Tom Finney and several other experienced professionals. 'It took us away from the routines of daily life and gave the troops something to enjoy as well,' Mee recalled.

Sergeant Mee's primary role, however, was to oversee physiotherapy and rehabilitation at the convalescent depot based in Natanya, a small coastal town midway between Tel Aviv and Haifa. Mee would receive troops from all over the Middle East, a combination of those who were seriously injured and others who were simply knackered. There were times when it was harrowing, disturbing work for a young medic. The physical disfiguration and mental wounds he dealt with enabled him to help footballers put their hamstring injuries into their proper context in later life. It made an unlikely setting in which to play a key role in the career of one of England's most celebrated footballers of the time, Wilf Mannion.

A blond-haired inside-forward with more than a touch of Paul Gascoigne about his play, Mannion would go on to win 26 international caps during his career with Middlesbrough and England. In later years, England teammate Nat Lofthouse, no less, would say, 'When I watched Pelé playing, I thought of Wilf.'

But the figure who presented himself before Bertie Mee in 1944 looked anything but a potential world-beater. Mannion had been a company runner in the Green Howards, a unit which had seen heavy fighting in Italy during the previous year. During one day's action, his battalion lost 80 men and suffered a further 75 injuries. Mannion had been with his captain, the former Yorkshire and England cricketer Hedley Verity, when Verity suffered what proved to be a fatal wounding.

Once Rome had fallen to the Allies, Mannion's unit was sent to Palestine to recover from its exertions. Interviewed by author Nick Varley for Mannion's biography *Golden Boy*, Mee recalled his meeting with a man he had seen play on several occasions but who was now a pale shadow of the fit, vibrant figure whose skills he so admired. Mannion had been downgraded from an A1, the healthiest physical specimen, to a B2, the lowest possible rating before one could be discharged on physical grounds.

'When you're in the line and someone next to you gets killed, I can understand you losing it,' said Mee, who, as well as nursing Mannion back from jaundice and malaria, placed him on an exercise programme aimed at restoring his general fitness and rekindling his interest in football. A whole range of sports, from football and cricket to horseriding and basketball, were prescribed. 'I took him out training and made him work,' said Mee. 'I just wanted him doing something to get him back again.'

Mee demonstrated early signs of the ruthless streak that injured

Arsenal players would come to fear, and respect, in later years. 'I wouldn't tolerate excuses of any kind. The mere fact that he played any football ever again gave me all the satisfaction I wanted.' Mee's care of Mannion also provides early evidence of his no-nonsense disciplinarian streak. When he found that star-struck colleagues were treating Mannion to nights out, he acted swiftly and ensured that the party-goers were transferred. Mee then arranged for Mannion to join the base's Military Police force so that he could keep him under his watchful eye and take advantage of his footballing skills.

Mee's own playing career was given an extra dimension when he turned out for the local League club, Maccabi Natanya. There, he forged a lifelong friendship with a young teammate, Elli Baram. 'Our club used to play friendly games against the team from the convalescent depot,' Baram recalls. 'My English was better than the other youngsters because I had been to a British school so I had the most contact with the troops. I ended up bringing in Bertie to play for us and he got Wilf Mannion to play as well. We were promoted to the First Division with them in our side! But Bertie didn't just come in for the games; he got involved in coaching the team as well. Then, one of the region's biggest clubs, Maccabi Tel Aviv, approached him and, from time to time, he went and worked with them.'

As well as his involvement with the local teams, Mee frequently socialised with Baram and his friends, and gave talks about his work to organisations in the area. The significance of an English soldier being accepted so completely by the community at a time of ongoing tension between the British and Palestinians should not be underestimated. Although all were fighting on the same side during the Second World War, this was the time of the British Mandate for Palestine, which meant that, since 1920, the region had been placed under the administrative control of the British. The mandate was the League of Nations' recognition of the stated purpose of 'establishing in Palestine a national home for the Jewish people' but in the meantime there was the inevitable friction resulting from the presence of an army of occupation.

Baram says, 'It was not the easiest of times and there were a lot of underground organisations that were against the British. But still Bertie was very popular. A lot of people admired him. The whole behaviour of Bertie was very different. He was distinguished, he would never offend anyone and he never ever got drunk. I doubt if he even used to have a beer. He was a gentleman.'

And Mee was not afraid to stand by his friend during a delicate situation. 'We always went out on Friday nights to a café where they had a dance place. My girlfriend, Carmella, who became my wife, also got to know Bertie,' Baram recalls. 'In 1943, I was arrested and put in an open prison because it was suspected that I was too nationalistic. Bertie was a great support to me, and he looked after Carmella and continued to take her dancing. There was a lot of feeling between them, just as there was later from me to Doris, Bertie's wife. We still consider them our best-ever friends.'

When the war was over, Mee finally headed for home early in January 1946. His commanding officer's assessment of Bertie at the time of discharge contains references to many of the qualities that would later become familiar in the football world:

> This Non-Commissioned Officer has been in this depot for three years. He has run his own department efficiently throughout. He is active in organisation of sport, confident and self-reliant in his dealings with men. He is very trustworthy and can be left to carry out his own job. Very highly recommended, both for organising ability and competence as masseur.

A back injury Mee had suffered in a gymnasium accident, plus his previous experiences with Mansfield, meant that he held no expectations of picking up his football career. Although he had played for the Wanderers, he admitted that he 'made up the numbers', adding that 'the injury was probably fortuitous'.

In an interview in *The Observer* in 1972, he described his injury as 'a great disappointment', but added:

> I hope I'm a realist as well as an optimist. The fact is, I was no good – not good enough anyway. I would have played League football at a low level but I'd never have made a First Division player and I like to be first in whatever I do.

Bertie and football were about to go their different ways, although it was only to be a temporary separation. His farewell to the military life, meanwhile, was to be permanent, even though friends and colleagues believe he could have forged a successful career in uniform. Fred Street, who worked for Mee in the health service and at Arsenal, says, 'I think if he had stayed in the army, he would have been commissioned because he had that about him. He was a little bit "cut above".'

Street also suggests, 'Bertie was lucky in timing in a sense. He was in the army – and you wouldn't wish that on anyone during a war – but it meant he got authority at a young age. He was a sergeant and he was able to use his personality to make people do things, whether they liked it or not. I think that was probably in him anyway, but the army helped to bring it out.'

And, as colleagues were to discover, you could take the man out of the army, but you couldn't take the military out of Sergeant Mee.

As civilian life awaited the return of the men it had lost to the services, the Ministry of Health saw an opportunity to take advantage of the skills of those who had been charged with the physical fitness and rehabilitation of the troops. These remedial gymnasts, as they had become known, had originally been the loud-voiced, vest-wearing physical training instructors beloved by Ealing comedies. Their task had been to maintain and increase the fitness levels of society's healthiest group. As the need arose to find more fit men to go and fight, many of those who had been deemed unsuitable for active service were recalled in an attempt to see if the physical training experts could make them battle-ready.

Harry Hopker, who was soon to cross paths with Mee, explains, 'We were physical instructors who were used to square-bashing, but then we started working with doctors to learn how to turn our physical training into remedial work. We had been used to making fit people fitter, but now we were moving into personal physical development, which was working with those who had been dismissed from recruitment because of illness or injury. We ran these nine-week courses which were absolute hell on earth, including ten-mile runs each day. Out of this, you got a core of physical training officers who had become medically orientated, able to do things like take blood pressure.'

The instructors' experience grew even more than expected with the war producing an escalating number of casualties in need of physical training and rehabilitation. 'By the end of the war, we knew how to handle handicapped people,' adds Hopker.

With the conflict over, these remedial gymnasts were seen as a valuable asset whose experience could now be used in the country's civilian hospitals. The Ministry of Health set up remedial gymnastic training courses to prepare the military instructors for civilian service, only to meet opposition from the country's chartered physiotherapists. Hopker explains, 'The established side was the Chartered Society of Massage and Medical Gymnastics, which was another way of saying remedial gymnastics. But their approach to physiotherapy at that time was a very passive one and they did not agree with the more robust army-type philosophy.'

Beginning in 1946, three separate six-month courses were staged at the School of Remedial Gymnastics in Pinderfields Hospital in Wakefield, Yorkshire. 'I was on the second course,' says Hopker, 'and they asked me to stay on and be an instructor on the third course, where Bertie Mee was one of my students.'

Mee, who had been completing further qualifications – for Membership of the Society of Remedial Gymnasts – at the West London School of Physiotherapy in Notting Hill, was invited to join Hopker on the Pinderfields staff when an additional training course was set up in 1948. When Harry met Bertie could hardly be described as a great reunion. 'I didn't really remember him at all as a student,' Hopker recounts. 'You only remember the cheeky ones and Bertie certainly wasn't one of those.'

Bertie did stand out, however, from his new colleagues in the team of instructors. 'Most of us were in white coats for the first time. We were all physical training instructors, but Bertie wasn't. He had been in the medical corps as a physio, so he was unusual in that respect. We had always been all "Left, right! Left, right!" and Bertie was a very calming influence indeed.'

Bertie and Harry shared a small cottage within the hospital grounds with a third colleague, John Colson. 'We spent hours together in the evenings,' says Hopker. 'Wakefield's nightlife at the time was the café on the corner. We didn't go out that much. We ate and slept in the hospital and played a bit of badminton.'

According to Hopker, Colson's literary projects helped to fill the hours. 'John was a very meticulous man who wrote a series of textbooks. They were full of the most annoying detail. The three of us would sit up until the small hours of the morning working out things like what the muscle action was when you bent down and picked up something from the floor. Bertie, John and I would stand and argue about those things for hours.'

The course over, Bertie was offered the position of chief rehabilitation officer at Etwall Rehabilitation Centre in Derbyshire, although he returned to Pinderfields to teach on another six-month course in 1950. It was during this break from Etwall that he encountered a man who would be by his side during his finest hours at Highbury, future Arsenal physiotherapist George Wright.

'It was 1950 and I had just come out of the Army Physical Training Corps,' Wright remembers. 'The National Health Service was in its infancy and was looking for instructors. Bertie was an instructor on the first remedial gymnastics course that I took as part of my resettlement. It was all academic work and everyone looked up to Bertie. He was the teacher, so you were accepting of what he was telling you. He was always very straight and very official. That continued throughout his life.'

Mee made enough of an impression on Wright that at the end of the course he approached him to ask for some career advice. Wright confessed to Mee, 'I have passed the course and have my qualifications, but I don't feel confident enough to go and work somewhere by myself.'

Mee's army background had taught him the importance of making quick decisions and he fired back, 'I will be having a vacancy soon at my place. Why don't you join me?'

Wright accepted the offer. 'I must have had some potential otherwise Bertie would not have wanted me, but at that stage he was the master and I was the pupil. I got on well with him but he always let you know he was in charge.'

Not only did Wright join Mee at work in Etwall, which was used in the main for the rehabilitation of injured miners, but he and his wife, Margaret, moved in with Bertie for two years. By that time, Bertie himself was a married man, having wed Doris Edwards, the daughter of an electrician, on 26 March 1949 in West Bridgford, Nottingham. Almost four years younger than her future husband, Doris, who worked as a secretary, had actually been dating one of his best friends,

Frank Cartwright, when they first met after the war. Just to prove there were no hard feelings over Bertie winning Doris's affections, Frank accepted the invitation to be best man at the wedding, although the nuptials had to be delayed while Doris overcame tuberculosis. The disease was not as prevalent as it had been following the First World War, but Doris was confined for a while to a hospital where many of those around her were dying. One doom-laden doctor warned her, 'There will be no wedding bells for you.'

Doris proved him wrong and she and Bertie settled down to enjoy village life in Etwall, where he played for the local cricket club and she was a prize-winning cake-maker at the Women's Institute. Together, they shared their love of ballroom dancing. Wright recalls, 'Bertie was not quite as regimented at home. He could unwind a bit. My overriding memory of him at home was that he was always a complete gentleman, very polite and courteous.'

3

KING OF CAMDEN ROAD

Bertie would inspect your hands to make sure they
were scrubbed, check that your shoes were clean
and that you had a crease in your trousers.
– Fred Street, Mee's colleague in the health service
and Arsenal physiotherapist

THE KIND OF REMEDIAL WORK IN WHICH BERTIE MEE HAD
specialised at Etwall was becoming increasingly popular by the early
1950s. His old friend and colleague Harry Hopker explains, 'Remedial
gymnasts were becoming more important in hospitals. A lot of the
doctors had been in the war and liked the new robust approach. Society
generally was more receptive to group work. At Pinderfields Hospital,
a questionnaire went round asking patients if they would like an open
ward or a private room. Everyone chose the open ward. So patients
loved to come and join a group of 30 other people. It made it
enjoyable.'

The Ministry of Health decided a new rehabilitation centre was
needed in the capital and established a facility in Camden Road in
north-west London. Hopker continues, 'There had been some of these
rehab centres before. Organisations like the Miners' Welfare
Commission in the Midlands set up some to try to get coal miners

back to work. This was an extension of that idea. This kind of thing didn't really exist in the hospitals, so Camden was a pioneering centre.'

Hopker says that it was no accident that Mee was selected to run the facility in the role of rehabilitation officer. 'Bertie was one of the country's pioneers on a paramedical level. There was a chap called Captain C.J.F. O'Malley who managed to persuade the Ministry of Health to set up these rehabilitation centres, including the one at Camden. He had a lot of influence and Bertie was hand-picked by him, I am sure. Bertie was a very good manager and organiser.'

The set-up at Camden Road provided Mee with a severe test of his abilities. 'It was a horrible place,' says Hopker. 'It was all stairs, steps and slopes. It was the last place on earth you would want to have a rehabilitation centre. To keep that place ticking over was a very skilful job. Of course, when you are working with physios, occupational therapists, speech therapists and people like that, everyone has their own priorities and they are not always that willing to cooperate. It needs a good manager to coordinate it all so that it works for the patient, and Bertie was supremely skilful at that.'

At Camden, Mee had his first real experience of running a staff. He and his team of 30 were responsible for the rehabilitation of patients with injuries ranging from the relatively minor, like backaches and broken legs, to more traumatic conditions, such as strokes or multiple sclerosis, or victims of industrial injuries, including amputees. It was in 1956 that a former RAF physical training instructor called Fred Street came into Bertie's life. Street was to spend the best part of two decades working for Mee, including as physiotherapist at Arsenal. 'He runs like a gold thread through my life,' says Street, who retains sufficient objectivity to provide an enlightening description of the somewhat tyrannical style of leadership that Mee was to take from the health service into professional football.

Sitting in his consulting room at London's Park Lane Clinic, Street chuckles and smiles his way through his memories of the man who helped shape his working life, even when the tales he recounts are not the most complimentary to his former boss. 'You have to remember,' he says, 'that everything I say is with affection. I might have been a lorry driver without Bertie.' And, in a statement that could easily refer to the success Mee achieved with players who were mostly good, solid professionals without being uniquely gifted, Street adds, 'He pushed people to get the best out of themselves.'

In Street's case, Mee's pushing took the form of virtually bullying him into a career in physiotherapy. Having spent five years in the RAF working with injured servicemen, Street was considering a return to civilian life. 'I had extended my national service and I was at the end of five years' service. What do you do next as a PT instructor? I saw the chief medical officer at Henley Court in Surrey, and he suggested going to see Bertie Mee. I had never heard of him.'

Street was told that Mee ran a civilian rehabilitation centre that operated along the same principles as his own RAF experience. He duly turned up to meet Mee and was greeted by a man whose manner was 'very short and sharp'. Street's first impressions were to be validated over the years. 'A lot of people have said it, but he was a dead ringer for Captain Mainwaring from *Dad's Army*. He was pompous, short, slightly bullying and full of opinions. He could be rather pedantic and would split hairs. But they were all good qualities for what he did and the way he went about it.'

Street was exposed at once to Mee's knack of quickly getting his wishes fulfilled. 'I had only been there a few minutes and he said, "You are just the right sort of person we need, a military person." Bertie felt that military men were the right material; there was something about their training and the background of dealing with serious injuries. He said, "You can start here tomorrow. We'll organise for you to get your civilian qualifications." It wasn't a question of what I would like to do. I told him I would think about it and went back home. Next morning, I got a letter in the post from him saying, "It was good to meet you" and so on, and "This is what we are going to do." And in the same post there was a letter from the Ministry of Labour with a travel warrant and an interview time with the governors at the remedial gymnastics school in Pinderfields.

'I was doing a bit of filling-in work at Burton's, the clothes shop, so I took the day off and went up and sat in front of this committee of governors. There was a priority in those days for ex-servicemen and they said I'd come highly recommended. It was obviously just a rubber-stamp job. Bertie Mee had said I was the right man and he had that kind of clout, those contacts.

'I told Bertie I had been accepted and that I was to start in September. He said, "In the meantime, come and work here." I knew what I was doing but I didn't have the qualifications, so Bertie put me on the books as a porter. I actually worked in the gym with the patients. He made the proviso that I would come back and work with him once I was qualified.'

Several years later, Mee, not for the first or last time, placed another controlling hand on the destiny of Street's career, deciding it was time for him to undertake his chartered physiotherapist's training. 'I was in my late 20s and there was no measurable advantage in doing another qualification,' says Street. 'It just gave you another string to your bow. Bertie suddenly says to me, "The principal up at St Mary's wants to see you." That was Bertie again, telling me what to do. I had to give my notice in at Camden and pack up my job. To be fair, I ended up thanking him for it because it opened up a lot of doors.'

Street's picture of life at Camden features Mee prowling the corridors and treatment rooms ensuring a regimental precision in the organisation. Future players and football colleagues would easily recognise the energy and attention to detail that Street describes. 'He was very much, "Do as I tell you, not as I do." A strict disciplinarian to the point of making it like the services. In the '50s, you could get away with it. He would inspect your hands to make sure they were scrubbed, check that your shoes were clean and that you had a crease in your trousers. He was like that with the patients as well, but they put up with it.'

But behind the bluster and the bullying lay the mind of someone who was still prepared to be innovative in his approach to his job. The Camden Road centre became renowned for championing various ground-breaking methods, most notably the kind of group therapy that enabled patients to feed off collective energy rather than working alone with one physiotherapist or instructor.

Street explains, 'When Bertie got the OBE, I wrote to him and said that I hoped some of it was for his work in the health service. I think that, in a sense, it was more important than what he achieved in football. He was ahead of his time in the organisation of the centre and the philosophy of bringing different disabilities together and working them in classes. I suppose it was a product of the services, where you have so many people that you can't have one-on-ones. He created a tremendous atmosphere – a bit like Butlins – with a dozen of us working together in the gym. We had fun and patients would encourage each other. It was a major breakaway from the more traditional, gentle style of physiotherapy; the world of quiet massage. Bertie's world was about getting people going; getting them back to work.'

Mee watched such sessions with satisfaction, understanding the benefits being derived by the patients, but he kept a safe distance. There would be no emotional attachment, no striding onto the gymnasium floor to end a session with a group hug. No one could ever accuse Bertie of being 'touchy-feely'. In fact, Street recalls, 'In the '50s, it was very austere, everyone was "Mister". Bertie said he didn't think I should allow my patients to call me "Fred". He used to have the staff in his office for meetings and one day he said, "I don't want patients using your first names."

'I was head of the gym so I said to him, "Bert, can you let us do it our way? The day you find it causes problems, then you can jump on me for it, but in the meantime I get a benefit out of it."

'He just muttered something like, "Mmm. Maybe you're right." That was the nearest you would get to an apology, or Bertie admitting he was wrong.'

Street recalls another incident where he had to speak up on the staff's behalf in the face of a tirade from their boss. 'It was a Friday and he wanted to go shopping at lunchtime and we came back a couple of minutes past two. On Friday, just for fun, the patients would take the warm-up instead of the staff. We did it to music. That was another thing he introduced at Camden, before they called it aerobics. We used to do it to Russ Conway! Anyway, the staff were just stood around having cups of tea or playing table tennis. He was a stickler for time and he said he wanted to see the staff in the office. When the staff came in, he went on and on about them standing about and everything, and in the end I interrupted him and said, "You've made your point." I told the staff to go. He didn't like that, but I said to him, "Bertie, you are right in principle, but it's Friday and the staff are good people who are earning buttons. It's not as if they are layabouts. And we were late too."

'He said, "You're right. Maybe I need a holiday."

'And he went off for two weeks that Monday!'

Mee maintained strong and significant connections with professional football throughout his time at Camden Road. Various London clubs, including Arsenal, Tottenham and Queens Park Rangers, used the centre to help rehabilitate injured players. 'Clubs used to bring their more serious injuries to us because they didn't have much in the way of in-house facilities,' says Street.

Mee also worked closely with the Football Association. He would lecture apprentice professionals during release courses at the FA's centre at Lilleshall and he helped to establish the Football and Injuries Training Badge, a two-week course for potential trainers run at Carnegie College in Leeds before it moved to Bisham Abbey in Buckinghamshire and eventually found a permanent home at Lilleshall. 'It wouldn't give you a job outside football, but it offered a good grounding,' says Street. 'Bertie used to lead the lectures. The course is still running.'

Mee's exposure in the football world meant that his methods were gaining more and more followers, enhancing his growing reputation in the game. Street explains, 'Bertie brought a lot of things into football, things he had picked up from other areas. He took a fresh look at what was done in terms of preparation, particularly on match day. Bertie was very advanced. Teams would just turn up at the ground, but Bertie introduced the idea of stretching routines and he looked at what players ate before matches. The tradition was a well-done steak, but Bertie introduced the high carbohydrates – cornflakes, poached eggs on toast, that kind of thing. It gets a lot of press now, but Bertie was the initiator of much of that.'

With his background as a professional player, albeit short-lived and low-key, and his burgeoning reputation in the sport, it was only a matter of time before the chance came for Mee to move into football on a full-time basis. It was Arsenal, whose club doctor, Alan Bass, had worked with Bertie at Camden Road, who presented such an opportunity. Asked by BBC Television a few years later why Arsenal had chosen him for such a position, the modest Mee gave an embarrassed smile and replied, 'Presumably they liked the shape of my nose or had heard something of my reputation.'

Ron Goodman, who worked for Arsenal's kit suppliers and would befriend Mee in future years, adds, 'I suppose the person really responsible for Bertie going to Arsenal was Mel Charles, who had a knee problem when he was brought to Highbury. Somebody suggested he try the Camden Road centre and Alan Bass, or somebody at

Arsenal, said, "If this man is so good, why don't we employ him?" And they did. Football clubs then were paying much more than the National Health Service.'

Despite his love of the game, Mee, according to Street, went to Arsenal 'largely for a few quid'. Street explains, 'To say he took it "reluctantly" would perhaps be the wrong phrase, but Bertie was working in the health service in a one-off kind of job as rehabilitation officer – there was no grading for it. He was the boss, probably just a few quid above the rest. He was supposedly under the doctors, but he used to run them as well. Alan Bass was one of them. So here he was trying to get a little bit of a pay rise. He and Doris were scratching along on health service money. He was looking for just a hundred quid more a year. It sounds silly, doesn't it? It would have put him up to perhaps £1,200 a year. Arsenal were looking for a new physio and Alan Bass wanted qualified staff. He was beyond the days of the old trainer with a wet sponge. So Bertie was asked if he would take the job for about £1,800, which almost doubled his money. It was partly down to him wanting to work in football, but mostly he took the job because of the money. You see, when you go to a football club, you are an auxiliary; you are not what the club is about. Part of Bertie did have a problem with that, but he loved the game and knew a lot of people in it. With all those elements, plus the fact he wasn't getting anywhere with his hundred quid, he took the job.'

George Wright, his former colleague and housemate in Derbyshire and future trainer at Arsenal, agrees with Street's opinion of Mee's motives. 'When he was living in Mill Hill, my wife and I visited him on several occasions and we had the feeling that he was down on his uppers a bit. So when the chance came along to go to Arsenal, he grabbed it.'

Mee himself never hid the fact that the increased wages had indeed influenced his decision. His elder daughter, Beverley, recalls, 'Mum always used to tell me that he said he had only taken the job at Arsenal so he could afford to buy me my first pair of proper shoes!' And in *Arsenal in the Blood*, an oral history of the club published in 1988, Bertie told author David Lemmon:

> Arsenal came to me and said, 'What about it?' And I said, 'Make me an offer and I am there.' Because I was getting very

frustrated for various reasons, mostly financial. I was married by then and when I found it difficult to buy my wife a winter coat, I felt that it was time to move on.

But he also made clear in the same interview that Arsenal had long featured prominently in his professional plans:

It was my ambition to work for Arsenal and, of course, my ambition came about. I had had the ambition since the early part of the war when I got my physio qualifications, and I was looking to come back into football.

Harry Hopker confirms that it was more than just the money that appealed to his friend. 'He always aspired to Arsenal. He always wanted to be with them. They were the Manchester United of that time and he was very proud of that.'

In truth, however, the club that Bertie Mee was to join was at that time very far from being comparable to Manchester United, or any of the country's leading teams. Unpacking his medical kit in the Highbury treatment room and taking a look around him, what Mee would have seen was a club in danger of falling apart at the seams, held together only by the threads of its illustrious reputation.

4

THE BIG SLEEP

Arsenal is the greatest club in the world. It breaks my heart to see them struggling now. They are too good for this.

– former Arsenal captain Joe Mercer,
speaking in 1958

ARSENAL EMERGED FROM THE SECOND WORLD WAR IN A STATE of considerable ill health. Highbury had suffered bomb damage, the club had estimated debts of £200,000 and, on the field, the team that contested the 1946–47 season clearly had little chance of emulating the triumphs of their 1930s equivalent. For a time, relegation looked more likely than another Championship. Struggling under such a burden, manager George Allison enlisted the help of team physiotherapist Tom Whittaker as his assistant. The cheerful, shirt-sleeved Whittaker's influence was credited with helping Arsenal to preserve their First Division status and offered evidence – significant for Bertie Mee's career – that it was possible for someone of Whittaker's profession to contribute beyond the treatment room. Even before Whittaker, though, Arsenal hadn't been afraid to give responsibility for footballing matters to those apparently unqualified. Allison had been a journalist and broadcaster before undertaking the seemingly impossible task of succeeding Herbert Chapman, the man who built Arsenal into one of the world's most revered clubs before his sudden death in 1934.

Apart from Whittaker's promotion, the most significant move of the first post-war season at Highbury was the signing of former England wing-half Joe Mercer, whose knee injury had led to his demotion from the first team at Everton. Whittaker, who had seen the state of Mercer's leg during a visit to Highbury, persuaded Allison to sign him up for £7,000. Arsenal even allowed him to continue living on the Wirral where he ran his newly acquired grocery business. He would train with Liverpool and commute to matches. It was an inspired move. In 1947–48, with Whittaker installed as manager, the First Division was won under the galvanising on-field leadership of the supposedly crocked Mercer.

Forced to leave his attacking tendencies on the physio's table, Mercer's injury helped Arsenal introduce the formation that was to become the accepted form of defence for most English clubs. His reduced mobility necessitated that he play as a defensive half-back, stationed next to the centre-half in a back four. Mercer's training partner, Liverpool striker Albert Stubbins, highlighted Arsenal's defensive mentality when he said, 'Joe told me that he was told never to cross the halfway line. They would say, "Let them come, let them come," and they would back up and pack the defence further back.' Arsenal had been accused of playing defensively in the past, claims that would be heard again in the future.

The FA Cup was won for the third time in the club's history in 1950 and two years later they reached the final again, but were unlucky to lose. There was one more triumphant season to come – 1952–53, which culminated in the dramatic title-clinching Friday night finale against Burnley – before the victories suddenly dried up. Hollywood may have released *The Big Sleep* seven years earlier, but it was just reaching Highbury. And it would last for 17 years.

By the time Arsenal were preparing to defend their crown, Joe Mercer had gone back on his emotional retirement announcement, even though he was about to turn 39. Within two months, he must have been regretting Tom Whittaker's powers of persuasion. Arsenal lost six and drew two of their first eight games, and when Sunderland stuck seven past them, the Gunners were bottom of the First Division. No champions had ever made such a woeful start. In fairness, they had led 2–1 at Roker Park before goalkeeper George Swindin, in what turned out to be his final game for the club, was injured. But, whatever the mitigating circumstances in one particular game, the prevailing pattern for the coming years had been established: frustration, mishap and downright incompetence.

Whittaker's response to the crisis was to sign former England centre-forward Tommy Lawton, who was unhappy as the struggling player–manager at Brentford. But Lawton, who had turned down the opportunity to join Arsenal 17 years earlier, was a shadow of the dominant presence that made defences cower when he wore the blue of Everton and Chelsea, and it was seven months before he scored the one First Division goal he managed during 1953–54. Despite dragging themselves up to 12th place, Arsenal suffered further humiliation at home to Norwich in the fourth round of the FA Cup.

As for Mercer, who was in and out of the team all season, he broke his leg in a match against Liverpool when he collided with teammate Joe Wade. His poignant wave of the hand while being carried off on a stretcher was recognised by the Highbury crowd for what it was: a sign that, this time, it really was the end. It would not be long before Mercer embarked on a managerial career that, had it taken an alternate course several years later, could have changed Highbury history.

The 1954–55 season saw Arsenal move up to ninth in the table, but the team was in a state of flux. Stalwarts of previous successes departed, while Derek Tapscott, a young Welsh forward, was attempting to establish himself as the spearhead of the Arsenal forward line. Peter Goring and Cliff Holton were converted from centre-forwards to wing-halves, the former successfully and the latter less so, leaving the long-serving Doug Lishman and Don Roper as the leading scorers. At least Welshman Jack Kelsey was now established as one of the best goalkeepers in the Football League.

Lawton thrilled Highbury by scoring a hat-trick against Cardiff in the first home game of the following season, but had left the club by the first month of 1956. Whittaker, despite suffering from increasingly poor health, remained active in his attempts to find a winning combination, bringing in wingers Mike Tiddy and Gordon Nutt from Cardiff, and defender Stan Charlton and utility man Vic Groves from Leyton Orient. Lishman's service to the club was terminated by a transfer to Nottingham Forest, while full-back Walley Barnes gave up his ongoing battle with a knee injury when he joined the BBC's football broadcasting team. Seven wins in the final eight games lifted the team into fifth position in Division One, while the Gunners' FA Cup hopes remained alive until a quarter-final defeat by Birmingham. It had hardly been a glorious march to the last eight, however. In the third round, Arsenal were held at home by Southern League Bedford and in the replay – the first game ever broadcast by independent television – found themselves five minutes from defeat before winning in extra time.

A 4–1 victory against Blackpool produced an incident that illustrates the way that the tradition and standards of the past could encroach on the needs of the day. Gunners left-back Dennis Evans recalled Whittaker warning him to take it easy on Blackpool's national treasure, Stanley Matthews. 'He told me not to set out to kick Stan off the pitch. He said, "Even your own fans will hate you if you do that."'

As well as being indicative of Matthews' stature in the game, it also illuminates the importance the club placed on old-fashioned virtues like honour and sportsmanship, to the point where it could potentially affect what happened on the field. One of Bertie Mee's achievements as Arsenal manager would be his ability to walk that particular tightrope. As much as he would believe in upholding the club's established standards, it is impossible to imagine him disapproving of Peter Storey kicking George Best if the need arose. Mee would prove it was possible to impose levels of off-field behaviour that honoured the club's reputation but did not detract from the business of grinding out results. Heaven knows what Whittaker would have made of some of Arsenal's future battles with Leeds.

Another interesting comparison between Whittaker and the man who would be the next Gunners manager to win a trophy can be shown in the story of Alec Stock's brief employment at Highbury. Stock, who had played for Yeovil in the non-League team's famous victory against Sunderland in the FA Cup, left his job at Leyton Orient to become Arsenal's coach and share Whittaker's workload. But less than two months after his arrival, he returned to his former position following several disagreements with his boss. He revealed later, 'When I went as Tom Whittaker's assistant, the nature of the job was not clearly defined to me and I never felt fully occupied in so big an organisation.'

If there was one thread running through Bertie Mee's working life, it was his ability to organise; that any coach of his would be unsure of his duties was unthinkable. Stock's comments reveal much about the state of chaos infiltrating Highbury. What they don't allow for, however, is the declining state of Whittaker's health during 1956. Whittaker had managed to keep his problems secret from his players, but over Easter, he was taken into hospital for heart surgery. On 24 October, he died from a heart attack at London's University College Hospital.

For the second time in little more than two decades, the club had seen its manager die on the job. Whittaker had illustrated his awareness of the dangers inherent in his position when he said, 'Someone has to drive himself too hard for Arsenal. Herbert Chapman worked himself to death for the club and if it is my fate, I am happy to accept it.'

Bertie Mee would acknowledge the pressures that had certainly contributed to, if not caused, the deaths of Chapman and Whittaker. In fact, comments he made in the *Arsenal Football Book* published in 1969, hauntingly hark back to Whittaker's statement:

> It doesn't matter if I get ulcers. My job is to see there are no distractions. I often feel like letting off steam but I've got to keep it bottled up. I must keep calm so that the boys can lean on me in moments of crisis.

Next in line to inherit the pressure of the Arsenal manager's chair was England international Jack Crayston. A powerful wing-half, he had been a member of two of Arsenal's Championship-winning teams in the '30s and had picked up an FA Cup medal in 1936. Once again, the club decided that the continuity of appointing an Arsenal man was more important than whether the candidate's position at that time was a relevant preparation for management. In Crayston's case, as in Allison's and Whittaker's, it wasn't. As well as carrying out some scouting, 'Gentleman Jack' was a trained accountant and was assisting with the club's bookkeeping.

Arsenal managed a fifth-place finish in 1956–57 and another quarter-final berth in the FA Cup. Tapscott was the top scorer with 25 League goals, and a sharp-shooting youngster, David Herd, the son of pre-war Scottish international Alec Herd, emerged from the reserves to score 12 goals.

Another step was taken towards strengthening the club structure in December 1957 when Ron Greenwood, who would go on to manage West Ham and England, was appointed coach. The former manager of Eastbourne United – a post that, bizarrely, he maintained during the first few months of his Arsenal appointment – was one of a new breed of tactical innovators finding their way into the country's dressing-rooms. Yet the best coaching methods require good players in order to achieve success. Arsenal did not have enough of them and their 12th-place finish saw them achieve the club's lowest points total since 1930. A 3–1 loss at Third Division Northampton in the third round of the FA Cup compounded the gloom.

After one home defeat, a group of supporters protested outside the stadium and even the Arsenal match programme was running the team down. The notes for the game against Blackpool read, 'The present position is the culmination of an insidious trend dating back to 1952 when the team, beginning to wilt in skill, was carried forward to reasonable success by its determination and the superb captaincy of Joe Mercer.' It is interesting to note that a League Championship was only classed as 'reasonable success'. As well as criticism of the spirit in the team, there was an implicit suggestion that maybe the wrong man was in charge. Mercer was interviewed by journalists about the position and said diplomatically that he hoped Arsenal would work their way out of their predicament.

Over the years, a thick veil would have been drawn over the entire 1957–58 season at Highbury had it not been for the fact that it staged what, at the time, was considered the most remarkable game of the season. Events of a few days later would ensure that this particular match, a 5–4 defeat against League champions Manchester United, would assume mythical status. It was the final League game played by the 'Busby Babes' before eight members of the team were wiped out in the Munich air crash. Arsenal played their full part in an incredible afternoon. The game reached half-time with United apparently on their way to an easy victory after goals by Duncan Edwards, Bobby Charlton and Tommy Taylor. But an astonishing three-minute spell around the hour mark saw Arsenal score through Herd and then draw level with two goals by the elegant and popular Jimmy Bloomfield.

Dennis Viollet scored a well-taken fourth for United and Taylor added a fifth, but Tapscott pulled back a goal to complete the scoreline.

Until tragedy decimated a young team with seemingly limitless potential, United were setting new standards for teams like Arsenal to match. Jack Crayston knew it was an impossible task without new players, but his attempts to get money out of the board to strengthen the team proved unsuccessful. Swansea winger Cliff Jones had been a target, but without the directors' support, Crayston saw the Welshman go to Tottenham.

An Arsenal programme outlined the club's policy of not bidding for a player's signature, explaining, 'We always ask the fee required and, having been told, make up our mind whether the player is worth that fee.' In other words, if a player was good enough to interest more than one team, Arsenal would stand aside. Such frustrations were too much for Crayston, who resigned at the end of the season.

The Arsenal directors looked again to the club's history to find their managerial candidate. As reporters had been speculating, Joe Mercer, manager of Sheffield United at the time, was the target. Arsenal chairman Sir Bracewell Smith offered him £3,000 a year to return to Highbury, but Mercer, having consulted his family, decided to stay in the North. 'I've made my decision and I feel happy about it,' he said. 'I have been extremely happy with the Sheffield club. But beyond that I am not prepared to say one word. You can understand this is very delicate.'

The best Mercer could offer his former team were words of sympathy. He never did fully explain a decision that, according to most of the football world, was inexplicable. Sure, he was happily settled in the Sheffield area, but he loved Arsenal. And he had found problematic the United directors' reluctance to give him a free hand to run the club. The obvious conclusion was that things must have been even worse at Arsenal than was apparent.

Arsenal claimed that Sheffield United had refused to release Mercer from his five-year contract, which, ironically, was cancelled after the Arsenal affair. Presumably, Mercer's employers felt he wouldn't be going anywhere if he hadn't left for Arsenal. By the end of 1958, however, Mercer had taken the vacant job at Aston Villa, adding to Arsenal's suspicions that the Blades had deliberately blocked Mercer's potential move to Highbury. He remained too much of a gentleman to spill the beans. But, whatever the real story, his decision changed the course of Arsenal history. It is conceivable, if not probable, that Bertie Mee's subsequent role in that history would have been greatly diminished had Mercer ventured south.

By the time Mercer was taking over at Villa Park, George Swindin was the new manager of Arsenal. A confident and courageous goalkeeper, Swindin had been manager at Midland League Peterborough United, where he had achieved some eye-catching FA Cup results. Typical of his Yorkshire background, Swindin could be stubborn and was not afraid to speak his mind, a big change from the genial figures of Whittaker and Crayston. The first season under Swindin proved the most successful since the title victory of 1953. In fact, the third place achieved by Arsenal would not be bettered for more than a decade.

If Crayston was watching from his new office at Doncaster Rovers, he must have been frustrated to see money to strengthen the team suddenly materialising for his successor. Wing-half Tommy Docherty arrived from Preston for £27,000, having defied archaic club orders to go on a summer tour of South Africa. He had preferred, not unnaturally, to travel to Sweden with Scotland's World Cup squad. Docherty announced his Highbury arrival by scoring on his debut against Burnley, although he never again found the net for Arsenal. Docherty, an extrovert character who took a little time to win over the reserved Highbury crowd, was joined by another Scotland international, Jackie Henderson, signed from Wolverhampton.

As the personnel changes continued, Mel Charles, brother of Welsh legend John, was signed from Swansea. While not in the same class as his sibling, he did share many of his qualities, but needed two knee operations within a year. A total of 17 professionals left Highbury during the season, including combative Welsh wing-half Dave Bowen, who returned to Northampton and was succeeded as captain by Groves. 'It was a strange period because there was a lot of turmoil on the playing side,' recalls Docherty. 'Players wanted to leave and had become unsettled and we never really took off as a team.'

Arsenal were in a challenging position in the table in October 1959 when Docherty broke his ankle in a match against his former Preston teammates. The Gunners responded by slumping into relegation form. They made an offer of £50,000 to Huddersfield for young Scottish striker Denis Law, but when Manchester City topped that amount, Arsenal reverted to their former policy of refusing to participate in bidding wars. Law was destined for Maine Road and one of the most storied careers of his generation. The '50s ended with Arsenal on their way to finishing 13th in the First Division. Already, the memory of the club's last major honour seemed a distant one.

The end of the 1959–60 season saw Billy Milne retire as team trainer. A friendly Scotsman, Milne had won medals during the war and had taken over from Tom Whittaker following his promotion to manager. 'He was the toughest, hardest and bravest person but he knew nothing about physiology and anatomy,' Joe Mercer had said of him. Recalling his broken leg, he added, 'Fortunately, the Liverpool trainer got there first. Otherwise I might not have had any leg left.'

It's a funny story and told with affection, but it does not say much for the professionalism of Arsenal, one of the country's top clubs at that time. That would all change with the appointment of a new physiotherapist, Bertie Mee.

5

MANAGER IN WAITING

You wouldn't fake injury when Bertie was the physio.
For one thing, you knew you wouldn't get away with
it and, for another, you were scared of how hard he
worked players to get them fit again.

                – former Arsenal winger Alan Skirton

BERTIE MEE FOUND A NEW TRAINING GROUND WAITING FOR HIM
when he arrived at Arsenal in the summer of 1960. Instead of relying
on the stadium at Highbury or the facilities in Hendon, the Gunners
had established a new centre in the University College grounds at
London Colney, just north of London in Hertfordshire's stretch of
green belt. But even before pre-season training began in bright new
surroundings, there was an important project for the team's incoming
physiotherapist to undertake.

Winger Alan Skirton had made such an impression as a teenage
player for his local team, Southern League Bath City, that both
Arsenal and Chelsea battled for his signature. In 1958, George
Swindin paid £5,000, then a record for a non-League player, to secure
the services of a man who would become known as the 'Highbury
Express'. While completing his national service in the Army Pay
Corps, Skirton played a pair of reserve games in Arsenal colours. But,

as the chance of a first-team debut approached during the 1958–59 season, Skirton's health was clearly not up to the rigours of the First Division.

'I'd had flu a couple of times and generally felt unwell,' he says. 'On one Friday, I had played in an Army Cup game at Catterick and I travelled back down to London because I was in the 12 to play Manchester United on Saturday. I was sharing a room with John Barnwell and I was really embarrassed when I woke up in the morning because my bed was soaked through with sweat. I went to the ground and George Swindin said he wasn't going to play me because I had not been well. I said, "Do you know what? I don't feel too clever now." I watched the game and went on to Bath because I had 48 hours' leave. By Monday, I was in hospital with pneumonia and what turned out to be tuberculosis of the right lung. People were dying from it back then, so I guess I was very lucky.'

By the time Skirton was declared fit enough to attempt to resume his football career, having been discharged from the army, 18 months had gone by and Bertie Mee was preparing for his first season at Arsenal. Mee welcomed Skirton to Highbury two weeks before the rest of the squad reported for pre-season training. 'I owe the fellow such a lot,' says Skirton. 'It was a relief to go back to football, but I was a long way from being fit enough to play.'

Mee worked with Skirton twice every day, setting up a gruelling circuit of drills, sprints and exercises around the Highbury pitch. 'Bertie used to chase me round it, encouraging me, bullying me. It was very traumatic and I was physically sick every morning and afternoon. The club gave you a luncheon voucher and most people would go to the Wimpy at Finsbury Park, but I couldn't face it. I used to sit in the local park dreading going back. I just remember looking at the bloody stadium clock and wishing those sessions were over. But Bertie was there with me the whole time. I was ready to take part in pre-season training and was picked for the first game against Burnley.'

By November of 1960, Highbury had a new hero following the controversial signing of former Newcastle inside-forward George Eastham, a man who had dared to challenge the feudal system that existed in English football. Under the 'retain and transfer' rules, clubs held all the power and players were no better than slaves. By the time 1959–60 rolled around, Eastham wanted out of St James' Park. He was dissatisfied with the club house in which he was stationed, upset at Newcastle's attempts to prevent him touring with the England Under-23s and uncomfortable with the part-time job organised for him to supplement his wages. But because Newcastle didn't want to sell him, he was going nowhere. Never mind that his contract had expired. The choice was a stark one: play for Newcastle or play nowhere. Eastham chose the latter, moving to Surrey to work as a cork salesman for Ernie Clay (who would later become chairman of Fulham). His employment was more than just a gesture. Without Newcastle paying his wages, he needed to feed his family.

It appeared as though Eastham's career had reached a roadblock. George Swindin, however, decided that Arsenal could provide an alternative route and offered to buy him. Newcastle's price was £25,000 plus two players, at which point Swindin indicated that striker David Herd might be available. In the end, a straight fee of £47,500 was agreed. Yet, for Eastham, the matter was far from closed. With the backing of the Professional Footballers' Association, he took Newcastle to court for having made him a football outlaw. The case took until 1963 to be heard, at which time Mr Justice Wilberforce made a historic ruling in Eastham's favour, stating that Newcastle's failure to release him at the end of his contract was 'restraint of trade'.

This pivotal moment in English football lay in the future, though. Of more immediate import for Arsenal at the end of 1960 was that they had acquired an exciting new signing to parade in front of their expectant fans. Optimism soared when he scored two goals on his first-team debut in December, a 5–1 win against Bolton, although by that time the Gunners had settled into mid-table anonymity.

Three significant figures departed the club in the early months of 1961. Tommy Docherty went to coach Chelsea under former Highbury hero Ted Drake, coach Ron Greenwood left to become manager of West Ham, and Sir Bracewell Smith was succeeded as chairman by Denis Hill-Wood, who became the second of three family members to hold the position, following his father, Samuel, and preceding his own son, Peter.

The completion of the season saw David Herd, top scorer with 30 goals, leave for Manchester United. Herd had not been amused by the club's attempt to offload him as part of the Eastham deal, especially as he'd previously been mentioned in the same context when the Gunners expressed interest in Denis Law. It was a move that did nothing to improve the mood of the increasingly disgruntled Highbury faithful. It was bad enough, after all, having to suffer the arch-enemy, Tottenham, carrying off both the League title and the FA Cup without the club selling a player who had become a favourite through his effort, enthusiasm and goals.

Away from Highbury, the summer saw an event that was to change the face of the game even before the resolution of the Eastham case: the abolition of the maximum wage. The players' latest battle for improved status had provided a backdrop to the season's action. It was nothing new, however. The struggle had been ongoing since the war, although for many years it attracted little attention from a British public far more interested in its own entertainment than the players' wages. During the 1950s, by which time the immediate post-war boom in attendance had levelled out and clubs were weighing up mounting costs against falling gates, the players made slow, halting strides. Five times they earned an increase in their maximum weekly wage, which stuttered from £10 to the £20 they were awarded in 1958–59 (£17 during the summer off-season). But now it was time for the players to win more than just another couple of pounds. The decision of leading international players like Jimmy Greaves, Gerry Hitchens, Joe Baker and Denis Law to accept greater rewards in Italy persuaded football's authorities to accede to the players' wishes for no wage limit.

While the Fulham chairman, comedian Tommy Trinder, was awarding England captain Johnny Haynes an astronomical £100 per week, the members of Arsenal's first-team squad were offered £30, plus £10 for first-team appearances, £4 per win and £1 for every thousand on the gate between 35,000 and 45,000. Eastham and Mel Charles initially refused the offer, but both duly signed on the dotted line. Later in the decade, the Arsenal board would change their bonus system, removing the clause relating to attendance and allowing players who had been with the club for longer to reap greater benefits. As manager, Bertie Mee would discover that it was a policy fraught with problems.

The new season, 1961–62, began with the annual hope for an Arsenal improvement. They went up precisely one place, from eleventh to tenth, and progressed one further round in the FA Cup, losing at Manchester United in the fourth. It was hardly what had been expected after Swindin had spent £40,000 on Hibernian winger Johnny MacLeod and £34,500 on tough-tackling Wolverhampton wing-half Eddie Clamp. Neither proved an inspired signing. MacLeod would never add to his four Scotland caps, while Clamp was gone early the following season.

One can only assume that Clamp is the subject of a story that Fred Street recounts. 'Bertie told me once that he was watching from the directors' box and a player did an almighty awful over-the-top tackle. The chairman apparently bent over to Bertie and said, "He does not play for the Arsenal again." And they sold him that week. That wouldn't happen today. They would turn a blind eye.' Street's story echoes that of Clamp himself, who, playing only his fourth game in his second season at Arsenal, made an ugly challenge on Aston Villa's Charlie Aitken. He was immediately dropped and sold to Stoke.

Arsenal's new signings seemed only to make them even more disjointed. They missed Herd's goalscoring, and speculation grew throughout the season that the summer would see a managerial change. The plain-speaking Swindin decided not to wait until then, tendering his resignation in March.

For the first time since the appointment of Herbert Chapman, Arsenal gave the manager's position to someone with no previous connection to the club, unless you count the fact that Billy Wright had grown up as a Gunners fan. The former England captain was a popular choice to guide the club's fortunes, his reputation more than making up for his lack of managerial experience. A total of one hundred and five England caps, including ninety as captain, three League Championships as captain of Wolves, an FA Cup triumph and a Footballer of the Year award were reason enough for Arsenal fans to expect great things.

Wright was a national institution. When he married Joy Beverley, of the chart-topping Beverley Sisters, thousands went to Poole in Dorset to witness that era's equivalent of David Beckham marrying a Spice Girl. Since retiring as a player in 1959, Wright had turned down offers of club management and focused on his position in charge of the England Under-23 and youth teams. But the opportunity to run the club of his boyhood dreams diverted him from a course that many felt was destined to take him into the England manager's seat.

While watching the comings and goings with interest, Bertie Mee contented himself with turning Arsenal's treatment room into the most efficient in the country. With the use of Highbury's high-tech facilities, the equal of any health service hospital, few doubt that he did just that. In 1998, Mee explained himself in *Arsenal in the Blood*:

> It really didn't make much difference to me who was manager, I just got on with my job. I was respected and I think they found me helpful in as much that, unlike the prima donnas of today whom I read and hear say, 'I'll declare myself fit on Saturday,' there was no question of that with me. I said, 'I will tell you when you are fit.' The managers appreciated that and the players were kept under close control from that point of view, plus the fact is you work harder when you are injured than when you're fit, which is not commonplace in football. There was no question of coming in for treatment in the morning and then 'off' in the afternoon. They came back in the afternoon and, if I thought it appropriate, they came back in the evening.

David Court, a young utility player who would be given an opportunity in the first team under Wright, remembers, 'Bertie was very much a new broom. He was very organised and ran a tight ship. It was a very businesslike atmosphere. He was a nice man, but when he was working, he was working. It had maybe been a fairly easy-going set-up until then, but he transformed it into a professional outfit.

'Bertie believed his job was to get players fit as quickly as possible and as safely as possible. He didn't make it a particularly comfortable experience. He looked after the actual injury with great professional ability and for the rest of the time players probably had to work harder than they would have in training. He used to exercise other parts of the body far more to ensure levels of fitness didn't drop. Some players who thought they might go to the physio for a couple of days' break soon got different ideas, although he would never do anything that would jeopardise your recovery from the injury.'

Midfielder Jon Sammels, who arrived at the club from Suffolk as an apprentice and made his debut in Wright's first season, says, 'He was the best physio in the country. He had a lot of experience in other fields and you believed what he said. If he said you had to run up the stands as part of your treatment, you trusted that it was the right thing to do. If you were fit enough to get your basic strength back again, he would make you piggyback guys up the East Stand. And if there were two of you injured, he would set one of you off on the track at the bottom of the North Bank and you'd have to run all the way round the pitch. Your partner would be seeing how many times he could run up and down the terrace. Then you'd change over and keep going until Bertie thought you'd done enough. He'd test your pulse and if it wasn't up enough, he'd send you round again.

'It meant you didn't look forward to being injured. I think Bertie knew that and he didn't want malingerers. His army background was evident. He had the respect of the players and it was strictly business in the treatment room. You went in there to get treated and to get back to work. It was not a place for sitting around having a chat. If you weren't needed, Bertie didn't want you in there.

'Bertie knew more about the players than we did ourselves. When you have treated people for broken legs and torn ligaments, when you have nursed them through lonely hours of rehabilitation, taught them to run and kick a ball again, you are bound to get to know them pretty well. Bertie knew us through our most defenceless moments.'

Court recalls that, despite Mee's officious ways, the younger players found him to have a humane side. 'Outside of his military exterior, he was an approachable person. He was somebody I felt I could talk to if I needed to. It would be a confidential conversation and any problems would be addressed without embarrassment – and there often are potentially embarrassing things when you are dealing with a group of young men.'

Bob Wilson, then Arsenal's goalkeeper-in-waiting, continues, 'When you are injured, you get worried and a bit jealous and a bit scared. Physios are so important because they know what the players are feeling. Bertie was like that, even though he was so military in his approach.'

Striker John Radford, another who would force his way into Wright's first-team set-up, remembers Mee being an approachable character in the treatment room. 'Bertie worked with another physio, Bert Owen, and strangely enough, even though Bertie was the senior man, us kids all feared Bert Owen more because he seemed so strict with the youngsters. He was not as friendly as Bertie. I had a few problems with my back when I was younger and I always found it easier to go to Bertie and talk about it because he seemed so knowledgeable. You always felt that Bert Owen thought you were faking it. As time went on, we found out how strict Bertie could be.'

Mee's approach reflected the needs of the increasingly professional era of football that followed the abolition of the maximum wage and the advent of regular television coverage. And he was as excited as anyone at Highbury about the prospect of Arsenal embracing the new age by throwing off the shackles of the past under their new manager. The smouldering anticipation was stoked further by Wright's first move into the transfer market. Joe Baker was signed from Torino for £70,000, having followed the example of fellow Italian exiles Jimmy Greaves and Denis Law by returning to the new restriction-free salary structure of English football. Before going to Italy from Edinburgh club Hibernian, Baker – a Scot in all but his birthplace of Liverpool – had become the first player to be capped for England while playing outside the country. He had become a 'victim' of regulations of the time that forced you to play for the land in which you were born. Wright then paid Dundee £62,500, a world record for a centre-half, to acquire Ian Ure, a genuine Scot playing for Scotland. Blond, strong-jawed and known for his fiery temperament, Ure had helped his club win the Scottish League Championship and reach the semi-finals of the European Cup.

Terry Neill, a 20 year old from Northern Ireland, was appointed Arsenal's youngest-ever captain after two seasons of fighting to establish himself in the number 4 shirt. Skirton and George Armstrong, a teenager from County Durham who had joined Arsenal a year earlier, filled the wing positions for the first game at Leyton Orient and, with George Eastham injured, Geoff Strong and John Barnwell supported Baker from the inside-forward positions. Baker scored a goal in each of the first two games, wins against Orient and Birmingham, but Arsenal won only one of their next eleven games.

Jack Kelsey's career in the Arsenal goal was coming to an end because of a back injury and his place initially went to Ian McKechnie, who had been signed as an outside-left by George Swindin but caught his eye as a goalkeeper in training sessions. Dogged by weight problems and injuries, McKechnie soon gave way to Irishman Jack McClelland.

The Arsenal team of the time were encapsulated in the space of four autumn games when they drew 4–4 at Tottenham and then, after a 1–1 draw against West Ham, beat Wolves 5–4 and drew 5–5 with Blackburn. Fifteen times during the 1962–63 season Arsenal scored three or more goals but conceded that many on thirteen occasions. New signing Ure struggled in a team in which he identified a lack of unity. Four decades later, he recalls, 'Arsenal were desperate for success and were hoping that guys like me would spark things off. They were trying to get a wee bit of stability. But it was a slow process. We were a load of individuals; we didn't work as a team. Unless your inside-forwards, or midfield players, are working back, your defence is going to give goals away. It was like that. It just wasn't a team and there was no proper leadership. George Eastham had magnificent skill and Joe Baker could score goals, but the defence and attack were like two different teams.'

Greater consistency in the second half of the season took Arsenal to seventh place, although their FA Cup run ended with a fifth-round defeat against Liverpool. Baker, with 31 goals in League and Cup, and Strong, with 21, had proved effective and their goals continued the following season. Playing as a twin strike force, they each scored 26 League goals, but the same old defensive frailties condemned Arsenal to finish in eighth place.

There was a new diversion for the Gunners in their first invitation to compete in the European Inter-Cities Fairs Cup, the competition later known as the UEFA Cup. As its name suggests, it was originally set up to foster improved relations between cities that staged trade fairs. Only one club was allowed per competing city – in fact, a representative London team had featured in the early tournaments – and Arsenal were given the task of representing the capital city by virtue of their finishing position the previous season.

The club's first venture into competitive European football proved an anti-climax, with no hint that this same competition would eventually be the club's route back to glory. Johnny MacLeod scored the club's first European goal against Danish part-timers Staevnet. Five up at half-time, Arsenal won 7–1, but, as if to prove their maddening inconsistency, lost the return leg 3–2 at Highbury, where only 10,000 fans showed up. The adventure ended in the second round when Belgium's RFC Liège held Arsenal 1–1 in London before winning 3–1 on their own ground. Given the low attendance at Highbury and the travelling costs, Arsenal's first taste of the supposedly lucrative world of European football had actually cost them money.

At least there were some encouraging signs of talent emerging from the Highbury system: amateur goalkeeper Bob Wilson made his Arsenal debut while still teaching at a local school; and others, including John Radford and defender Peter Simpson, got their first Arsenal game. The goalkeeping position, however, continued to be problematic. McClelland broke his collar bone at Leicester, while Wilson and McKechnie were considered too inexperienced for regular action. Wright's solution was to sign Jim Furnell from Liverpool, the club that once again dumped Arsenal out of the FA Cup in the fifth round.

In April, Wright made a signing that was to prove of long-term benefit to Bertie Mee when he paid £35,000 to West Bromwich for Don Howe, an accomplished full-back who had played alongside his new manager in the England team. His skills might have been diminishing, but Wright foresaw him bringing much-needed fire and fight to the dressing-room.

Arsenal kicked off the 1964–65 season amid a buzz of excitement at Liverpool, a city basking in the feel-good atmosphere created by The Beatles' conquest of America. Added to this was the fact that the home team were kicking off as League champions and that Anfield was the first ground to play host to *Match of the Day* cameras. It was hard not to view Arsenal as uninvited guests at a civic party when, later that evening, Kenneth Wolstenholme introduced the BBC's new football highlights show. From a Gunners point of view, the action put before the BBC2 viewers could not have offered the nation a better snapshot of their predicament. Wearing their all-white change strip, they went two goals down, pulled back to 2–2 and then threw away a point by conceding a last-minute winner. Howe was given a torrid time on his debut by Liverpool winger Peter Thompson, while Geoff Strong, who scored one of the goals, clearly impressed Bill Shankly. By November, the Liverpool manager had signed the Arsenal forward, who later said, 'I could not see any future at Highbury in terms of success. Everything at the club was marvellous in so many ways, but it was too good really. It lacked the spark that was necessary to win trophies. I had just a few weeks at the club with Frank McLintock and I could see that maybe he was bringing the drive that was needed.'

McLintock, born in Glasgow in 1939, was signed for an £80,000 fee in October after playing on the losing Leicester side in two FA Cup finals. He felt that a move to Highbury would bring him the winner's medal that had eluded him, but was shocked by what he found. He recalls, 'Billy Wright told me on the phone he was going to get Gordon Banks and Ray Wilson at the club and I thought, "Bloody hell, that will be terrific."' As history relates, neither signing materialised. 'The team wasn't properly balanced,' McLintock continues. 'It was a mishmash.'

Without Strong, there was little support for Baker, although Radford scored seven times when he was given a run of thirteen First Division games. Arsenal finished two places below halfway in the League and worse befell them in the FA Cup, beaten 2–1 at Third Division Peterborough.

Of the younger players, David Court established himself as a useful all-rounder and Jon Sammels played almost half of Arsenal's League games. Meanwhile, with Radford leading the attack, Arsenal reached the FA Youth Cup final, beating Everton 1–0 at home before losing the away leg 3–1. The next season, with Irish full-backs Pat Rice and Sammy Nelson in the team, Arsenal would win the competition, beating Sunderland 5–3 on aggregate. Wright's legacy to Bertie Mee – apart from a dressing-room wracked with problems – would be those young players – Simpson and Sammels, Radford and Rice – who were to be an integral part of the club's future success.

For the present, however, Wright was confronted by a problem that, he later admitted, he was too inexperienced to solve: how to get the more established players pulling in the same direction. 'I began to realise that I had some senior players who did not want to play for Arsenal. They wanted to do well for themselves, but they weren't Arsenal through and through.'

Ian Ure argues, 'I don't think Billy was a very good manager. What the club needed was discipline and we didn't get that. Players were in cliques. The star players were never criticised, even when they had bad games. Billy didn't get the best out of players. He was in awe of the stars, but they weren't pulling as part of a team.'

Even the younger players could see the trouble Wright was being given by his own stars. Radford recalls, 'The senior players took the mickey out of Billy, who was a nice bloke. I got the impression that guys like Joe Baker and George Eastham had little respect for him. You could tell by the way they talked during training and didn't get on with what they were supposed to do. Billy didn't have the strength to deal with them.'

David Court puts Wright's problems down to him being a newcomer to management. 'It was his first managerial appointment and one could argue he was not ready for that type of job. He was happier working with younger players purely and simply because a lot of the older players were people he played with or against and it is not easy to manage in that situation if you don't have the experience. Young players like me got our opportunities because he felt comfortable with us.'

Many observers expected Wright to use the Peterborough result as an excuse to shake up the team, but he declined the opportunity, saying, 'I selected the team. I must take the flak. The side will be unchanged for next Saturday's League match.' Which Arsenal promptly lost.

With his team doing him no favours, Wright felt the pressure increasing, much of it exerted by the ghosts of the past. In his official biography, *A Hero for all Seasons*, Wright told Norman Giller, 'I got to hate the bust of Herbert Chapman in the marble halls. It was always there as a reminder of the glory years and underlined that we were winning nothing at all.'

Wright confessed to being physically sick before games and revealed that 'several times, I quietly cried my eyes out in sheer frustration'. More serious was his later confession that 'I discovered how comforting a drink or three could be.' Post-game boozing with reporters gradually developed into a dependence on alcohol that continued well beyond his time at Highbury. The problem, which he eventually fought to overcome, was not acknowledged for some years, although Peter Storey claims to have noticed that 'he was drunk some of the time'.

Storey, a tough-tackling full-back who was establishing himself in the first team, also recalls a pre-season trip to the Caribbean that highlighted the problems confronting Wright. 'We never did a day's training. We had a riot in Jamaica. Joe Baker head-butted one of the

Jamaican players and the game got abandoned and we all came off. In another game, Joe slung his boots at Billy and said, "You do better." There was terrible friction; a terrible rift. On one side of the changing-room were the big signings and on the other were the young guys like me. We tended to get the blame for everything. There were arguments during training and games. Frank was always arguing with [Billy] and it was a terrible atmosphere. Billy was a nice bloke, but the pressure was too much. It all went wrong and he started hitting the bottle a bit.'

As the 1965–66 season approached, it was increasingly obvious that changes were needed; more than just abandoning their traditional white-sleeved shirts for an all-red version. McLintock, who was becoming so frustrated at the apparent lack of ambition at Highbury that he made an unsuccessful transfer request, admits to instigating the change of kit. 'Dopey,' he says. 'It wasn't new shirts we needed. It was new players.'

There was much anticipation in the country about the World Cup that would be staged in England the following summer. Catching the wave of excitement, Arsenal lost only twice in their first twelve games and even beat champions Manchester United 4–2 at Highbury, but just when it looked like McLintock had perhaps been right about those new shirts, they lost their mystical powers and the team won only six more League games all season.

Bob Wilson's Highbury career had another false start when he forced his way into the team and dislocated his shoulder, his place reverting back to Furnell. Meanwhile, Don Howe's playing days came to an end with an injury that, while causing an initial concern for physio Bertie Mee, would ultimately benefit him as manager. Howe broke his leg in a collision with Blackpool goalkeeper Tony Waiters. Sammels recalled that 'his bone was sticking through his sock'.

The incident leads Howe to recall how advanced Arsenal's treatment of injuries had become under Mee. 'Arsenal were at the forefront in modern techniques. I broke my left leg – a compound fracture of the tibia. The normal procedure in those days was to stick the leg in plaster for ten weeks and, if it was still not healing, stick on some more plaster. Bertie and Dr Alan Bass gave me the latest thing that had come from skiers. More people were going skiing on holiday and falling down slopes and in Switzerland, instead of using plaster, they were putting a metal plate into the bone. That was real modern technology back then.'

Back on the field, Sammels was established alongside McLintock in the centre of the Arsenal midfield. Wright had moved Eastham out to the wing, believing his slight physique and skill on the ball were becoming a risk in the increasingly physical world of First Division midfield play. Scoring goals had never been Arsenal's problem in the '60s, but now even they were slowing down. Baker struck 13 times before being sold to Nottingham Forest for £70,000 in February, but was the only Arsenal player to reach double figures. Faltering League form led Wright to call a crisis meeting with the players after a defeat to Blackburn. A third-round FA Cup tie against the same team was next on the fixture list and Wright emerged to tell the press, 'The Cup is all we've got left. We must knock Blackburn out. We have let the title slip away, so the match at Blackburn means everything to us. And we are going to win it. I have a team of talented players who thoroughly deserve success this season.' Those deserving and talented players went out and lost 3–0.

If the writing had not been on the wall already, it stood out in large capital letters after the events of Thursday, 5 May, the day of Arsenal's final League game. The visitors to Highbury were Don Revie's Leeds United, on their way to finishing as runners-up in the First Division for the second time in successive seasons. Arsenal had scheduled the game for the same night that Liverpool were playing Borussia Dortmund in the televised final of the European Cup Winners' Cup. When given a choice of football offerings, and with the rain pouring down outside, the Arsenal fans voted with their TV sets. Only 4,544, Highbury's smallest crowd, turned up. 'I was sat in the paddock watching because I was injured,' says Alan Skirton. 'At one point a guy with a trumpet started playing "The Last Post".'

The embarrassment of the night – which ended in a 3–0 defeat that condemned Arsenal to 14th place, their lowest First Division finish since 1930 – meant that Billy Wright's time was up. The club, however, managed to make things unnecessarily messy. The first inkling he had of what was afoot came while he was taking a holiday before returning to work on the BBC's World Cup coverage. He received a call from assistant manager Les Shannon, who informed him that he, Shannon, had been fired. It was a strange move to make while the manager was away and Wright accepted that the same fate must be awaiting him on his return. Sure enough, he got home to find a message that the club chairman, Denis Hill-Wood, wanted to see him. The inevitable followed, although the first reports from the club suggested that Wright had resigned. He soon put that straight, saying, 'I have never walked out on anything in my life. I have been sacked.'

Hill-Wood explained that 'Billy had to go because of the intolerable pressure from outside,' and expanded on that theme some years later. 'You have a bad run and the players start thinking they are not getting the best coaching or the best advice. The supporters start writing hostile letters. When things were going badly, I would easily get 200–300 letters a week. They start demonstrations outside the ground: so-and-so must go. The pressures that build up on a manager are quite intolerable.'

Looking back, Wright said, 'It was heartbreaking for me. Maybe I was too nice, but that is the way I am. But I wanted so much to make Arsenal great again and I did feel that with the young players we were moving along the right lines.'

Sammels supports that comment, saying, 'I feel a bit sorry for Billy because he didn't get a lot of thanks for what his work led to in the future. Many of the Double squad were home-grown lads who Billy helped bring through. He left out Joe Baker and George Eastham, who were hero-worshipped by the fans, and brought in two youngsters, me and John Radford, to replace them. It was a brave decision.'

Don Howe also speaks up for his former teammate. 'I knew Billy well from my England days and he really felt the pressure at Arsenal. The press were building it up and more was expected of Billy than some other managers because he had been a great England captain. People didn't give Billy the amount of time he deserved. The club were bringing in new players and some of the players that Billy brought in went on to be successful in the Bertie Mee era. That's the way it often goes – one manager brings in new players and ideas, and another manager gets the benefit of what he has done.'

David Court, now a youth-team coach at Arsenal, goes even further in his acknowledgement of the club's debt to Wright – and his predecessor, George Swindin. 'I believe that in many ways the period from 1959 – when they really upgraded the youth set-up and established a kind of 'centre of excellence' environment – until 1969 could be argued to be the most successful ten years in Arsenal's history. We went on to win the Double with three-quarters of the team having come through the system. The club's power over the last thirty or forty years is in no small manner due to that ten-year period of building.

'You can criticise certain elements of the situation at the club before Bertie Mee became manager – and when Bertie took over he moved the club on apace. But there were not that many personnel changes. Bertie took that raw talent, gave it its chance and galvanised it into a successful team.'

Such success would bear out Wright's confidence in the set-up he was leaving, although it is difficult to imagine the talent at the club flourishing under his discredited leadership and without the kind of top-level coaching that Bertie Mee introduced. As Terry Neill said, 'We all liked Billy, but you cannot help taking advantage. Footballers are tough competitors by nature. They are trained to walk over people. If he lets them, they'll make a doormat of the manager as well as opponents.'

6

IN THE HOT SEAT

A good manager is best when people barely know that he exists.

— LaoTzu, sixth-century BC Chinese philosopher

All managers are losers. They are the most expendable piece of furniture on the face of the earth.

— Ted Williams, Boston Red Sox outfielder

ARSENAL HAD LEARNED THEIR LESSON FROM THE APPOINTMENT, and subsequent failure, of Billy Wright as manager. The club would acknowledge as much a few years later in the first-ever *Arsenal Football Book*, published in 1969, in which it was admitted that they had 'strayed from the path which had led them to so many triumphs in the past'. The decision to place the club's fortunes in the hands of Wright, a man with no attachment to Highbury other than the emotional ties of his boyhood, was now viewed as the mistaken act of bringing in an outsider to solve a family crisis. No matter that the two previous managerial appointments, Jack Crayston and George Swindin, both former Arsenal players, had also failed to deliver the desired results. Wright's failure meant that it was time to look within once more. And, just as the club had done when they'd appointed Tom Whittaker, they ventured down to the treatment room to find their man.

On 20 June, a couple of weeks before the World Cup kicked off and ten days after Wright's departure, Bertie Mee was named as Arsenal's new manager, with the proviso that it was initially for an undetermined trial period. The club had approached him upon his return from a holiday in Jersey and he'd had to wait until Doris returned from a driving lesson to give her the news. After taking the weekend to consider the offer, he had accepted.

The appointment was greeted with little fanfare, especially with many of the leading London football writers engaged on pre-World Cup duties. These days a press conference to announce an Arsenal manager would be covered live on Sky Sports, with fans following proceedings online or by text messages and no one able to move for sponsor boards. Mee's introduction to the media involved him sitting round a table with four journalists. Only two national newspapers were represented.

John Goodbody, now of *The Times* but then with the *North London Press*, was one of those in attendance. 'It was the summer and in those days football did not get much attention at that time of year. Nevertheless, the fact that there were only four of us is indicative of the lack of awareness of Bertie Mee. That would be unthinkable now. One of my clear memories of the press conference was Bertie warning that he was not going to do post-match press conferences because he wanted to consider the ramifications of the game before speaking. I remember Norman Giller of the *Daily Express* saying, "Tuesday morning's papers will make interesting reading then."'

Even those with memories long enough to remember the achievements of former club trainer Whittaker were surprised at a move that seemed to belong to a bygone age. Surely, in the days of tracksuit managers and increasing tactical dependency, the club could not strike lucky again. Up at Liverpool, where the League Championship trophy had recently arrived, Bill Shankly scoffed, 'They've appointed the medicine man.' (Ironically, Shankly would eventually be succeeded by his trainer, Bob Paisley, and that particular medicine man would eclipse even Shanks's triumphs. Paisley, unlike Mee, had at least been a top-flight player.)

Most football fans around the country, and even some in the vicinity of Highbury, had never heard of Bertie Mee, the man being entrusted with one of the most prestigious jobs in the game. It was different, however, in football's inner circles. Shankly may have questioned the appointment, but he certainly knew of Mee's reputation in his specialist field. Don Howe recalls, 'Bertie was looked upon then as the top physio in the country. He had new ideas and was very knowledgeable. In the physiotherapy room, the attention the injured player was getting was really up to date, plus he was very good at getting injured players back to training and getting them fit. He had brought all his organisational skills from the health service to Highbury and I think that is what got him the job of manager. The directors looked at Bertie and said, "At least we are going to get an organised club."'

Mee made no secret of his surprise that such an opportunity should befall a man with limited experience of playing professional football and whose only managerial experience was organising military exhibition games during the war. Featured in an edition of the BBC documentary series *Man Alive*, aired in March 1969, he looked back at his appointment. 'I was very flattered; nevertheless it did come as a surprise to me. Because of my lack of background in terms of a playing career, and a club such as this – one of the greatest in the country – I was surprised they should offer this post to me. I thought there were quite a lot of people in the country who were definitely better qualified to do the job than I was.'

Long-time Arsenal director Ken Friar, who was then assistant secretary under Bob Wall, recollects the discussions that led to Mee's appointment. 'Clearly, we had come to know Bertie very well as club physiotherapist. We felt his man-management skills would be sufficient, along with the overall organisation and structure at the club, to bring us success.'

Friar acknowledges the club's change of direction following the previous hiring of an outsider, Billy Wright. 'Bertie knew all the people at the club, all the players. When making such decisions, what one is trying to do is reduce the risk. By getting someone you know, you don't have such a dramatic change.'

According to Wall, the Arsenal board felt that they had a man whose shortcomings in the strict football sense would be outweighed by his ability to introduce discipline and direction into an often chaotic environment – just what was needed to solve the crisis of confidence and cliques that existed in the dressing-room. 'At the rehabilitation unit, he must have grown accustomed to controlling people,' Wall commented in *Arsenal from the Heart*, his phraseology being a clear indication of the nature of leader that the club desired. And while Friar describes Mee's elevation as being, to a certain extent, a safety measure, Wall recognised the risk that was being taken. 'He was taking on a task entirely new in his experience and the board were anxious that he should be free to return to his original work without losing face should he not enjoy the challenge of management. Or if they felt he wasn't going to fulfil their requirements as manager.'

In a subsequent interview, Mee confessed, 'I had not planned to become a football club manager. I was very happy in the career of my special interest, and I was enjoying a great deal of job satisfaction from it. But I was used to positions of responsibility. I had run organisations of various types. So my response was that if that's what the board would like, then I would give it a go.

'The first thing I realised was that I knew nothing about the job even though I had practically been the right-hand man to George Swindin and Billy Wright. I took my time before accepting it because I didn't want to let down a club with great traditions.'

In the book *Arsenal in the Blood*, Mee looked back three decades to offer further insight into his motivation for taking a position that had never previously occupied a place on his intended career path:

> Mediocrity was being perpetuated. That was painfully obvious to me, and that's why I went into management because I thought I could change it. The standard needed raising 30 to 40 per cent. I had no ambitions in that direction when I first went to Arsenal but, having been with George Swindin for two years and with Billy Wright for four, I knew in my heart of hearts that I had been involved in management in the wider sense. I was a teacher for five years, teaching physiotherapy. Obviously, I had ideas of how I would do things.

The players received word about their new manager via letters from the club or from reading the newspapers. Had the word 'gobsmacked' been around in 1966, it would have applied to most of them. Bob Wilson recalls, 'We did laugh at the time. We got a letter from the board saying that Mr Wright had relinquished his position – no mention of him being sacked – and that Bertie was the new manager. They said, "We hope you will give Bertie the cooperation he deserves." Bertie was a great organiser and we thought he'd just been put in charge for a short while to get affairs in order until someone else took over.'

The same sense of disbelief prevailed among the journalists who covered Arsenal. Many proffered the theory that Mee was keeping the seat warm throughout the summer for Alf Ramsey, forcing chairman Denis Hill-Wood to come out and deny such a far-fetched notion in the days immediately following England's World Cup success.

John Radford confirms that Mee himself had never suggested that the position would interest him. 'The treatment room is often the place where you pick up on vibes about what is going on at a club. But Bertie never pushed for the job and we could never have imagined him being considered.'

Alan Skirton was one of the players who immediately saw the sense of the appointment. 'I had spent more time with Bertie than many of them. I'd had a complete fortnight with him when I was recovering from my illness. I knew the general feeling was that he was such a disciplinarian that you would never go out there and cheat him. He knew when you were giving 100 per cent. So it wasn't a surprise to me that he was made manager.'

If Arsenal fans were awaiting extravagant promises and a gung-ho rallying cry from their new manager, they were to be disappointed. That kind of stuff, Bertie Mee believed, was better left to men like Bill Shankly. Mee's first statement in his new position was full of the calm realism that was to become the mark of his public statements. 'I am as interested as everybody else to see how this works out. All I can promise is I shall do my very best for a great club. The club came to me and asked if I would take over in an acting capacity. I consider it a great honour and a great challenge. We have excellent players here, but I appreciate that it is desirable to strengthen the team in some positions.'

If Bertie Mee was, as Frank McLintock is fond of saying, 'a pompous little man, like Captain Mainwaring in *Dad's Army*', then there is no doubt that his predecessor was the soft-touch Sergeant Wilson. While Mainwaring would bark at the Walmington-on-Sea volunteers to 'quick march', Wilson would ask if they would 'mind awfully stepping this way'. That sums up perfectly the different approach of the two Arsenal managers. Mee was well aware of the problems that had been bequeathed to him by the leniency of Wright, even if he was too much of an officer and a gentleman to make critical comments. 'I was very sorry Billy Wright had to go,' he said instead. 'We were good friends and there was never any friction between us. All I hope is that I can have the luck that seemed to evade him.'

Mee did, however, hint that a stricter regime was on its way. 'I can be a tough man when necessary; firm but fair. I want to have a state of enlightened, rather than authoritarian, discipline at Arsenal.'

With Bertie Mee settling into the manager's seat, it is worth looking briefly at the profession he had entered, especially as the most illustrious of his Highbury predecessors had done so much to shape it.

It was a role that effectively did not exist in the early days of the Football League – the late nineteenth and early twentieth centuries – when clubs were run by professional businessmen who formed a board of directors, responsible for finance, administration and selection of players, who were their social inferiors. It was usually down to the club secretary, a paid employee, to act as liaison between the board and players.

In the years approaching the First World War, as the game grew more popular, the task of running the club became too big for the directors, so more responsibility for the team and players passed to the secretary. Thus the role of secretary–manager was born, which also gave the directors a convenient scapegoat when things went wrong on the field. In fact, it was only when blame needed to be apportioned that the secretary–manager was projected as a public figure, normally to announce his 'resignation'. Arsenal had appointed their first secretary–manager late in the nineteenth century and went through three in quick succession as lack of success on the field and poor crowds led to the club's move from Woolwich to Highbury.

As the working classes, who had come to comprise the majority of the game's fan base, began to care more passionately about their team, they increasingly demanded a figure to be their club's focal point. This development helped to drag the secretary–manager out of the directors' shadows. Those in power at the clubs, recognising the risk that their companies or products could be tarnished by their association with an unsuccessful club, were happy to allow this shift of public focus.

When football resumed after 1918, a new breed of secretary–manager began to emerge: men who felt that if they were to be judged by the team's results, then perhaps they should attempt to influence events on the field. Suddenly, hitherto alien concepts like coaching, training and tactics entered the game. One of the men at the forefront of this development was Herbert Chapman, the man whose bronze bust Bertie Mee would end up walking past in Highbury's marble hall on his way to work – and whose overbearing spiritual presence so unsettled Billy Wright.

Chapman is correctly acknowledged as one of football's visionaries. In 1934, he commented, 'Football today is too big a job to be a director's hobby. In my opinion, the club manager ought to pick the team.' Such statements were radical for a time when the secretary–manager's increased responsibility still didn't usually extend to choosing which players could be entrusted with the fate of his own employment. He, of course, had ensured that he was given such power when he arrived at Highbury.

Chapman would have been content to have become a mining engineer at the conclusion of his modest career as a player had he not been offered the position of player–manager of Southern League club Northampton. He moved up in the football world by becoming manager of Leeds City in 1912, but saw the club fold shortly after the First World War amid the scandal of illegal payments to players. Huddersfield Town were quick to offer him a new position and were rewarded when he led them to an FA Cup win and successive First Division titles. It was after the second of those Championships that Arsenal approached Chapman to replace the sacked Leslie Knighton.

Arsenal, who hadn't won a major honour before Chapman's arrival, were to be winners or runners-up in the League or FA Cup in all but two of his eight years at Highbury. And Chapman used Arsenal's success on the field to establish the club's global reputation, which Bertie Mee would protect so vigorously in years to come. Chapman drove the club to create one of the country's finest stadiums, with its art deco stands and giant terracing; he pioneered the use of floodlights; and even forced the name of Gillespie Road station to be changed to that of the club outside whose gates its entrance was situated.

Chapman was the type who would have endorsed Arsène Wenger's signing of a Japanese player, Junichi Inamoto, to coincide with the launch of Arsenal's Asian Internet site and applauded the sound commercial thinking behind the naming of Emirates Stadium.

Chapman was one of the first managers to take tactics seriously, developing the custom of pre-game team talks. He spurred players to study the game, to discuss it with teammates, to share ideas in meetings and to think about their own contribution to the collective effort. Tactically, his most notable role was as one of the first managers to introduce the stopper centre-half, signalling the beginning of the 'Boring Arsenal' label that would persist on and off right through to, and beyond, the Mee era. The move was a practical solution to the problem posed by the new offside law, which stated that only two, not three, defenders had to be between the attacker and the goal for him to remain onside. Recognising the advantage that the forwards now had against the traditional formation of two defensive full-backs and three midfield-dwelling half-backs, Chapman pulled back the centre-half to become a third defender.

Chapman emphasised the importance of defensive solidity with comments that Bertie Mee and his team would echo almost 40 years later. 'Before you go on the field for any League match, you have been given a point for doing nothing. If you stop the other side scoring, you will finish with that point.' Chapman did stop short, publicly at least, of espousing a win-at-all-costs brand of football. 'Can it be believed,' he asked, 'that the Arsenal, in order to produce results, would cultivate a style that did not appeal to the crowd?'

What Chapman and Mee knew, of course, was that nothing was as entertaining for a fan as seeing his team win, even if the score was 1–0. Asked by interviewer Jeremy James in the *Man Alive* documentary whether he felt football teams should view themselves as entertainers, Mee replied, 'Yes, I certainly do. I am very conscious of this and we should definitely provide as much entertainment for the public as we possibly can. What is difficult to decide is whether the public want entertainment, pure and simple, or whether they want a winning team irrespective. And the indications are that primarily they want a winning team. If they can have an entertaining team as well, that's fine, but primarily winning is the first requisite from the spectators' point of view.'

Having established himself as the leading authority figure at his clubs, Chapman ruled with a strict code of conduct. Like Mee, he was not afraid to administer discipline. One of the most celebrated stories illustrating his authoritarian nature followed Arsenal's 2–0 humiliation by Walsall in the 1933 FA Cup. Tommy Black, who kicked out at an opponent and gave away a penalty, was promptly sent home by Chapman and transferred to Plymouth. Alex James, the little Scot who controlled Arsenal's midfield, was the only man occasionally brave enough to stand up to the manager, enjoying the sport of goading him about training routines or tactics. But Chapman would not be swayed from his rigid path. 'I will never tolerate slackness. If it enters a team, there can be no success that is worthwhile. I cannot be bothered with any man unless he is prepared to give his whole mind to the job.' It could have been Bertie Mee speaking.

One can only speculate about what other achievements may have been listed against Herbert Chapman's name had the sudden onset of pneumonia not taken his life early in 1934. He had already done enough, though, to speed along the evolution of his profession and helped to shape the role that Bertie Mee inherited in the summer of 1966. Before Chapman, the secretary–manager had been a marginalised figure, bereft of real responsibility. Post-Chapman, the manager would become the most important single person at a club, in charge of tactics, contracts, player psychology, even the material for the team's kit. In fact, the burden of responsibility in Mee's era was arguably even heavier than in the modern age of round-the-clock media scrutiny.

Mee, who had hardly been groomed for the role, was learning on the job. Later, in an interview that appeared in the *London Soccer Annual 1970*, he would discuss the demands of his position:

> As everyone knows, there are many pitfalls in management and some kind of training in what I would call 'man management' is obviously desirable. There is intense competition in the game and the manager has to be an administrator, have knowledge of finance, contracts – the responsibilities of the club to the player and the player to his club; all of this, as well as producing the results on the field. The pressures are greater as football becomes big business rather than just a sport. You have to learn

to cope with every kind of situation yourself, and in addition teach others to cope as well.

Steve Burtenshaw, one of the coaches to work under Mee, points out, 'If you go back to the 1966–76 period when Bertie was manager, he would oversee the whole lot. It was a much more intense working week for the manager back then. Nowadays, you have more people to lighten the load.'

In the memorable summer of '66, while his players enjoyed their holidays and watched the World Cup on television, Mee got down to the business of preparing the club for a new era. His subsequent explanation of his thinking that summer demonstrated that, even though he was on trial, he was focusing on long-term success:

> I began by approaching the task in terms of management, from a purely management point of view. It was my belief that there was nothing radically wrong, but the club had to be more professional from all angles. We needed a general tightening up. The players were a good crowd, but I felt they could be more dedicated to the job, and certainly could care more about Arsenal. The danger was that mediocrity was being perpetuated.
>
> It would be easy to say that the team was the most important factor. But when you are starting from scratch – as I did – then that is not necessarily correct. One must look into the future and build a background organisation capable of backing up a successful team. Of course, during this period you must never neglect the team. But surely it is better to have a lopsided club for the first few years with the balance weighing heavily for the backroom organisation against the limited success of the team. There will never be long-term success for Arsenal, or any other club for that matter, if the coaching, scouting, administration is not of the highest order. I can safely say that in this department Arsenal are now second to none.

The initial task was to choose a first-team coach, a decision that Mee could not afford to get wrong given his own limited and specialised football experience. He settled on Fulham coach Dave Sexton, a former forward with several London clubs who had gone on to work under Tommy Docherty at Chelsea. 'I had got to know Bertie some years before,' Sexton explains. 'I was trying to get my coaching badge at Lilleshall on a course run by the FA. Bertie was one of the staff there, giving us talks about the physiotherapy and the medical side. My first impression was that he seemed a nice bloke, had an attractive personality and spoke very sensibly. I attended more courses and struck up a good friendship with him.'

Sexton had no hesitation in accepting Mee's job offer. 'Because I liked Bertie and because he was an intelligent man, I felt I couldn't go wrong. Plus, of course, Arsenal was a huge club. With Bertie's background, he gave me my head as a coach, which doesn't always happen in our business. He gave me the responsibility and I felt I could trust him to give me his support.'

Having recovered from the shock of Mee's appointment, the players would soon respond to Sexton's coaching. Defender Peter Simpson recalls, 'When Billy Wright was manager, there were no real tactics and the training was totally different, a bit of running and five-a-side. Dave Sexton was fantastic. He was one of those coaches who encouraged you so much.'

Bob Wilson's admiration remains untainted decades later. 'I went to his home in Brighton after he had left club management. He took me into the loft and he had loops and loops of films: passing off the outside of the foot, passing off the inside of the foot, body control. Every spare minute of every day he would put together these loops.'

Mee's first-season brief to Sexton was simply to get the club moving in the right direction while he himself went about creating the professional, organised atmosphere in which the club had the potential to thrive. 'As far as tactics and our playing style were concerned, we did it together,' says Sexton. 'If we were discussing anything, I could say what I thought and then he decided either to do things his way or take on board what I was saying. He gave me the chance to put in my two pennies' worth and I don't remember us ever falling out over anything. I felt he respected me and I certainly respected him.'

Sexton's journey to the Arsenal training ground at London Colney ended up forming an important part of the working relationship between the two men. 'All the time I was there, I was coming from

Brighton. I got the train to Victoria and then the Tube out to Cockfosters. Bertie used to pick me up at Cockfosters every morning and I used to look forward to it. It was an interesting routine. We could talk one-on-one without the distractions of the training ground. We got a lot done and became close.'

7

OPENING SHOTS

I must admit that during my first year as boss I sometimes wondered if I was the right man for the job and I quickly realised that instant success is impossible in football.

– Bertie Mee

BERTIE MEE'S COMMENT AT THE TIME OF HIS APPOINTMENT about needing new players was given instant pertinence when, three days later, he was informed of Manchester United's decision to put Denis Law on the transfer list. Since Arsenal's unsuccessful bid six years earlier, the flamboyant Scot had found his way across Manchester from Maine Road to Old Trafford by way of Torino. Now, he was stating his dissatisfaction at the new contract terms offered by United. Pressed about possible Arsenal interest, secretary Bob Wall gave the time-honoured phrase: 'We are always interested in any player put on the transfer list.' Law and United soon kissed and made up and Arsenal's 'interest' was never put to the test. In fact, it was to be two months into Mee's reign before he made his initial signing.

Before that, however, there were players to be discarded. Bob Wilson recalls, 'There was a big core of people at the club who you knew were more interested in the bookies or the snooker hall. Bertie got together a group of players who he knew were ambitious and who were trying to prove to each other that they could play.'

George Wright, who took over Mee's role as club trainer and physiotherapist, says, 'When Bertie succeeded Billy Wright, the administration of the playing side of the club was very slapdash. Bertie changed the staff and changed the players a lot. He knew who the troublemakers were and who was not fitting into the total team effort.'

Bob McNab, who arrived at the club in the early weeks of Mee's reign, adds, 'The dressing-room was in a bit of upheaval. A couple of the players Bertie was letting go were still around, which did not help the atmosphere. Players were looking over their shoulder and appeared a bit insecure. After a while, things started to improve, in large part due to the influence of Dave Sexton and Bertie's discipline, which set standards much higher.'

With Joe Baker having already departed, the other big name of the Billy Wright era appeared bound for pastures new as Mee's first season approached. George Eastham, who had two spells as Arsenal captain, had been dropped and transfer-listed during Wright's final year, only to win back his place on a wave of public outcry. Eastham had been unhappy at Wright's efforts to turn him into a winger and one of Mee's first acts as manager was to make him available for transfer once again. Stoke City manager Tony Waddington, who was prepared to place Eastham in the heart of his midfield, caught a late-afternoon train to London to agree a £30,000 fee for a man who, for the second time, had spent his summer as a non-playing member of England's World Cup squad.

On the same day, across London, George Graham was telling Chelsea that he wanted to leave Stamford Bridge. The Scotland Under-23 international had been the club's top scorer during the previous season with 17 goals, but, for now, was not considered an Arsenal target. Instead, reports centred on Mee's possible approach to Rotherham for winger Barry Lyons or to Swindon for outside-left Don Rogers. Taking a broader look at the club's playing staff, Mee had decided that fewer professionals would make for a more efficient operation, eliminating the need to pay third-team players who had little chance of making the grade. He announced plans to scrap the club's Metropolitan League team after the forthcoming season.

Arsenal opened their League programme at Sunderland, where

Mee's first selection included only six players who had featured in Wright's final game. The team sheet read: Furnell, Court, Storey, McLintock, Ure, Neill, Skirton, Baldwin, Radford, Sammels, Armstrong. Sub: McGill. The first goal of a new era came after five minutes when Alan Skirton scored from a Sammels free-kick. Jim Baxter, the former Rangers midfielder, equalised, but Skirton headed a second Arsenal goal and George Armstrong wrapped up a 3–1 victory. After the game, captain Terry Neill stressed the improved physical condition of the Arsenal players under Mee's guidance.

Arsenal were less impressive in beating West Ham 2–1 in their first home game, where a crowd of 40,533 represented an improvement of 10,000 on the previous season's Highbury opener. After two more games unbeaten, Mee stressed the importance of the next match, at Tottenham. 'It is extremely crucial,' he said. 'We can convince north London people we are worth following. I expect our players to win back the support they have lost to Spurs over the last few years.' It appeared that the stampede of returning fans would have to wait. Arsenal were outplayed and lost 3–1. Later in the season, Arsenal's followers would see their team lose at White Hart Lane and witness Spurs winning the FA Cup, their fifth major trophy since Arsenal last won anything.

It was finally time for Mee to make his first signing. The target was 26-year-old Nottingham Forest inside-forward Colin Addison, his team's leading scorer in three of the four previous seasons but who was now unsure of his place following the arrival of Joe Baker. Mee's offer of £45,000 was accepted, and he and Addison were pictured shaking hands. Perhaps it was a sign of things to come that both men wore worried looks, with only Addison's wife, Jean, appearing to enjoy the moment.

Mee recouped £30,000 of his outlay with the sale of Alan Skirton to Blackpool. After scoring the first two goals under Mee, Skirton had gone off injured in the next game. His transfer, he recalls, was the result of what he felt were unfulfilled promises made by Billy Wright the previous season after he scored twice in a 3–3 draw against Aston Villa. 'The crowd were baying for Billy's head at that time. After I scored two in the last ten minutes, Billy offered me a pay rise, which I am still waiting for. When the season finished, my contract arrived on the same day as the newspaper with headlines of Billy being sacked. Instead of a two-year contract with a two-year option and a £5 rise on the basic salary – which was what I had been promised – I was offered a one-year deal, one-year option and a £10 appearance fee. I realised it was not Billy Wright who did that contract. Bertie said he wanted me to stay and that he would sort out the basic wage. In fairness to Arsenal, I'd had nothing in writing. Billy Wright stitched me up. So I asked for a transfer. It was the worst thing I ever did. Words can't really express what I think about Bertie Mee. The man was great. I got on so well with him. He did it his way and it didn't surprise me that he was successful. Asking to leave Arsenal was the biggest mistake of my life.'

A quirk of the fixture list saw Addison making his Arsenal debut against Blackpool, who arrived at Highbury bottom of the First Division and without a single away point. Skirton, inevitably, proceeded to put them a goal up. Addison responded by setting up McLintock's equaliser with a piece of strong running, having had a goal disallowed and seen another shot cleared off the line.

Arsenal entered the League Cup for the first time in 1966–67, finally embracing the six-year-old competition after it was given the prestige of a Wembley final and its winners the offer of entry to the Fairs Cup. Mee, however, preceded Arsène Wenger's selection policy for the tournament by three decades when he named several fringe players for the second-round game against Gillingham. The Gunners needed a 70th-minute equaliser by Tommy Baldwin to snatch a replay.

Unable to win a regular place in the Arsenal attack, Baldwin was attracting interest from Huddersfield. Through a thick fog, the Yorkshire club watched him score another equaliser in the replay against Gillingham and declared themselves ready to accept him in part-exchange for left-back Bob McNab, an accomplished defender whose growing reputation had alerted several First Division teams. Meanwhile, another transfer race was lost when Blackburn agreed a fee of £40,000 to sign Manchester United winger John Connelly.

September drew towards its close with Gillingham finally overcome in the League Cup and negotiations beginning over the transfer of George Graham. The Scot had been so unhappy with his early season form that he'd asked Tommy Docherty to drop him. His relationship with his manager had been strained since an incident more than a year earlier when Docherty discovered that eight players, including Graham, had broken a midnight curfew before a vital game against

Burnley. The group had stayed out in Blackpool until four in the morning and the next day, Graham, skipper Terry Venables, John Hollins, Barry Bridges, Eddie McCreadie, Bert Murray, Marvin Hinton and Joe Fascione were put on a train back to London. A depleted Chelsea side lost 6–2, ending their hopes for the League Championship. 'It looked as though the team was going to break up,' says Graham. 'I had already worked with Dave Sexton and thought he was one of the best people I had ever worked for, so when Arsenal came in with an offer, I joined them.'

A deal was concluded quickly, valued at £75,000. A third of that amount was the price placed on Baldwin, who, rather than heading to Huddersfield, made a shorter trip across London. Docherty stirred things up by crowing, 'Baldwin has a bit of the Joe Baker about him. I believe I have got the best of the bargain in these negotiations.'

Mee remained intent on signing McNab, but faced competition from Liverpool, who invited the player for an interview and medical at Anfield. Shankly flattered McNab for his ability, but sent his blood pressure racing by prodding his near-naked body and noting, 'I never realised you were such a strong wee man.' After travelling south to meet with the courteous and correct Bertie Mee, McNab opted to sign for Arsenal. 'I knew very little about the Arsenal or their manager,' says McNab. 'My first impression of Bertie was that he seemed to be quiet, unassuming and well-spoken – a bit like a doctor. He was a complete contrast to Bill Shankly, who was so intimidating.'

McNab would soon see the harder side of his new manager, though, as he fought to recover from a thigh injury he had brought with him from Huddersfield. 'Once it was healed enough to resume training, Bertie worked with me for about ten days. I was so tired after the morning sessions I used to go back to my hotel and sleep. Bertie had become famous for this in his time as physio and I wondered if he'd learned some of his techniques from books on torture! It taught me something I kept my entire career: that tremendous feeling of strength and explosive power, which I always attempted to maintain. He also showed me how to overcome the potential thigh-strain issue, showing me a group of exercises designed to strengthen the muscles. I did them before every practice and every game. I cannot imagine me having the career I had if I hadn't made the decision to join Bertie and Arsenal.'

McNab would also come to thank Mee for the faith he showed in him during his early months at Highbury. 'The first nine months at Arsenal were a nightmare. I had injuries, flu, pleurisy and a complete loss of confidence and form. At no time did Bertie or Dave Sexton do anything other than support me. How they did it as I struggled from one bad game to another I will never know.'

With his first three signings completed, Mee reflected with satisfaction on his transactions. 'I think I can close the Arsenal chequebook for a while. I have completed in three months a rebuilding move I anticipated would take a year.'

Recalling how those transfers took shape, Dave Sexton says, 'Bertie and I would sit and discuss everything together. If we were interested in someone and I hadn't really seen him play, I would go and watch him. Then we would discuss it some more. In the end, though, the final decision was Bertie's.'

Don Howe, who was to succeed Sexton as coach, continues, 'The actual buying of the player was left to Bertie. We both always knew the areas of the team that needed strengthening and I might know who we were looking at, but when the time came to buy, I had no input. Bertie listened to what our chief scout, Gordon Clark, said about players he had looked at. Often, I would just hear that so-and-so was coming to the club.'

Although there would be more players coming and going over the next few years, it is interesting to note that by October 1966 all of the players who would be first choices in the triumphs of 1970 and 1971 were already attached to Arsenal, as first-teamers, reserves, youth players or apprentices. That says much about Mee's ability and that of his coaches to recognise and nurture the talent at their disposal without needless tinkering, as well as bearing testament to the production line put in place by the much-maligned Billy Wright.

McNab's signing was concluded after he watched Arsenal lose 4–2 at home to Leicester, the visitors' first two goals coming inside the first five minutes. The new boy clearly didn't see much barring his way into the first team. Mee's response to the defeat was to send a message to the reporters herding outside the Arsenal changing-room that he was unable to speak with them. Here was the Bertie that would become familiar to the hacks.

In his early weeks as manager, Mee had made comments that served only to place additional pressure upon his team. Following remarks about Arsenal's rivalry with Tottenham, he had prefaced a game against Chelsea by condemning Wright's tactics during a 0–0 draw between the sides the previous February. Mee had stated, 'There is no danger of us repeating the defensive tactics that caused so much controversy. We did overdo the defensive stuff, but that will not happen tomorrow. Tight defence is an essential part of modern football, but it must be used to reinforce an attacking policy.' Arsenal lost 3–1 after taking an early lead.

Mee appears on those occasions to have allowed himself to be drawn into the media's agenda, but as he settled into his new role it became clear, often to the frustration of the press, that he would in future be setting his own terms and conditions. Friend and former health-service colleague Harry Hopker puts it bluntly. 'Bertie detested the press. He said everything was stage-managed. He thought you never got an exact representation of what you said and felt it was manipulated. Even on television he knew that very rarely were things broadcast live, so most of what you said would end up on the floor.'

Steve Burtenshaw, who would later serve as coach under Mee, recalls, 'He wouldn't talk about the game immediately afterwards. It drove the Sunday newspaper boys mad. But he was clever with the press and understood how it could affect the team. If there were four games in a week, he wouldn't say to the press that he was worried about tiredness. His thought was "we don't have any tired players", as he believed that having the press talking about it would make the players discuss it and therefore start feeling it. It was part of the way he went about things. He didn't ever give people the chance to make an excuse because he knew they would take it.'

Ron Goodman, who became friends with Mee while working for Arsenal's kit suppliers, adds, 'Bertie could take the pressures of the media better than anyone else because he simply never got involved with journalists. He didn't want to have long conversations with them. Funnily enough, though, he was never ex-directory. People, including those from the press, used to ask me if I could give them Bertie's number. I told them to look it up in the phone book. He always said that if he didn't want to speak to them, he wouldn't.'

Don Howe recalls conversations during his time as Arsenal coach in which the nature of the London media was the main topic. 'Bertie didn't trust the press. He said they were always trying to stir something up. When we talked about things like that, which wasn't too often, he said, "We are in London and this is the Arsenal. You have got to be aware that they want an Arsenal story every day. If they can get one by trying to stir things up, they would rather have that than a complimentary story. Out of every ten stories, they would like nine to be critical. They would love to drive a wedge between you and me, and between me and the chairman. You have got to be careful and so have I."

'He was very shrewd like that. He didn't want any big mates in the press and kept them away. He said that you might think some of them are friendly, but you have to ask why. It is because they want inroads into the club. Lots of times I would be quoted, and there were times when things did not come out in the context I wanted and I would have to explain it to Bertie. I might have told a reporter we were working on Charlie George's left foot and it came out as, "Arsenal are unhappy with Charlie George's left foot." That was the reason why Bertie felt you couldn't win with them. It was not a nasty thing. He just knew it was their strategy and their job.'

Graham Perry, a friend of Mee's in his latter years, says, 'I asked Bertie once how he felt about how football was portrayed in the media. He resented the intrusiveness of the press and the atmosphere in which football was reported. It often brought him into conflict with the modern way in which football was handled, and led him to be positioned by the press as someone of some reticence.'

Jeff Powell, the long-serving *Daily Mail* journalist, was one of the writers closest to the Arsenal camp. He remembers Mee as 'a little hard nut with good manners', but someone who was smart enough to allow members of the press to get on with their jobs. 'You could call him up for a story, as long as you didn't want salacious stuff. If you talked specifically about football, he was fine, although he didn't give away anything he didn't want to. Of course, you would sometimes write things he didn't like and he would bridle a bit if you criticised him. If people deliberately turned him over, he would just be cold and cut people off for a while, but he didn't hold grudges. Confrontation wasn't his game. Of course, we had disagreements, but if he thought you'd got something wrong, he would explain.'

Journalist John Goodbody, who covered Arsenal throughout Mee's reign, adds, 'I think managers generally had been far more reticent anyway. We were brought up on people like Bill Nicholson, who was against the press and more difficult to deal with. Bertie was very courteous and eminently sensible, but he was a very withdrawn man, not effusive in any way. He would be friendly and chat with you, but you couldn't compare him to other people of that era, like Malcolm Allison.'

In the days when journalists frequently travelled with the official club party, Powell saw Arsenal's players on 'some pretty substantial binges' after games. But as long as they reported back at the prescribed time ready for training, Mee allowed them that freedom and did not fret about reporters being around his team at such times. Powell continues, 'He never complained about us mixing with the players. He knew I had a good relationship with many of them and it was not a problem. In fact, there were a couple of times when I had been sharply critical and would be greeted by some long faces, but Bertie and the senior players would tell people to behave themselves, keep their tempers and act like men.'

Friend Elli Baram recalls that it was not in Mee's nature to court the press or use them to deliver messages of criticism to his players. 'He was very modest with regard to public relations. I don't think he knew how to do it, so he didn't try. And he would never talk of somebody behind their back. Whatever he had to say to somebody, he would say it to their face.'

Midway through his reign as Arsenal manager, Mee turned down the opportunity to have his team feature in Hunter Davies's ground-breaking book *The Glory Game*; the author instead spent a season observing Tottenham at close quarters. 'Bertie was not a man who liked the public spotlight; he preferred to enjoy success on his own terms,' adds Graham Perry. On one occasion, however, Mee did allow the media to get close, with fascinating results. After being approached by the BBC during the 1968–69 season, he consented to feature in an episode of the *Man Alive* series entitled 'Football Manager'. The one-hour documentary offered viewers a peek into the worlds of Mee and former Arsenal player Laurie Brown, who was then player–manager at Bradford Park Avenue. In the days before reality television became a broadcasting staple, it was pretty revolutionary stuff. Mee allowed himself to be filmed at work and was interviewed in the Highbury changing-room, on a train to an away game and behind his busy, yet well-ordered, desk, offering views on various aspects of managerial life.

Most intriguingly, he allowed the cameras into his home on the day after a game and he sat at the foot of his stairs chatting to his interviewer. Always smartly dressed, Mee's one concession to it being a Sunday is that he wore a casual cardigan over his crisp white shirt and tie instead of a jacket. The family segment also demonstrated Mee's method of screening his calls. Wearing dresses in vivid Arsenal red, made specially for the occasion by their mother, daughters Allyson and Beverley were seen in the kitchen helping Doris prepare the lunch when the telephone rang. Beverley walked briskly into the hall, picked up the receiver and enquired, 'Who shall I say is calling? . . . I'll get him for you.' (It was the late Reg Drury, stalwart of the London media pack.)

A documentary with the broadcasting establishment, the BBC, is one thing; appearing as a pundit or voicing opinions in newspaper columns was an entirely different matter however. This was an era in which the cult of celebrity was growing rapidly, not just in football, but in society as a whole. Football's leading characters were being projected into living rooms twice a weekend via highlights programmes, while the sport's presence in other media – be it the increasing number of youth-orientated magazines and sticker collections or petrol-station giveaways – helped to further elevate them towards the status previously reserved for stars of screen or show business. Managers like Malcolm Allison, Brian Clough and Bill Shankly – Big Mal, Cloughie and Shanks – had personae that fed the public's appetite for larger-than-life characters.

Hand in hand with this phenomenon was the changing nature of football journalism. There were fewer writers whose opinions still carried the clout of old-school scribes like Desmond Hackett of the *Daily Express*. Increasingly, the journalist's job was to provide sketchy details of what had happened on the field, devote the bulk of his story to quotes from the main protagonists and leave the analysis to the high-profile columnist – former or current players, or managers whose experience of what went on in the dressing-room and on the field could provide an insight that no reporter could match.

There was money to be made and profile to be gained for those who were interested. Mee was not. For him, there was a fine dividing line between character and caricature, and he was happy to let others run the risk of stepping across it. Of course, he would never have cut the same engaging, controversial figure on television as Shankly and Clough, but his reluctance to push himself into the limelight also perhaps stemmed from his awareness that he was not as steeped in the game, and therefore not considered as knowledgeable, as those men.

Former health-service colleague George Wright believes that Bertie was considered something of an outsider to those who never got close enough to see beyond their own prejudices. 'During all that time in football with Bertie, I had the opinion that others resented it a bit that he wasn't a player. He was quite aloof in relation to media, players and to other managers. If you are not a player, the rest of the football world thinks less of you. It's unfortunate, but that's the way it goes.'

Fred Street ventures, 'I think he probably knew he wasn't accepted by the media because he was not from the traditional background of a manager. It was based on that nonsense that you have got to be a great player to be a great manager. Bollocks. Some of the best managers have been players from the Third or Fourth Divisions, so it doesn't follow. I think, though, he must have been conscious of that. He was never in the frame with the big names, even when he won Manager of the Year. Others would be mentioned as possible England managers, but not Bertie. Maybe today he would be. Sven-Göran Eriksson wasn't a great player. Arsène Wenger did not have a great track record as a player. The job has changed. Back then, you were an outsider if you didn't play at a high level.'

Steve Burtenshaw continues, 'People like Clough and Allison had their way of doing things and Bertie would do his thing. He wouldn't change his ways. But he would not admit that he did not know enough. He knew enough to talk to people. He had his own views on football.'

Don Howe would work alongside Mee for long enough to have no doubts about his boss's football knowledge, 'A lot of what's said about him is unfair. People didn't give him enough credit for his football knowledge. There was never a time when he couldn't join in and make points to players. His football intelligence was very high. His strength was that he let people get on with their jobs, but we knew we couldn't get away with anything by saying something and thinking that Bertie wouldn't understand. A lot of managers would have been too proud to bring in people like Dave Sexton and Bobby Campbell and me. He had no ego.'

Harry Hopker says, 'Bertie appeared once or twice on sports interview shows but he wasn't comfortable doing it. It was a bit of an alien culture to him. He was a very intelligent chap, you know, and, without reflecting badly on the football world, it is a macho world – and he was a bit too refined for that.'

Mee, therefore, reserved extensive interviews mostly for Arsenal's own publications or one of the many football annuals published at that time (every major player, it seemed, had one named after him). It was in one such book, an edition of the short-lived *London Soccer Annual*, that Mee explained his reticence with the media:

> I think the essential thing is for a person to be what they are and not try and project a separate personality. While many people think I am a quiet man, it is not because I am consciously trying to project any particular image. A football manager must adapt himself to many situations and I assure you that I am quite capable of becoming very involved and committed to situations and, indeed, presenting an air of assumed rage as and when appropriate. Perhaps by nature I am not such an extrovert as some managers and I try to consider the many aspects of situations before making public comment. I consider it is my job both to protect and support my players and if any difference exists between myself and the players, this should be settled in private rather than to expose the situation publicly.

In 1972, Mee would shed further light on his relationship with the media in an interview with *Goal* magazine:

> I'm not gagged, but what I say is consistent with my own responsibility to my particular community. I gagged myself for a year, and my players too, until I felt I was mature enough to speak freely. If a manager says what he wants, he must allow his players to say what they want. But he should set an example of the way in which it should be done. The media are out to exploit them (the players) and they have to learn to make sensible, restrained comments.

Mee's views would change little throughout his Highbury reign. In Peter Douglas's 1973 book *The Football Industry*, it was stated that Arsenal were not among the 25 clubs reported to be improving their public relations efforts. Douglas wrote, 'It is interesting to note that Arsenal, for example, steadfastly refuse to make any concession in this direction, in spite of requests by their supporters (during disputes in the 1969–70 season) for "better public relations".' Clearly, that comment stemmed from the manager's refusal to play the media's games.

As it happened, there was little happy news to report from Highbury throughout the remainder of the 1966–67 season. An injury-hit team lost 3–1 at home to West Ham in the League Cup with youth-teamers John Woodward and Michael Boot making their debuts. David Jenkins, a 19 year old from Bristol, making his second first-team appearance, got the Gunners' goal. Having taken six points from the first three games – these were, of course, the days of two points for a win – Arsenal took another ten matches to double their total. When the new signings all played together for the first time in a 1–0 loss at Manchester United, the *Daily Express* defined their performance as a 'shambles of mediocre, ill-defined soccer'.

Mee's response was to take Arsenal to Lilleshall for four days to work on new team tactics, a punishing break that saw the players embarking on two-mile runs before breakfast and training until 9.30 at night. Mee enjoyed the atmosphere and working environment of such trips and would repeat them regularly over the next decade. 'We had no distractions and everybody worked extremely hard,' he said of them.

Arsenal's first game back saw them lose 1–0 to a defensively minded Leeds team bent on their first away win of the season. This time, the *Daily Express* rejoiced in highlighting the Arsenal players' 'lack of energy' and added cheekily that, instead of dwelling on past glories, it was time for the club to discuss the present – 'Arsenal's brave battle against relegation.'

With the Gunners apparently struggling again, it was open season. Ken Bates, chairman of Oldham at the time, showed a glimpse of the outspoken manner that would mark his years as Chelsea chairman when he bristled at Arsenal's £20,000 demand for an 'unknown' reserve defender. 'They must be living in a dream world,' he said. 'If they have financial problems, I hope they don't expect Oldham to solve them.'

Mee then had to fight off interest for one of his best players, winger George Armstrong, for whom both Sunderland and Newcastle were prepared to pay £50,000 to relocate him to his native North-east. Armstrong had requested a transfer a month earlier, but Mee responded: 'Where could I possibly find somebody to replace him? The final decision rests with the board, but, from my own point of view, I feel it would be impossible to let Armstrong go.' Previous managers had experienced differences of opinion with the Arsenal directors when it came to transfers, but on this occasion Mee's refusal to sell was supported from above and within a month Armstrong asked to be removed from the transfer list.

Early in February, Arsenal announced that they were ready to confirm Mee's position as manager. 'We shall offer Bertie the manager's job within the next month,' chairman Denis Hill-Wood declared. 'We have been delighted with what he has achieved.' The second day of March saw Arsenal fulfil that promise, and Sexton was promoted from coach to assistant manager. Bob Wall said, 'Bertie has now accepted the position of full manager. There will be no contract, at his request.'

Arsenal's progress in the FA Cup included a 3–0 victory over Bristol Rovers on the back of another team-building break, this time at Hove in Sussex, near coach Dave Sexton's home. After a 0–0 draw at Bolton in the fourth round, a 3–0 replay victory at Highbury was notable for a John Radford hat-trick and the return of Arsenal's traditional white sleeves. Football League regulations forbade them from changing from the all-red version mid-season, but the club made it known that a permanent change was on its way. Mee might not have felt that the past had much relevance to what was happening in the present, but he also recognised the importance of certain traditions at a club like Arsenal. The Bolton result led visiting striker Francis Lee, later to be transferred to Manchester City, to comment, 'Playing Arsenal used to be a picnic, but Bertie Mee has worked wonders with their spirit. This side can go all the way.'

Proving Lee wrong, Arsenal were unable to go any further, losing at Birmingham. Without the injured Ian Ure and Frank McLintock, and posing little attacking threat to the home side, Arsenal would have been pleased to have escaped with a draw but were beaten by an 83rd-minute goal by Geoff Vowden. The season was effectively over, but

Arsenal's response to their FA Cup disappointment was to go unbeaten through the final twelve games of the season to finish in seventh position. The final table showed that Arsenal had conceded 47 goals, compared with 75 the previous year, proof of the improved organisation of the team under its new management.

Sexton, who would be identified in later years with innovative, attack-minded teams like Chelsea, QPR and Manchester United, had quickly recognised that Arsenal's major problem was in defence – although that hardly required Superman's X-ray vision – and had made the introduction of a man-to-man marking system one of his first priorities. The system, as basic as it was, ensured that everyone knew his responsibility. If the opposition scored, a culprit could be identified. For a team for whom conceding goals had become a fatal habit, it was a start, like getting a heroin addict onto methadone.

Arsenal were becoming a tighter unit all over the field, as McLintock explains, 'Dave started working on closing down as a team, like a chain reaction: the right-back would push forward; the right-sided centre-half would push over. We always used to try to keep the line. As soon as the ball was cleared and the forwards pushed upfield, we would all push up as well.'

And as the players grew closer to their dynamic young coach – who would travel to Italy on Sundays to watch games and pick up new ideas – so their respect for Mee as a manager developed. 'At Huddersfield, our coach just told us to run around the field,' says McNab. 'Dave's coaching sessions were great; always interesting, well thought out and usually fun, but hard and intense. He was innovative, a great fellow, an absolute diamond.'

According to McLintock, 'Dave's impact made us respect Bert even more. After all, it was he who brought Dave in. He must have recognised his talent. I felt we could trust both of them and have some success.'

8

LOOKING FORWARD

Bertie knew what he wanted and he drove towards it.
Not ruthlessly, but with a bit of humanity.
              – former Arsenal coach Dave Sexton

WHEN BERTIE MEE STUDIED THE ARSENAL SQUAD THAT assembled for the 1967–68 season, it wasn't difficult to spot the major deficiency: his team badly needed a goalscorer. Under the tutelage of Dave Sexton, and with the addition of key personnel, Arsenal's defensive performance had improved beyond recognition, but now they needed someone to poach some goals. Mee made no secret of the fact and Arsenal were soon linked with just about every unsettled forward in the land. The former Chelsea and England striker Barry Bridges, rumoured to be unhappy at Birmingham, was, according to the Arsenal manager, 'only one of several forwards I have made enquiries about'.

The Bridges story circulated on the day that Arsenal beat Rangers 3–0 in a pre-season game at Highbury, before which Mee had announced that he was installing Frank McLintock as club captain instead of Terry Neill. Another Arsenal player in the news was centre-back Ian Ure, for whom Mee was willing to accept £125,000 after the Scotland international expressed his dissatisfaction at his weekly wage packet. 'Arsenal couldn't do enough for us in many ways,' Ure says. 'Throughout the hardship and adversity of the '60s, they treated us like grown-ups. But they could have given us more money.'

Stoke expressed a willingness to part with £70,000, plus defender Calvin Palmer, for Ure, while Mee stated that his ability to purchase a centre-forward did not depend on balancing the books by selling anyone. On the eve of the new campaign, Mee explained, 'We are interested in a forward. I think we'll have a good season but until we get him I don't think we'll hit the jackpot.'

After scoring a late pre-season winner against Israeli side Maccabi Tel Aviv, George Johnston, a Scottish forward signed six months earlier from Cardiff for £15,000, was given a place in the team for the opening game against Stoke. The versatile David Court, on the transfer list at £35,000, lined up at full-back for the injured Bob McNab. A powerful header by George Graham and a goal by Jon Sammels led to a 2–0 victory, but Mee was unhappy with Graham, who picked up two five-inch cuts in his shin. After Colin Addison had suffered a similar injury at the tail end of the previous season, Mee had made the wearing of shinpads compulsory. Graham had flouted the rule and, as well as being ruled out of the midweek game at Liverpool, was fined £10.

In the following weeks, the London papers continued to mix debate over whether Colin Cowdrey would take over from Brian Close as England cricket captain for the upcoming tour of the West Indies (he did) with speculation about whether Mee would sign any of the forwards he'd been trailing (he didn't). After watching Bridges score twice against Hull City, Mee admitted he had made 30 enquiries about strikers. 'My greatest joy,' he said, 'would be to say that out of so many enquiries one has been successful. But that has not been true.'

When Arsenal scored seven goals in successive away wins at West Bromwich (3–1) and Sheffield United (4–2), the urgency of Mee's quest seemed to abate temporarily. The goals continued to flow in the next League game, a 4–0 home win against Tottenham on the day that George Graham married his fiancée, Marie Zia. Spurs rival Terry Venables was his best man. There were to be no such games of happy families when, three weeks later, Mee took his men to Manchester.

Games between Arsenal and Manchester United at Old Trafford have caused their fair share of problems for Gunners managers over the years. After a brawl in the 1990–91 contest, Arsenal were docked points by the Football League, while the ugly scenes at the end of the 0–0 draw in 2003 led to the suspension of four Arsenal players. A year later, United's victory degenerated into confrontation on the pitch and recriminations off it. But even before George Graham and Arsène Wenger would be required to answer for their teams' indiscipline, Bertie Mee found himself staring at the same hysterical headlines that would greet his successors.

Neither United striker Denis Law nor his former Scotland teammate Ian Ure could be described as angels on the field. Both had been sent off three times before they launched into a running battle during Arsenal's 1–0 defeat on the first Saturday of October. Eventually referee George McCabe had seen one punch and one kick too many, and sent both players to the dressing-room. The public inquest that followed the game was partly due to the players' previous records and partly a result of the prevailing wind of concern about on-field discipline that was blowing through football. It was noted that sixteen players had been sent off during the 1967–68 season already, compared with only six at the same stage a year earlier. With the worrying increase in battles between rival sets of supporters inside and outside of grounds up and down the country, football was under pressure to ensure that the players were setting the best possible example: a theme that would continue to dog Arsenal as the season progressed.

Mee may have been a strict disciplinarian, but at the same time he displayed fierce public support for his players. On this occasion, the media felt it was blind loyalty, the kind of which Wenger has frequently been accused. Mee's reaction to the Ure incident was not so different in tone and content to the Frenchman's support of Martin Keown and company a quarter of a century later.

'If you want players who don't create any problems, you won't win anything,' Mee told reporters. 'You become a bottom-half-of-the-table team. I have no quarrel with the referee's decision. Naturally, I am disappointed, but you must also consider that [Ure and Law] are both tremendously talented players, both with volatile temperaments. It is one of the reasons why they are such good players. I don't condone what happened at all. Ian himself regretted it bitterly. But he had a great game. I can't take that away from him.'

Sound familiar? Colleagues of Mee believe that he would have handled the 2003 Old Trafford incident in much the same way as Wenger. 'Bertie wouldn't have liked it but he would have remained supportive of his players publicly and dealt with it in a quiet way,' says Steve Burtenshaw. 'Nothing was allowed to go outside the club when players were disciplined. That kind of incident could easily have happened in the 1971 season because they were a very competitive bunch of lads. But Bertie would have let them know it could not happen again. He was big on team discipline. He told players they owed it to the group. There was no question of any player saying, "Sod it. I want to do it my way." It's not being creepy to the manager; it is just showing respect for the rest of the team. You had to put the group's interest ahead of your own. I am not sure it applies so much today.'

Don Howe adds, 'Bertie was keen to make sure the players behaved the right way on the field. "No vendettas" was one of his great sayings. He would tell them to forget it and get on with the game. If we lost, he expected us to lose with dignity.'

Mee felt strongly his own responsibility to be calm, to set an example in the face of frustration. In the *London Soccer Annual*, published in 1969, he explained:

> This is something I hope to try and pass on to my players. It is important that I look at both sides of any particular problem and not become too emotionally involved with either individuals or situations. The latter tends to result in hasty comments which can produce many problems to the individual and the organisation. I hope that a little of this approach rubs off on the players and it is important that my staff also practises this philosophy. I, in turn, have a responsibility to them to help them to create the mature environment which fulfils (this) point. Obviously I'm older than the players and the staff and it is important that I help both groups in every possible way.

If the 'Voice of Arsenal' column in the club's official programme was supposed to present the official Highbury view of events, then the comments about the next home game after the Old Trafford incident are remarkable. There was neither support nor condemnation of the men involved, nor any hint of the 'responsibility' towards the behaviour of players that Mee obviously felt. Just simple dissociation. Pontius Pilate could not have washed his hands any cleaner than whoever wrote:

> It was one of the hardest and cleanest games we have played in this season, and if individual players evoked the wrath of the referee, that is their personal responsibility, for which they are accountable to the Disciplinary Committee of the Football Association.

With the authorities increasingly determined to demonstrate their willingness to get tough with the game's offenders, Ure and Law were each banned for six weeks, the heaviest sentences the game had handed out for more than twenty years and the most severe ever imposed on an Arsenal player. Both clubs were warned not to compensate the players for loss of earnings.

In stating that Arsenal would not consider any additional punishment, Mee offered an interesting insight into his views on the handling of players. 'There is no question of Arsenal taking any private action in this affair because I am against imposing financial discipline on senior players. With young people it is a different matter. I fined two of my youth players last season because of misconduct and it has had the desired effect. But I want my first-team men to be responsible and you can't expect them to become responsible if you treat them with the same heavy authority you would use with, say, your children. Ian is a professional and a very good one. I couldn't wish for a better record of playing consistency than he has given me. I have to consider that players react differently to situations. Some are more placid than others.'

Ure may have escaped internal discipline on this occasion, but not because Mee took lightly the issue of players falling foul of the referee. On one occasion, he told a player who had been dismissed in an important game that he wanted to fine him two weeks' wages but, in accordance with Professional Footballers' Association guidelines, needed the individual's compliance. When the player, believing he could thwart his manager's plans, refused to give his approval, Mee told him he would invoke the alternative measure of withholding the six tickets the player received per home game, along with his allocation of

FA Cup final and England–Scotland tickets. The player agreed to the fine.

Back in the more mundane world of his search for a striker, Mee announced after a 2–1 defeat of Sunderland that he was going to meet with his Scottish scouts to get reports on their efforts to solve the problem. 'We can't go on like this,' he said. 'Jim Montgomery was in great form, but that does not excuse our misses.'

Having announced his intention to intensify the search for a goalscorer, Mee was distracted by another problem. This one came out of the blue – the Blues, actually – when Chelsea summoned Dave Sexton to succeed Tommy Docherty as manager. After joining the west London club as coach in the spring of 1961, former Gunner Docherty had been made to wait only a few months before taking the top job following the dismissal of Ted Drake, a Highbury legend who, in 1955, had led Chelsea to their only First Division title. Under 'The Doc', Chelsea played with flair and daring to finish fifth, third and fifth in successive Division One seasons. Cup success came their way in the League Cup in 1965, and they reached the FA Cup final against Tottenham two years later.

The Chelsea board had backed Docherty over his disciplinary stance following the late-night drinking episode in Blackpool, but after the death of chairman Joe Mears in 1966, relations between the club's directors and its manager were never the same again. Docherty had run-ins with new chairman Charles Pratt over the allocation of Cup tickets to players, newspaper articles he had written and a £100 fine he'd incurred for calling the referee of a youth match a 'bloody disgrace'. The incident that finally led to Docherty's departure from Stamford Bridge occurred on a club tour to Bermuda, where – after seeing two players sent off – Docherty told the match official, 'You should be swinging from a tree, not refereeing.' The remark earned him a one-month ban from football. In October of 1967, depressed at the direction in which his career appeared to be heading, Docherty resigned.

Chelsea swiftly contacted Sexton and on Monday, 23 October he returned to Stamford Bridge as one of the game's youngest managers at the age of 37. 'It was a difficult decision to make,' he admits, 'although I had strong ties with Chelsea because I had been there quite a long time. I was reluctant to break the bond between me and Bertie, and I had worked with all the younger players. I left Arsenal with a heavy heart because I had been very happy.'

Bob Wall explained that there had been nothing he or Mee could do to prevent Sexton's departure. 'We knew a man of his calibre and ability would not stay as a number two for very long.'

Mee spoke of Sexton's desire to 'paddle his own canoe', but the players, many of whom felt they were receiving worthwhile coaching for the first time in their careers, did not accept the situation so readily. Frank McLintock says, 'We were furious when Bertie let Dave go. Maybe he couldn't have stopped him, or maybe he should have done more to keep him there, but it was the first time we had found somebody we felt could do what was a very difficult job.'

Mee opted to hand first-team coaching duties to Don Howe, who had been in charge of the reserves since suffering his career-ending broken leg. Howe recalls Mee's original offer of a position on the club's backroom staff. 'I had been struggling to get back to First Division fitness,' he says. 'One day Bertie called me in and said, "I don't know what you are doing in the future, but how would you like to be manager of the reserves? We would just let you get on with it. We all agree that it would be a step forward." Bertie laid down some ground rules. He said he wanted the young reserve players to work harder. He wanted them back for training in the afternoons, sometimes as a group, sometimes as individuals. I said, "Fine," and then got on with it. And there was no interference from Bertie. We would have meetings on Monday and Friday, but he left everything to me. It wasn't because he was not interested; he just believed in letting people do their jobs.'

Bob Wilson believes that Mee's appointment of Howe as Sexton's successor shows his confidence in the 'delicate area of accepting your own strengths and weaknesses'. He continues, 'It takes self-belief to give power to someone and not feel as though they will threaten you. But if you want to be successful, you put in the best man you think you can. You shouldn't put a guy in there because you used to share a room with him as a player or he is your best mate. Bertie went to people because he thought they were the best for the job.'

Initially, Howe's appointment did little to stop the fretting among the Arsenal players. 'We all felt a great sense of loss after Dave left,' says Bob McNab. 'I heard many times the players feeling the club had no ambition. The first couple of weeks under Don were strained, with quite a number of players sulking and not putting much out in training.'

Mee's belief in allowing staff to solve their own problems meant that it was down to Howe to win over his charges by himself. He did so with an explosion a couple of weeks into his new role, interrupting a training session in the club gymnasium to shout, 'Right, I have fucking had enough of you lot. I am Don Howe. Dave Sexton has gone. I am the coach and from now on you will do what I say.'

McLintock says, 'From then on you could tell he was in charge. Don grabbed us by the scruff of the neck, and gave himself a good kick up the bollocks as well. He just got better and better.'

If Arsenal needed an important game to make them focus after the upheaval, they didn't have to wait very long. After John Radford scored a hat-trick in a 5–3 win against Fulham, Blackburn were coming to town for a fourth-round League Cup tie. Victory would put Arsenal in the last eight, only two ties away from their first Wembley appearance for sixteen years.

The run had started with a 2–1 win at Coventry in the second round, Graham having set up the first for Sammels before giving Arsenal a two-goal lead. In the third round, Reading proved stubborn opponents at Highbury after going behind in the 19th minute when Peter Simpson shot home. The Third Division side had the better of the second half and it was with some relief that the home supporters heard the final whistle.

A night of torrential rain and high winds greeted the 20,002 hardy souls who ventured to Highbury to see the Blackburn tie. As players splashed through puddles, Arsenal took the lead when Graham headed in from Armstrong's corner. Colin Addison scored a second, but once again the Gunners were left clinging to a single-goal lead after Blackburn found the net 13 minutes from time.

Addison's goal was his last for Arsenal. In the final week of November, Mee conceded that his first signing as Arsenal manager had not paid off when he sold him to Sheffield United for £40,000. There was still no sign of an incoming transfer. Mee announced that no bid would be made for Swindon winger Don Rogers, who had been rated at £110,000 after telling his club he wanted First Division football. 'We made three enquiries last season and two this,' said Mee, 'but were told he was not for sale. Since then we have examined the situation closely and come to the conclusion that he lacks the consistency to be a First Division player.' How Rogers would ram those words down Mee's throat 16 months later.

Along with the relentless search for a striker, the physical nature of Arsenal's football remained a recurring theme of Mee's second season in charge. The unwanted headlines of Old Trafford were still fresh in the memory when a three-game series against Burnley produced more ugly incidents for Mee to mitigate. The first match was the League Cup quarter-final at Turf Moor, where Arsenal found themselves two goals down after nine minutes. The game turned, however, in a ten-minute spell in which the visitors scored three times – through Graham, McLintock and Graham again. The opening stages of the second half passed relatively serenely for the Gunners, but full-back Bob McNab was sent off by referee Ken Burns after 57 minutes for striking Burnley's balding centre-forward Andy Lochhead. From then on, Arsenal came under increasing pressure, eventually conceding an equaliser five minutes from time.

The bad feeling of the tie carried over into the following Saturday's League game at Highbury, where Arsenal had McLintock and Storey dismissed. The captain went for allegedly hitting Burnley forward Frank Casper, while Storey argued too vehemently about a free-kick that had led to the visitors' winning goal. Mee, angry at his players for being drawn into such incidents and far from pleased with the officiating of Jim Carr, ordered that no one should speak to the press after the game. Monday's *Daily Mirror*, however, found Ken Jones reporting an unnamed Gunners player voicing his anger at their opponents' approach. 'Someone should take a good look at this Burnley side,' said the anonymous Arsenal man. 'As soon as they have been touched, they go down as if they have been hit by Henry Cooper's left hook. They are the biggest actors in the business. McLintock did no more than tap Casper's face with the flat of his hand.' (After testimony by Mee, McLintock would subsequently be exonerated by the FA's disciplinary committee, who suspended Storey for two weeks.)

Arsenal chairman Denis Hill-Wood, presumably not having received Mee's instructions, also weighed in. 'I will not tolerate dirty players at Arsenal and I do not believe we have one on the club's books. I have not discussed the game with our manager, Bertie Mee.

Discipline is his job.' A few weeks later, Mee would have to discharge those responsibilities again when reportedly telling his players at half-time to cut out the rough stuff during a 1–1 draw at Coventry, by which time two scuffles behind the referee's back had gone unpunished.

For the League Cup replay at Highbury, the experienced David Smith was named as match official. In the end, he had an uneventful evening. The closest he came to meting out punishment was when he called rival captains McLintock and Gordon Harris together after they clashed shortly before half-time. The game followed the pattern of Arsenal's earlier ties, the Gunners establishing a lead but being unable to put the opposition away without some late-game nerves. John Radford squeezed the ball in at the far post after 29 minutes and Terry Neill, the newly elected chairman of the Professional Footballers' Association, stretched to convert Graham's header after 57 minutes. But only 60 seconds later, Neill was beaten in the air as Willie Irvine headed Burnley back into the game. Arsenal held out for the last third of the game, earning a two-legged semi-final tie against Huddersfield.

As 1967 came to a close, a teenager called Charlie George attracted headlines by scoring four goals in a cup-tie for the Arsenal youth team; former Peterborough manager Gordon Clark was appointed by Mee as chief scout; and Southampton centre-forward Martin Chivers became the latest striker to be linked with Arsenal. Increasingly frustrated at his failure to get his man, Mee limited his comments to, 'We are interested in any good players who come on the market. But, in more specific terms, I would not want to reveal my attitude towards Chivers.' The player would soon reveal his attitude towards Arsenal by choosing instead to sign for Tottenham in a £125,000 deal.

When Arsenal had last played at Wembley – their 1952 FA Cup final defeat against Newcastle – the League Cup was still almost a decade from inception. As 1968 dawned, there was no doubting the place the competition now held in Bertie Mee's priorities following the decision to grant its winners European football. 'Arsenal have taken a back seat in recent years while Tottenham and West Ham have reaped the benefit of competition in Europe. It is important for the climate of the club. The players take on new-found status.'

It is interesting that, not for the first time, Mee placed the emphasis on making up lost ground on their London rivals as opposed to placing their challenge in a wider context. In the modern day of football clubs as 'global brands' and the population's increased geographical flexibility, many local rivalries no longer carry the same intensity – certainly for Arsenal fans who have become used to Tottenham being unable to mount a serious challenge to their superiority. In the '60s, however, Mee, who lived in the heart of the north London battlefield in Southgate, was acutely aware of the importance of Arsenal taking the limelight away from their neighbours.

At Highbury against a Huddersfield team that had knocked out First Division clubs West Ham and Fulham in earlier rounds, Mee brought back McLintock after a two-week absence with a knee injury. As early as the fourth minute, the skipper was forced to rouse his troops after a faltering defence allowed Colin Dobson to score for the underdogs. But, once again, Arsenal responded with a three-goal burst before half-time. Jon Sammels's penetrating pass enabled George Graham to score with a powerful header and the head of strike partner John Radford gave the Gunners the lead. Then Bob McNab stunned his former team by firing in from 30 yards. It was Huddersfield who scored the second half's only goal when a young Frank Worthington set up Trevor Cherry. At 3–2 ahead, there was still some work for Arsenal to do before preparing for Wembley.

Their cause was not helped when the FA passed judgement on McNab's sending off at Burnley, banning him for two weeks and fining him £50. The punishment was made more galling by the apparent inconsistency of football's disciplinarians, who on the same day merely fined Liverpool striker Ian St John for a Boxing Day dismissal at Coventry. McNab claimed that two witnesses, including Burnley captain Gordon Harris, had let him down by declining to give evidence on his behalf. 'I set my heart on playing at Huddersfield,' said the full-back, who would now be a spectator for the return match at Leeds Road.

Arsenal's preparation for the second leg included a 1–1 draw in the FA Cup at Shrewsbury, earned by a disputed Radford goal, and an unimpressive replay victory. The real news, however, was that at long last Bertie Mee was outlaying a club record £90,000 for a striker. It was hardly the big name that Highbury fans had been expecting. One season earlier, Bobby Gould had been playing in the Second Division for Coventry, scoring 24 goals in their promotion campaign under the dynamic management of Jimmy Hill. Even the Highfield Road crowd had been slow to take to a man whose skill did not always match his enthusiasm and he had temporarily lost his place in the team after becoming a target for terrace abuse. Now 21, he had scored eight goals in thirteen games in Division One, including, significantly, one in each game against Arsenal. Mee had also seen him score a hat-trick against Burnley in a comeback game after injury. The shock of the Arsenal supporters could not match that of Gould himself, who said of Mee's interest, 'There wasn't a more surprised player in England than me.'

Gould was an interested spectator as Arsenal took the field to defend their precarious advantage against Huddersfield. On a snow-covered surface, Mee's team seemed ill at ease as the home side tore into them and it was no surprise when they conceded a goal after 17 minutes. But the Gunners settled to their task and, after thirty-four minutes, Graham clipped a pass to Sammels, who scored from five yards. Superior skill and fitness turned the game in their favour and David Jenkins scored on eighty minutes after Arsenal broke down another weary Huddersfield attack. Five minutes later, McLintock raced thirty yards to meet Storey's cross with a goal-bound header. The final whistle sounded on a 6–3 aggregate victory and Arsenal's players hurled themselves into joyful somersaults at the club's biggest achievement in years.

It was appropriate that Arsenal's first final of the Bertie Mee era – the first of five in successive years – should be against Leeds, the team against whom all other English sides would be measured during that period. Arsenal's ambitions would more often than not be entwined with Don Revie's team, with whom they shared some crucial, and brutal, games. It was clear that when the sides met at Wembley both would be desperate for victory: Arsenal to end their years in the wilderness, Leeds to continue their Revie-driven march to the top of the English game and to end a series of second-place finishes that had begun to earn them the tag 'chokers'.

In the next couple of years, Leeds would go on to complete their evolution into the apparently indestructible force that cast a dark menace over Saturday afternoons. They were like the Daleks: a team to watch from behind the sofa. Yes, the deadly dustbins regularly got their come-uppance at the hands of William Hartnell, Patrick Troughton or whoever was the Dr Who of the day; likewise the football universe was frequently saved by the likes of Liverpool, Manchester United, Everton and, eventually, Arsenal. But the monsters would be back in the next series, more frightening and seemingly more invincible than ever.

Revie, of course, was Leeds United's Davros, the evil creator, although he could hardly be accused of having designed a team in his own image. As a player, he had been a thoughtful, creative force. It had been the 'Revie Plan' – the adoption of the Hungarians' ploy of playing the number 9, Revie, as a deep-lying schemer – that helped Manchester City win the FA Cup in 1956. As a manager, taking over the pitiful Leeds team with whom he had ended his playing career, he had other ideas. He might have put Leeds into all-white strips, directly impersonating Real Madrid, and stated his intention of ruling Europe, but the way in which Leeds had rough-housed their way out of the Second Division had been more Burnley Town Hall on wrestling night than the Bernabéu Stadium. Revie didn't mind how many toes, literally, his team stepped on. Even one of his own, Eddie Gray, admitted in his autobiography, *Marching on Together*, 'Some of our tackling in those days made me cringe. I would think, "How are they being allowed to get away with this?"'

But the end justified the means. Division Two was won in 1963–64, the season in which Revie secured the vital signing of Johnny Giles from Manchester United to team up with fiery Scots Billy Bremner and Bobby Collins in midfield. Giles was no angel and embraced the Leeds mantra. 'You had to establish a reputation that would make people think twice about messing with you,' he admitted. The Double was nearly secured the very next season when Leeds finished runners-up to their great Manchester rivals and lost the FA Cup final against Liverpool. After more near misses in the League and Cup, both domestic and European, the trophies would at last begin to accumulate, although there would still be plenty of examples of underachievement – FA Cup shocks against Colchester and Sunderland to name but two. And as the victories mounted, so Revie would at last release his team from their shackles, allowing the sublime skills of Gray, the vision and touch of Giles and the drive of Bremner to be seen at their creative best. Interestingly, Mee would also attempt to change his team's methods, and public image, once it had achieved the success for which an efficient system – rather than eye-catching style – had been adopted.

All of that lay in the future as the 1968 League Cup final loomed, marking the start of an Arsenal–Leeds bloodletting that would last five years. No one was expecting a pretty game. Mee's men were not relevant enough at that time to attract the level of criticism that Leeds had suffered, but – as the incidents in the Manchester United and Burnley games demonstrated – they were not exactly loveable themselves. Mee's response was to give a realistic appraisal of English football's pervading mood in the new era of television coverage and burgeoning commercialism. After all, no one had complained when Alf Ramsey won the World Cup with a functional approach to achieving victory. In a subsequent interview, Mee stated:

> It comes back to the competition of the modern game. Success is demanded by the fans, the directors, all of us – and I have to produce an adaptable set-up within which success can be achieved. Sometimes it is hard to reconcile principles that may be dear to me, but situations have to be coped with in this as in any other job.

And he would also later give a nod in the direction of Leeds when discussing the maturation of his own team:

> We are not consciously aware of having looked at Leeds and said, 'Yes, that's what we must do,' but one would accept that Leeds have done the right and proper thing and hope that we are on the same lines.

The edition of the *Football League Review* that was to be included as part of the official Wembley programme would carry an article in which Mee spoke further of the realities of the modern game, hinting clearly at the kind of contest in store in the final:

> Today's top teams are teams that want to win . . . teams who are prepared to do something about a game no matter how it is going. 'That,' explains Arsenal FC manager Bertie Mee, 'means teams who will work for each other collectively and individually. Obviously every football team goes out to try to win as its basic incentive,' he agrees, 'but it is the team whose

players are prepared to adapt their determination to any suggestion which battle through.'

The Arsenal manager agrees that this approach can make a team targets for critics who complain that they are too physical. 'You cannot have it both ways,' he says emphatically. 'Players who are prepared to slog it out for 90 minutes, no matter that they are unable to produce their "football" through the dictates of the opposition, players who make the process of winning a personal thing ... these are the players and the teams who are raising the standards of the British game to something of which we are all proud. If, in this process, we get tensions boiling over on occasions, if we get incidents, these should not be misinterpreted as anything more than the consequence of the hard and professional approach.'

The Arsenal manager stresses he is not defending dirty play. 'I hold no brief for players going over the ball and the like,' he makes clear. 'I am referring only to the hard, determined challenging which is so often misinterpreted as dirty play by people who should know better.'

After a 0–0 draw against Newcastle in the build-up to Wembley, journalist Desmond Hackett noted, in typically acerbic style, 'The only people who could have extracted any joy from this affront to football must have been Leeds United, who have the good fortune to oppose Arsenal in the League Cup final next month.' His view of new signing Bobby Gould, by the way, was, 'If this is the best of Gould, then Coventry have perpetrated the biggest take-off since Lady Godiva – but so much less interesting.'

Arsenal's 3–1 defeat in the League at Elland Road earlier in the season had seen them grumbling all the way back to London about Jack Charlton's apparent foul on goalkeeper Jim Furnell at a corner and their own unsuccessful claims for a penalty. The Charlton incident was to be a portent of things to come. The long-legged England centre-half, 'The Giraffe' as he was known, had been getting defences hot under the collar ever since he, brother Bobby and Jimmy Greaves had discovered during an England training session what a pest he could be if he stood directly in front of the goalkeeper at corner kicks. As a masterpiece of tactical planning, it may not have ranked much higher than one of Baldrick's 'cunning plans', but it was certainly effective.

Bob Wilson, who spent the week of the final waiting for medical updates about an injured Jim Furnell, recalls the verbal battering that accompanied Leeds's physical intimidation at those set pieces. 'I always remember Paul Madeley saying things about my wife or family. They would try anything. Leeds had a defining part in my growth as a goalie because they used those corner-kick tactics at the time I started in the first team.'

Once it became clear that Furnell, central defender Ian Ure and striker John Radford, the spine of the team, would all recover from various knocks, Mee's selection options for the club's big day centred on whether Terry Neill would get a game and if he should keep faith with David Jenkins. The 21-year-old winger, who had impressed Mee with his control and sharpness in the youth team and reserves, had taken the place of George Johnston in the second leg against Huddersfield and justified Mee's decision with a goal. Even though the final would mark only the eighth first-team start of his career, Jenkins was again preferred to Johnston, whose nineteen games to that point in the season had produced only two goals.

Jenkins recalls, 'I always felt as a young player that Bertie was prepared to give you a chance. He would come and talk to you even if you weren't in the first team. When I went to Tottenham the next season, I found that Bill Nicholson was very different. He was fine with you if you were in the first team, but if you weren't, I felt he didn't really want anything to do with you. You felt it would be the same 11 playing week in and week out. With Bertie, you were always waiting to see if you were picked in the next game. I never would have guessed that I would get the chance to play at Wembley because I was only young. The first team was going well, but I got in against Huddersfield and scored and played two or three more games. Bertie took a chance and Don Howe helped me along once I was in the first team.'

Most newspaper men correctly anticipated Mee's decision to leave Terry Neill on the bench. The Irishman had missed only one game all season, but with Ure and Simpson both fit, it was they who represented Mee's preferred pairing in the centre of defence. The manager broke the news to Neill in his office on the day before the game. It was not taken well and, on the way home from training, a distracted Neill drove into the back of another vehicle.

In the Wembley dressing-room the next day, Neill, still smarting, sat and read letters while Mee addressed the team. Even the disciplinarian manager could understand Neill's feelings sufficiently to turn a blind eye, although the Irishman admits his actions were 'petty and wrong'. Neill ended up missing the pre-game introductions to Princess Alexandra and, after the game, would not even collect his medal, telling reporters, 'This whole sickening business has set question marks flying around in my head about the future. Perhaps a change of clubs would be best all round.'

Arsenal's full line-up read: Furnell, Storey, McNab, McLintock, Simpson, Ure, Radford, Jenkins, Graham, Sammels, Armstrong. Sub: Neill, who would get on for the injured Jenkins in the second half. In the opponents' camp, Don Revie saw Giles and Jimmy Greenhoff pass fitness tests, enabling him to name a full-strength team.

Leeds, who had won all seven meetings between the teams since their promotion to the top flight and were playing in their third major final in less than three years, were the quicker team to settle, going ahead after 18 minutes. The goal came from a volley by Terry Cooper, the finest attacking left-back of the time, but the chance had, inevitably, been chiselled out of controversy. Arsenal insisted to referee Les Hamer that Jack Charlton had forced Furnell to the ground as they failed to clear Eddie Gray's corner. The relatively early goal did not lead to the open game that observers had craved, although not expected. George Armstrong missed a clear chance to turn the course of the game, but Mee's team seemed reluctant to press forward in search of an equaliser. Leeds, for their part, were intent on not letting another trophy slip through their grasp, bringing back wide midfield players Paul Madeley and Greenhoff to act as supplementary full-backs. When they did attack, their moves were dealt with comfortably by Ure and Simpson. The rest of the game was played out in a stalemate of tedium and tantrums, including a full-scale brawl that broke out after McLintock charged into Leeds goalkeeper Gary Sprake. Arsenal had the better of the second-half chances, Graham being crowded out when he took too long in preparing his shot. Physical assaults aside, Sprake's most difficult moment was when a shot by Radford forced him to save at full stretch.

The final whistle was a blessed relief to the neutrals in the stadium, although Leeds and the fans cared little about the manner of their victory as they at last celebrated a major success. As the Arsenal fans, in an act that earned additional condemnation, booed the Leeds players on their lap of honour, the press-box observers were clacking away on their poisoned typewriters. Desmond Hackett, not one to miss such a golden opportunity for vitriol, told *Daily Express* readers, 'This League Cup final will make history only as a game so bad it was little short of scandalous.'

Even the publications that had more time to take a fully considered view joined in the condemnation. *Football Monthly* coupled the Wembley events with a dull and bad-tempered 1–1 draw between Scotland and England under the headline, 'Shabby and Squalid – What have we come to?' Arsenal and Leeds were accused of a 'complete and cynical disregard for the £90,000 paid by real football supporters'. As bad as it may have been, the game offered a pretty accurate picture of the stage of development at which the two clubs stood: Leeds, supremely gifted in some areas but content to put the need for victory above all else; and Arsenal, an averagely talented, hard-working team unable to produce the inspiration to break down resolute opponents. To have expected anything different just because the game was played below the Twin Towers would have been naively optimistic.

The mood around Highbury in the aftermath of defeat was one of philosophical acceptance. Mee said to his players, 'Forget all about Saturday. Just remember how well we played to get there.' For a club starved of even the smallest taste of success, it did appear that having been invited to the banquet was more important than walking off with the silverware.

Sammels adds, 'We had just been thrilled to reach the final. It was not particularly good to play in, but at least we got something out of it. Bertie obviously wanted to win, but he did not seem too disappointed. He was very unflappable, always on a nice even keel. He must have had moments when he felt like blowing his top, but he never appeared to have many real highs and lows.'

Radford adds, 'Leeds at that time were dominating and bullying people. Losing to them in the League Cup was a good game for us in some ways because from then on we started to get a little bit like that ourselves and we were probably the first side to stand up to them.

Reaching Wembley that year was really the turning point. The club hadn't done anything, but 1968 was the beginning of it. Success breeds success. You get a feeling in the squad that you are capable of winning things and you can attract better players. We just started getting stronger from then on.'

9

GETTING ON WITH IT

Bertie's big saying was, 'Let's get on with it.' He felt that if you spent too much time talking about things, it was not productive.

– former Arsenal coach Don Howe

IN THE WAKE OF THEIR WEMBLEY DEFEAT AGAINST LEEDS, Arsenal's 1967–68 season drifted to an uneventful conclusion. A fifth-round FA Cup exit at the hands of Birmingham was most notable for Bertie Mee's decision before the replay at St Andrews to drop Jim Furnell, whose missed punch had allowed Geoff Vowden's header to cancel the Gunners' lead late in the first game. Mee instead selected Bob Wilson, who, injury apart, would maintain his position as Arsenal's number 1 for the next six years.

Cutting an eccentric figure with his college scarf, duffel coat and educated air, Wilson had been limited by fierce competition and a couple of untimely injuries to only ten first-team appearances in the five years since his Arsenal debut. Other than one abandoned game, he had not been selected since breaking his arm against Fulham two years earlier. He could not prevent a 2–1 defeat at Birmingham, but played well enough to force Furnell to demand a transfer, resulting in his eventual move to Rotherham.

With no further hope of success during the current campaign, crowds at Highbury slumped as low as the 11,262 who saw a late-season victory against Sheffield Wednesday. There must have been trepidation when the home fixture against Leeds had to be rearranged for the final midweek of the season. But on a night when the main television competition was the BBC's *Moira Anderson Sings* and an ITV production of *Dial M for Murder*, there was no repeat of the 1966 boycott and more than 25,000 witnessed an exciting 4–3 win.

Arsenal departed for their end-of-season trip to Japan and Malaysia in a mood of optimism after winning their final five games. But events in London in the last week of May served as a reminder of how far they remained behind the best in the country. While Arsenal were taking on mediocre Asian opposition, Manchester United were being crowned kings of Europe after their 4–1 defeat of Portugal's Benfica at Wembley.

It was towards the Continent that Mee had been looking as he attempted to create a new, fresh programme of pre-season training in anticipation of his third year in charge. He decided that Arsenal would conduct part of their preparation at a training camp in the German countryside at Hennef, near Cologne. As Steve Burtenshaw, who had become reserve-team coach following Don Howe's elevation to the first team, explains, 'Bertie liked to get a lot of the hard pre-season work done before you went away. Then you would go overseas and maybe play three games in a week before going home and easing down for a few days.'

Isolated among picturesque pine woods, the camp would, Mee believed, help to foster team spirit, as well as provide a test of endurance and fitness. The complex featured timber steps set into steep slopes, christened 'Cardiac Hill' by the players after they discovered that they were required to sprint up and down them. It also offered four football pitches, an Olympic-sized swimming pool and service equal to that of a first-class hotel.

Mee explained his philosophy in a later edition of the *Arsenal Football Book*:

> I went on a study course in Germany and Hennef impressed me
> with its facilities and position of relative isolation. Pre-season
> training, which usually lasts five weeks, is pretty intensive and

very hard work. If you are going through the work in the same surroundings, it can become pretty boring, but in different surroundings it is more acceptable. It was fundamental to establish togetherness – and living together for 24 hours a day gave us that. Perhaps one of the reasons we did so well in 1968–69 was because of the things we had gained there pre-season.

Those travelling to Germany included 16 first-team players, although reserves and youths would be added in future years. Mee, who did not believe in isolating players from families longer than necessary, identified ten days as the optimum length for the camp. The days began with an 8 a.m. breakfast and continued with two-hour training sessions in the morning and afternoon. Games were arranged against Aachen and Borussia Moenchengladbach, before Arsenal returned to Britain to draw against Rangers in Glasgow.

But it was activity on the training field that was more important than the results of friendlies. Don Howe had persuaded Mee to let him scrap the man-to-man marking installed by Dave Sexton two years earlier and introduce a zonal defence, where players were responsible for an area of the field rather than sticking doggedly to one man. Howe recalls Mee showing typical faith in his intentions. 'When we were in Germany I said, "I don't like the way we have players running around with their forwards, allowing themselves to be dragged all over the field. I'd like to change it." Bertie just said, in that way of his, "All right. Get on with it."'

Bob McNab recalls, 'It was a very brave decision, since only Don and myself had experience with the zonal system and the other defenders were not convinced that we should change. We'd had a bit of success with the man-for-man system.'

Frank McLintock, soon to become a key part of the zonal defence, explains, 'We used to pass men over. If my centre-forward was running out to the right wing, I could have ended up running into corner flags and we would be pulled all over the place. So when the centre-forward started his run, I would go with him for five or ten yards and then the right-back just used to come and get him. Peter Simpson would do the same with Bob on the left. It was carefully mapped out.'

With McLintock still charging around in midfield at that time and the number 5 jersey swapping according to fitness and form between Terry Neill and Ian Ure, the linchpin at the centre of defence was the unflappable Peter Simpson. Calm under pressure and an excellent reader of the game, it appeared to be only a lack of confidence and ruthlessness that prevented the dark-haired defender from Norfolk from playing for his country. It was a trait Bertie Mee had recognised even before taking over as manager. Cajoling Simpson to take a more positive approach to his career had become a pet project.

'I suppose I didn't have enough belief in myself,' Simpson admits. 'I have always been a pessimist, still am. In my early days at Highbury, I lacked the drive and determination to improve. I needed to be pushed in training all the time and I was content to remain an Arsenal reserve. Bertie was then the physiotherapist and occasionally after training he would take me aside to say something like, "If you got down to it, you could make the first team. You have the ability."'

Mee continued to drive home that message when he took responsibility for team selection and, having played only eight League games in Billy Wright's last season, Simpson missed only six in the first year under new management. 'Around that time I got married. The extra responsibility made me think of Bertie's words of warning. When I heard rumours I was available for transfer I finally realised I had to gee up. But for Bertie, I could have been in the Fourth Division.'

Having returned to England with a new defensive system, it was back to the usual training routine for the Arsenal players as they embarked on another season. For Bertie Mee that meant achieving the delicate balance between ball work, tactical organisation and the kind of fitness training that would add a defining element to his successful sides. Frank McLintock explains, 'We could play against anyone and they would be huffing and puffing and we never felt we were in any danger. We had a very athletic side. We could run all day and no one competed like we did. Actually, we probably trained three times harder than the modern Arsenal team.'

In a week where there was no Tuesday or Wednesday game, Monday would generally be a winding-down day for the players, an opportunity to work out any stiffness of joints. Games of one-touch football or five-a-side would be the norm. It was a day when, especially if the team had won at the weekend, London Colney was a happy place and football seemed like the greatest profession in the world.

Tuesday was different: a hard-working day at Highbury featuring circuit training and weightlifting in the gymnasium. With his background in physical rehabilitation, Mee prided himself in striking a compromise between the fatigue and staleness that could be caused by overworking his players and the retention of fitness levels that had been achieved during pre-season. Power and endurance were the end products that Mee hoped to achieve, which was why cross-country runs and 'doggies' – a series of forty-yard sprints at five-second intervals – featured prominently in the Arsenal routine.

Whenever possible, Wednesday was a rest day for the players, who would report back on Thursday to work on tactics and set pieces. On Friday, the emphasis would be on short, explosive work and fast-paced games of five-a-side, all aimed at getting the players sharp for the next day's game. The flow of a real game would be simulated with a sequence of six laps of the field, completed with a series of sprints, jogs and periods of walking. There would be no warning about when the players would change disciplines.

Films of previous Arsenal games did not figure highly in the weekly routine – and not just because of the technical constraints of the pre-video age. Howe said, 'We have tried closed-circuit television, but my feeling is that this tends to make you too critical of your play because all you can do is criticise a move that has broken down or a wrong tactic. We prefer to watch films showing what other teams are doing.'

Throughout the frenzy of activity at London Colney, the figure of Mee would often be seen walking between the first team's training area and the youth team's practice pitch. John Radford recalls, 'Bertie would be out there at training most days and when he wasn't you could tell that the lads were taking it just a little more easily. When Bert was out there, things went up 10 per cent.'

Frank McLintock adds, 'He would jump down hard on us if we needed it. We trained hard under Don Howe, so much that the modern player would wonder how the hell we did it. When you don't know any better, you just do it. Bertie wasn't at training all the time; sometimes he would have been tied up with some kind of administration. But we worked even harder when Bertie was there. He had this way about him that made you want to run and run and adopt a kind of "I'll show you" attitude.'

George Graham believes that Mee would be 'perfect' in the modern game with his approach to his staff and players. 'I think he would have been a successful manager today and a strong manager. I think the more successful and wealthy the players become, the stronger the manager needs to become. If the players today think you are a weak manager, you've got no chance. And I think all this stuff about foreign coaching is nonsense. What the majority of managers do now is hire a coach, discuss tactics with him and then stand back and let the coach get on with it. That is what Bertie did 30 or 40 years ago.'

Many years later, Mee explained to *Arsenal in the Blood* author David Lemmon:

> I left most of the coaching to Don Howe. That is what a dual situation is all about. Management, in those days, was, and still is, that your number one fitted into one of two categories. He was either, as in my case, an over-40 who'd been through the mill in more ways than one and understood people. And who was supported by a very good technical coach indeed, who could have a go, could shout his head off if need be. Then I could go in and pick them up. You could have a reverse situation – a young manager supported by a 45 year old who again had been through the mill.

Mee's morning staff meetings formed a vital part of the day's activities, as Steve Burtenshaw recalls. 'We would end every day with a chat about what was going on tomorrow and in the morning Bertie would have his nine o'clock cup of tea with the staff. Everything was organised then. You knew every day roughly what you were going to be working on, but you could alter it if you felt you were ahead of schedule or needed to work harder on something else. Bertie was flexible in that respect. Bertie didn't do the coaching himself, obviously. He would plan more of the physical and running activities and he would always be there for encouragement.'

Howe adds, 'In the staff meeting every morning, we would start off talking about football in general, maybe whether people had seen the game on the television the night before. We wouldn't spend very long analysing things. Bertie would ask everyone what they were doing that morning. You would tell him what you would be working on and he would ask why and then say, "Right, get on with it." Then he would put on his tracksuit and walk around. He would watch us working and kept in touch with all the coaches and their different sessions.'

Mee explained a little of his relationship with his staff, notably coach Don Howe, in an interview for the *London Soccer Annual*. Typically, he stressed his role as a creator of an environment in which the talents of his colleagues could be fully exploited:

> We have an extremely good working relationship. Not only between Don and myself, but I like to think all the members of our staff are involved. Indeed, we have a staff meeting every morning to discuss the numerous facets of the club's life, although when it comes to team selection and tactics for the occasion then it is a matter between Don and myself. Don obviously deals with the training and is completely in the picture regarding any decision I may make at a higher level. I like to think that my own contribution is to create a climate in which every member of the staff has maximum responsibility, is well aware of his own particular contribution, and he also knows that any constructive suggestions will be very welcome.

Tactics and training methods came together easily, according to Howe, without too much fretting and fussing. 'Most of the important conversations Bertie and I had were just before and after games. We didn't have long conversations every day. When the team was selected there were long discussions about who should be in, and then before the game we'd meet and talk over a glass of wine. But Bertie didn't ring my house and say, "Let's have a chat about football." In fact, I don't think he ever rang the house. He would say there was no need for long chats day after day.

'We would perhaps go together to watch a club that we would be playing. We would make a few comments and be aware of the opposition but we didn't change our side around. We would work on our own problems in training, not have long drawn-out sessions working on the opposition.'

Mee and Howe found it easy to present a united front on team issues, although players recall one infamous half-time in a game at Ipswich where Mee's 'well done' comment to the team was greeted by Howe screaming, 'Fucking well done?' Mayhem ensued as, confronted by Howe's in-your-face tirades, players attempted to avoid eye contact and one even hid in the toilets. 'Don, Don,' said Mee in an attempt to quell the storm before threatening to call security.

Mee may have tried to play peacemaker on that occasion, but many of those who worked on his staff recall a man who could be unforgiving if he felt that the required results were not being achieved. George Wright, the Gunners' physiotherapist during Mee's trophy-winning seasons, says, 'Bertie could be very sympathetic and want your help, but at other times he would let you know he was in charge and would pick fault with you. I remember he picked me up for wearing a polo neck instead of a collar and tie at one of our meetings. I think he suffered from small-man syndrome and could become a bit aggressive. When I was working with him, I was not so aware, but I became aware of it when I looked back.'

Dave Sexton is a little more forgiving in his memories. 'I thought he was a great man, a good teacher and he loved his football. He had a good heart. By that I mean he would give praise when it was due and could be firm if things weren't going right. I thought he was very fair. And he had a very good sense of humour. He made it fun to go to work. He was quick to smile and laugh and see the funny side of what we were doing. And he could laugh at himself sometimes. Life in football can be dramatic, with ups and downs, but he was a good man to work for. He was never daunted by the challenges and was always pushing his staff. To me, he was a loveable bloke and gave me a great chance.'

Fred Street, who had seen Mee's management methods in a non-football environment, found that little changed when he became a club manager. 'Bertie believed in a degree of fear as a controlling force. His chair behind his desk was a little bit higher than others to make people feel uncomfortable. Many of the staff at Arsenal were scared of Bertie. They used to disappear and hide if he was coming.

'He nit-picked. Tony Donnelly, our kit manager, used to make the tea every morning for the staff meeting. Bertie used to like sergeant major's tea: very strong with one sugar. He would come in at nine o'clock spot on. If his tea wasn't the right consistency or temperature, he would give Tony a bollocking – and Tony had probably been in since half past seven. "That's his job," Bertie would say.'

Another comment from some of Mee's colleagues is that he was too slow to offer praise. Street says, 'He never had much time for patting you on the back. He rarely gave you a "thank you", which I felt was a failure. I used to say to him that, with some of these staff, a little pat on the back goes further than a ten-quid pay rise. If you are the groundsman, it is great to hear, "The pitch is looking nice." Bertie could be quick to tell you if it wasn't looking nice, but he felt that was what you were paid to do.

'I remember a League Cup game when the drinks were not in place for the players before extra time and Bertie got angry with me. I felt he implied we weren't committed to the cause. I said, "Bert, we do our best. Cock-up? Yes, I accept that, but it was not with intent and I personally resent it if you feel that. The staff would walk through the bloody wall for you." So he did have that shortcoming, but his good points clearly outweighed his bad. He was like that all his life – organised – I think to the irritation of many people. You could do that in the army and, in principle, it isn't a bad way to run a place. It cuts through, even though it does step on a few toes.'

Steve Burtenshaw takes up the theme. 'If Bertie asked you to do something and you had not done it in the given time, he would want to know why and would not be pleased. If there was a problem, he would want you to go to him and explain. If you were the kit manager, it was no use turning up on Saturday with no change of shirts or not having the right number of cones at training. He allowed you the privilege of doing it in your own way but he expected you to be organised yourself.

'Of course, it was collar and tie every time you went to the training ground or stadium. You went into the ground and changed out of your tie after he'd had his meeting with the staff. For me, the nice thing about Bertie and Don was that they really listened to what you told them about the reserve team. I would put in a written report to Bertie and he would go through it with me and take a great interest. Bertie could be generous in his praise, but it didn't come very often. But if he said something like, "You have done a damn good job with Ray Kennedy," then you felt six-foot tall. It was not always possible for him to be like that. At times he was under intense pressure.'

Some of that pressure was simply due to the fact that, despite all of Mee's expertise in delegating and organising, a football environment could not always be managed to the extent that he would have liked. In an interview in the *Daily Telegraph* in September 1968 he said:

> I was brought up in organisations in which, if the influences within them could be controlled, there would be stability and progress. Football is not like that. It teems with factors the manager can't control: well-meaning friends, journalists, home influences, inter-personality problems between players and carrots dangled by other clubs. These things can arise in the outside world but never in such an explosive and emotional atmosphere.

Given the pressures he had to endure, plus the strength of his own personality and his background in physiotherapy, it is to Mee's credit that he was restrained enough to stay out of the treatment room once he became Arsenal manager. Street recalls, 'He never stuck his nose in or said, "I wouldn't do this," or, "Why are you doing this?" He would come in when I was doing an examination but he would never interfere. I never felt embarrassed or awkward or felt he was looking over my shoulder. We never had an argument over a player's fitness.'

George Wright has the same memories, although he took the precaution of laying his cards on the table before taking a job with Mee. 'There was no interference, but before I went to Arsenal I had it out with him. I told him that anything to do with physiotherapy would be down to me. I was a good organiser as well and I am sure he saw that. He never put pressure on me.'

Pressure, however, was something that Mee was accustomed to living with. He had seen the past bear down on Billy Wright and, over the next year or so, was to feel the full weight of it on his own shoulders.

10

TRADITION AND ILLUSION

History is more or less bunk. It is tradition. We want to live in the present, and the only history worth a tinker's damn is the history we make.

— Henry Ford

Tradition is the illusion of permanence.

— Woody Allen

THE WORLD OF FOOTBALL PUBLISHING ENTERED A NEW ERA AT the start of the 1968–69 season with the publication of *Goal*, a weekly stablemate to IPC's long-established *Charles Buchan's Football Monthly*. *Goal* would take football journalism further down the road – some would say slippery slope – towards youth culture than any of its predecessors with its mixture of colour posters, star columnists and instant life stories. Typically, one of those pieces would, in the space of a few hundred words, recount how some familiar figure of football's televised age had fought back from rejection or injury or suchlike to find himself banging in the goals that were the talk of the playgrounds. A year later, *Shoot!* would travel further along the same route with more colour, shorter features and interviews in the form of instantly digestible questionnaires. The number of posters that ended up on bedroom walls was of more interest to either publication than serious analysis.

The tabloids, meanwhile, were getting more heavily than ever into 'flyers' about possible record-breaking transfers, first-person 'buy-ups' and match reports that were sensationalised as much as possible through the use of quotes by the protagonists. It was a situation that would be lamented and lampooned when the anti-magazine *Foul* arrived for a brief yet eventful spell on the news racks from 1972 until its demise four years later.

For those football fans who did not read the broadsheets, it was *Charles Buchan's Football Monthly*, established in 1951 by the former Arsenal captain, that offered the most in-depth reporting on games. It may not have been Pulitzer Prize-winning material, but it did carry enough of a reputation that few at Arsenal would have been thrilled by the double-page examination of the club's 15 years of underachievement that ushered in the new season. Under the headline 'The Tarnished Image', the article stated that the club's 'retreat from glory' had been 'bedevilled by unfortunate managerial appointments and squalid disputes with players'.

The anonymous author described Arsenal as a 'dreadfully inept team' and referred to the perceived problems of Mee's predecessors by suggesting, 'Swindin found a new type of Arsenal player resenting measures his own contemporaries had accepted. Wright discovered he was short of the bravehearts he had been accustomed to at Molineux and was entitled to expect at Highbury.'

Given that without the achievements of the past there would be nothing newsworthy about the current drought, it was inevitable that such analysis would draw constant comparisons with previous Arsenal dynasties. 'You felt the pressure, and you felt it big-time because they'd had so much success,' says Frank McLintock. 'All the old names, like Cliff Bastin, Joe Mercer and Ted Drake, would come up and we felt, "Fuck it, we've achieved nothing."'

As proud as Mee was of the heritage of Arsenal Football Club, it irked him that judgement of his players always seemed to be based on how they measured up against their illustrious predecessors. What was important to him was the team's development in relation to their current rivals, not whether John Radford was another Ted Drake. To Mee, the issues of upholding tradition and creating a successful team were unrelated, which was why he so often downplayed the club's history. If he refused to be intimidated by the bust of Herbert Chapman, his players should not feel haunted by the photographs of great teams that hung on the walls inside Highbury.

Don Howe remembers, however, that some of those pictures were eventually removed. 'We had a little room by the side of the treatment room that was full of team photographs, going back to FA Cup wins and the like. We had them taken down because Bertie felt that we were building a new team and it was time to move on. It was not done to be disrespectful. In fact, he had great respect for tradition. His saying, "Remember who you are, what you are and who you represent," was rammed down the players' ears. Bertie knew the club was famous but he didn't want it to inhibit the players. He wanted them to express themselves and become great players, while maintaining the Arsenal standards.'

George Graham understands the pressure that tradition places on Arsenal managers, having inherited the position ten years after Mee's eventual departure from Highbury. 'It was always "the Arsenal" and things had to be done in the right way. You think of Arsenal and you think of the standards they have set. They were, and are still, recognised as one of the establishment clubs of the football world. Everything has to be the Arsenal way; from the code of conduct to the dress code. Things like that, the small things, add a certain pressure but they were important to me and they were certainly important to Bertie.'

Mee understood that it was a difficult balancing act to both honour and, at the same time, ignore the past, as illustrated by his comments on the subject in an interview around that time:

> I am not affected in any way by the traditions of the club. This represents history as far as I am concerned and it is the present and the future that I have always been concerned with. I think the important thing is to try to create new traditions that the present generations can associate themselves with, rather than just live in the past.

> I am, of course, grateful for the history. But we are in the process of building our own traditions. And these will be better than the old ones. There is a new generation of fans to

whom the names of Hapgood, Male, Copping and Drake have no meaning whatsoever. We cannot live in the past at Highbury.

Nobody has the birthright for success. It is something which has to be worked at, and worked hard at. But I will say this. If any team should succeed it is Arsenal. We are a great club which, on the field in recent years, has not lived up to its own testing standards. That is something I earnestly hope will be put right soon.

Even Mee was forced to admit that, as much as he might try to downplay the club's history, the players could not escape it. Quoted in *Goal* magazine, he confessed:

> There is an air of self-criticism and disappointment when things are going wrong, but when we take senior players on one side and discuss the situation they are at a loss to explain it. They talk about an atmosphere that is different to anything they have known with other clubs and they are terribly conscious of it. It prevents them from settling down to enjoy their game and it isn't easy to relax. We are not making excuses, but it could be that the club's past with its tremendous history of success works against us. Arsenal dominated English football in the '30s and became the most famous of our clubs. It is still a great club and I have tremendous faith in our future, but I cannot think of any club where players have to work so hard to win favour with the crowd.

With the 1968–69 season marking Arsenal's 50th year of unbroken tenure in the First Division, there was more retrospection than usual as the new campaign drew near. Every newspaper and magazine, it seemed, was using the anniversary as the hook for stories about the barren years. Club chairman Denis Hill-Wood would be moved to put pen to paper in the club's first home programme of the season, writing, 'There seems to be a misconception abroad that Arsenal managers, since Tom Whittaker, have been stifled and restricted by the Board of Directors and refused money with which to go into the transfer market. I can deny this absolutely.'

The *Sunday Telegraph* backed up the chairman's claims, but put forward its own reasons for Arsenal's decline:

> It has been said that three things were needed to restore prestige at Highbury: the removal of the legendary Herbert Chapman's bust from the main hall and with it the obsession with the past, the establishment of absolute authority in team matters with the manager at the expense of the secretary, and better relations with the press. This season journalists are admitted to the inner sanctum, but Chapman and the authority of secretary Bob Wall remain undislodged.

Such comments prompted the chairman to rush into print again in the next Arsenal programme, saying, 'It is despicable to suggest that the bust of Herbert Chapman should be removed.' But it was the implication that Mee was under the influence of the bow-tied Wall, the man who had risen from office clerk under Chapman, that particularly rankled. 'Bob Wall is just as much disturbed as I am that it should be said, if not widely thought, that he has any kind of authority over the manager. Arsenal managers, for at least the past 40 years, have had absolute control over their own department.'

Arsenal director Ken Friar supports that statement, commenting, 'Never has there been outside influence on the playing side of the club, not in Herbert Chapman's day, Arsène Wenger's or Bertie Mee's. Bertie, like other managers, had total control over the football side. Obviously he didn't have control of the whole club, nor would he have expected it. Sport is a business; there is always finance and administration involved and some prudence has to be exercised. In the matter of transfers, things operated then as they do now. Bertie would discuss with the board the players in whom he was interested and it would, in most cases, be me who handled the negotiations.'

Mee was undoubtedly his own man in the matter of team affairs. It is conceivable, however, that his reluctance to volunteer comment to the media on every little club matter could sometimes be misinterpreted as a lack of authority. It was, after all, often Wall who commented on transfer activity. Perhaps the suggestion that Mee did not have autonomy was a considered ploy to bring him more out into the open on such issues.

As the new season approached, the story occupying those members of the media whose job it was to record events at Highbury concerned the desire of Arsenal stalwarts Jon Sammels and Frank McLintock to leave the club. Late in 1967–68, Sammels had decided he'd had enough of being the Highbury crowd's scapegoat. An elegant midfielder with an explosive shot, his playing style made him a convenient target for the crowd when things went wrong, as they often did. Many fans still appeared to bear the grudge of Sammels displacing the popular George Eastham.

John Radford, who took over from another Highbury favourite, Joe Baker, adds, 'We were replacing popular players so it wasn't very enjoyable to play as kids. Even when we ran out there and were kicking in before the game, we were getting stick. I can understand it a little bit because we were replacing two superstars, but they were superstars who had never won anything for the team.'

That Sammels would consider leaving the club he had loved even before joining them as a wide-eyed schoolboy from Suffolk demonstrated the depth of his hurt. Denis Hill-Wood made it clear that Sammels would be going nowhere, but, in private, Mee had told his player, 'Let's see how you feel in a few months' time. If you feel the same way at the end of the season, come and tell me.' In the meantime, the compromise solution was that Sammels was left out of the team for half a dozen games. 'He is being rested by mutual consent,' said Mee, unaware that the problem would eventually return and place one of the few black marks against his greatest managerial triumph.

With the Sammels situation unresolved, Mee was to receive another shock when McLintock, his on-field general, explained on the eve of pre-season training that he no longer felt Arsenal was the club for him. After meeting the manager, McLintock told the press, 'I have been offered a contract that is very fair but I am desperately keen for success and think my chances may be better with a different club.'

Arsenal held a board meeting at which they decided that both McLintock and Sammels would be staying. Mee, hurt by the implied criticism of his management, clearly stated Arsenal's position. 'I don't think Frank was very judicious in his choice of words when discussing his transfer with the press. I like to think that we can and will have success next season. I am doing everything I possibly can to strengthen the side and hope to achieve that in the near future. We want Frank and Jon to stay with us and will do our best to convince them that Arsenal can offer them all they need. Frank and Jon are both intelligent, likeable men and I know they will continue to give of their best for Arsenal on the pitch.'

That may have been the case, but it did not stop McLintock threatening to take his case to the Football League, with the backing of the Professional Footballers' Association. The League quickly told him that there was nothing they could do, to which McLintock's response was to announce his intention to go before an independent tribunal 'in the hope of getting a fair hearing'. He said later, 'It wasn't easy asking to quit a club who had always treated me well but many people overlooked the fact that I was taking a gamble by moving and maybe dropping money.'

With his own players, as well as the media, pointing the finger of underachievement at him and his club, Mee could have hoped for a less pressurised opening to the season than a trip to White Hart Lane. But a 2–1 victory against Tottenham, earned by defending stoutly and attacking on the break, was to be the springboard to the club's best start to a season for many years and a spell at the top of the First Division. While the unsettled Sammels was Arsenal's most influential midfield player, it was John Radford who earned the headlines by harrying defender Phil Beal into an own goal and scoring one himself.

As Arsenal prepared to open their home season against Leicester, Mee, choosing to come clean with journalists, admitted that he was giving 'serious consideration' to bidding for Burnley winger Willie Morgan, rated at £100,000. But within 24 hours, he had decided that Morgan would 'not measure up to our requirements' and had seen his team beat Leicester 3–0 without him. Substitute Bobby Gould scored twice in a game that had McLintock saying, 'If we were to go on producing performances like this, I would reconsider my transfer plans.'

They did, winning seven and drawing two of their first nine League games. On a rain-soaked late-summer evening – the day that saw spinner Derek Underwood destroy Australia at The Oval after hundreds of fans helped the ground staff to soak up the puddles – the Gunners hammered reigning champions Manchester City 4–1 to top the League. David Jenkins scored twice in a display that had chants of, 'We are the champions,' rolling off the North Bank. Premature, but excusable. It had been a long time since Highbury had an excuse for a knees-up.

Inevitably, McLintock and Sammels offered further cause for celebration by announcing their intention to stay, although Sammels's fragile position in the fans' affections was not helped when news broke that he had signed a two-year contract that, according to press reports, 'could make him one of the country's highest-paid footballers'. Sammels explains, 'We had a lot of young lads there who were going to be the nucleus of the side for a long time. I said to Bertie, "I don't think you are looking after us very well." Players coming in had been given signing-on fees and I asked if the club could do something to bring Simmo, Geordie, Johnny Radford, Peter Storey and myself into line. I didn't go in thinking I was going to sort it all out for the lads; I just went in for selfish reasons. I got quite a lot of bad publicity out of that and it looked like I was trying to be bigger than the club, which wasn't the case.'

The biggest test of Arsenal's position at the top of the table came towards the end of September, when the Gunners ventured to Elland Road to face Leeds, the team fast becoming their nemesis. Naturally, the *Match of the Day* cameras were present to offer a potentially intriguing climax to a Saturday night BBC line-up that showcased *The Black and White Minstrel Show*, featuring Leslie Crowther, and *Marty*, starring bug-eyed comedian Marty Feldman. The football, however, was not exactly an all-singing, all-dancing affair.

Don Revie took the opportunity of rubbing Mee's and Arsenal's noses in it by parading the League Cup before the game, along with their other piece of recently acquired hardware, the Inter-Cities Fairs Cup. Then, already leading by one goal, they pulled their old corner-kick routine. As usual, Jack Charlton placed himself directly in front of Bob Wilson and rose from the middle of a mêlée to divert the ball past the now prone goalkeeper. Arsenal's defenders turned in disbelief towards the officials, convinced Charlton must have been guilty of something.

Arsenal had little to offer other than solid defensive work. 'It was not a catastrophe or major calamity,' offered Mee. While the Arsenal of old may not have responded well to such a setback, this team was beginning to show signs of the resolve that would become its trademark. In the space of four days, Arsenal ground out a 0–0 draw

Above: The young Bertie Mee in his days as a winger with Derby County (Colorsport)

Left: Bertie turns on the matinée idol charm in an off-duty moment during his army training (Family collection)

Right: Bertie astride the horse that would feature in one of his favourite wartime tales. He carried this picture in his wallet for many years
(Family collection)

Below: Ballroom dancing with Doris was one of Bertie's favourite pastimes until football management limited such opportunities
(Family collection)

Above: Bertie Mee (front row, fifth from right) in his physiotherapist's coat as part of the FA staff at a coaching course at Lilleshall. To his right are England manager of the day Walter Winterbottom and future national boss Ron Greenwood (Stephan Ottewill collection)

Left: Bertie Mee was not recognised as a 'tracksuit manager' but his presence at training would increase intensity levels among the Arsenal players (Colorsport)

Above: George Graham (left), Eddie Kelly, Peter Marinello and Pat Rice
enjoy a light-hearted moment with their manager (Getty Images)

Below: Bertie Mee poses proudly with the Fairs Cup, the trophy that
put Arsenal back into football's elite after 17 years in the wilderness
(Getty Images)

Above: A rare show of emotion as Mee celebrates victory in the 1971 FA Cup final with, from left, Peter Simpson, match-winner Charlie George and George Graham (Colorsport)

Left: Happy days with Frank McLintock after victory in an FA Cup semi-final. Mee's decision to let his club captain leave in 1973 was one of the most debated moves of his career (Colorsport)

Above: Bertie Mee completes the biggest signing of his career, the £220,000 capture of Alan Ball from Everton (Getty Images)

Below: Walking out at Wembley with arch-rival Don Revie, the Leeds manager, before the 1972 FA Cup final (Colorsport)

Above: Bertie Mee bids an emotional farewell to the Highbury crowd at the end of his ten-year reign as Arsenal manager. Contrary to his wishes, he was granted no subsequent role at the club (Colorsport)

Below: The Watford dream team pictured in 1981: manager Graham Taylor, chairman Elton John and assistant manager Bertie Mee (Colorsport)

Above left: Outside Buckingham Palace with daughters Beverley and Allyson and wife Doris after being made an OBE (Family collection)

Above right: Bertie and Doris with granddaughters Daniella and Jianna (Family collection)

Below: The final family photograph, taken at Bertie and Doris's golden wedding celebrations in 1999. Daniella, Beverley with husband Gianni Miserotti, Allyson and Jianna complete the group (Family collection)

at Manchester United and took a point from Maine Road in a 1–1 draw with Manchester City. The days of games finishing 5–4 were clearly in the past. But now they were facing criticism of another kind. Having claimed that Arsenal would be going all out for two points at Old Trafford, Mee's team performed in such a way that the *Daily Express* likened them to 'a bunch of thugs'. Ian Ure explains, 'We were a method side. It wasn't always pretty to watch but it was effective. Arsenal became a hard team to beat because we were so well coached and organised, and had a great blend of players.'

Mee was willing to adopt a realistic approach to the business of achieving success and, in a subsequent edition of the *Arsenal Football Book*, he explained:

> For me, people watch football for excitement and to see their team win. A 1–0 victory can be every bit as exciting and invigorating as a 6–5 victory and much more so than running off winners 6–0. Scoring has become increasingly difficult in the last few years. The striker's job is much more complicated than it has ever been. Its demands are as much mental as physical. So much more thought has to be put into scoring that a striker has to approach a game with tremendous guile. It would be a tragedy for the game in this country if clubs adopted the *catenaccio* system which has stifled the game in Italy. At the same time, I cannot see the day when teams will throw caution to the wind in an attempt for goals.

While recognising and applauding Arsenal's stubborn streak, a return of one goal in four games meant that media and fans were once again highlighting the need for a regular scorer to support the worthy Radford, who had contributed roughly half the team's goals and earned an England call-up. Mee stated, 'If Arsenal sign another striker, he will have to be a top-notcher in the Geoff Hurst–Ron Davies mould.'

Instead, Mee had the choice of Bobby Gould, who failed to score in 12 consecutive starts after his double as substitute against Leicester, or George Graham, whose lack of pace made him an increasingly bad risk up front. In fact, it was not until midfielder David Court found the net in a 3–0 Boxing Day win against Manchester United that the wearer of Arsenal's number 9 shirt got on the score sheet in a League game.

Another run of three scoreless games followed, prompting Mee to examine the problem from a new angle. For the next game, a goalless draw against West Ham, Mee had a cameraman stationed on the roof of the Highbury stand. 'It's an experiment worth persevering with,' he said. 'It gave us an elevated view of the game. This helps us considerably on the tactical side to thrash out any problems.'

One option that Mee did not have to be 100 feet up in the air to recognise was giving an opportunity to young reserve-team striker Charlie George, who had hit nine goals in a burst of four games. Mee, however, decided he was still a few months from being ready for the First Division.

Meanwhile, Gould became the latest player to consider his Arsenal future when he was dropped for a home game against Nottingham Forest, only to be talked out of it by Don Howe. Encouraged to work on improving his ability as a wide player, his efforts paid dividends and, having won back his place shortly before Christmas, Gould embarked on a run of eight goals in ten League games. Six consecutive victories, stretching between the last day of November and 11 January, kept Arsenal in the thick of the Championship race.

And there was another Wembley final to look forward to, one that surely could not be lost this time.

11

BURIED AT WEMBLEY

Soothsayer: Beware the ides of March.

Caesar: What man is that?

Brutus: A soothsayer bids you beware the ides of
March.

– Julius Caesar, Act I Scene II
(William Shakespeare)

ARSENAL'S RUN TO THE 1967–68 LEAGUE CUP FINAL HAD GIVEN
them a fresh respect for English football's newest major competition.
Now the profile of the tournament was raised further when the
Football League finalised a deal with ITV to broadcast the final, albeit
highlights aired 24 hours after the event.

The Gunners' first steps towards a return to Wembley were
surprisingly tentative. They displayed little of the confidence evident in
their League games as they struggled past a limited Sunderland team,
Terry Neill's glancing header being helped in by an uncharacteristic
Jim Montgomery error. It was a smoother passage in the third round,
where Arsenal won 6–1 at Scunthorpe, although the home side did
have their moments. They had the better of the first 20 minutes and it
was against the run of play when Bobby Gould scored a scrappy goal.
Scunthorpe equalised when Peter Simpson sliced into his own goal,

but David Jenkins restored the lead two minutes later and added two more in the second half as his team cruised home.

The game was Jenkins' last significant contribution in an Arsenal shirt. A couple of days after the Gunners beat Liverpool 2–1 at home in the fourth round, he was off down the Seven Sisters Road. Tottenham paid Arsenal £55,000 for him and, a day later, got their money back when the Scottish winger Jimmy Robertson, a scorer in Spurs' 1967 FA Cup final triumph, agreed to move in the opposite direction. History would prove that neither achieved much of note for his new club, although it is not just with hindsight that the signing of Robertson seems a strange move. Even at the time it was suggested that Mee, who seemingly had little intention of playing two wingers, was guilty of undervaluing the player many felt was one of the finest wide men in the game, George Armstrong. It would not be the last time such accusations would be aired.

Victory against the men from Anfield, which secured a place in the quarter-finals, was a hard-earned affair. Simpson chipped past Liverpool's keeper Tommy Lawrence, 'The Flying Pig', from the edge of the box and the lead was preserved by Bob Wilson's save at the feet of Tommy Smith and the failure of Alun Evans to hit the target. Earlier in the season, Bill Shankly had caused a stir by becoming the first manager to pay £100,000 for a teenager when he bought Evans, a frail looking 19-year-old striker with a shock of blond hair, from Wolves. Liverpool eventually equalised with 15 minutes to play when right-back Chris Lawler, who scored more goals than many midfielders, headed in a free-kick. But the dependable Radford fired in a loose ball to win the game with two minutes remaining.

By the time the quarter-final tie against Blackpool came around, Arsenal's goalscoring problems were at their worst, but the result was never in doubt. 'Arsenal Go Gay – Five' said one quaintly dated headline after the Gunners' victory. Armstrong and Radford stretched the Blackpool defence and scored the first two goals before Simpson's powerful shot made it 3–0 at half-time. A reply from Blackpool's talented but injury-prone midfielder, Tony Green, did nothing to throw Arsenal off course. Gould flicked in the fourth goal and Armstrong ended a strong run with number five.

The fates decreed that Arsenal's semi-final opponents would be Tottenham, the neighbour whose own success had served to underline

Arsenal's lack of achievement. 'We'd had a rough period at that time and Tottenham always seemed to be doing well,' says David Court. 'The rivalry is not as vitriolic now, certainly from Arsenal's point of view, but during that period of time Spurs had their most successful team ever so it didn't help the situation. The club and the crowd wanted their share of success.'

More than 55,000 packed into Highbury to endure what, for 88 minutes, proved to be a frustrating evening. Both teams appeared scared of giving up a first-leg advantage to their rivals, although Sammels threatened on occasions and Radford saw a header cleared off the line. Without Martin Chivers, a long-term absentee because of a knee injury, Spurs put Mike England up front alongside Jimmy Greaves, who was enjoying one of his most prolific seasons and was even the subject of a national campaign to earn his reinstatement to the England team. But Greaves's makeshift strike partner was well handled by Ian Ure, back in the team because of Terry Neill's ankle injury.

Radford gave Pat Jennings an uncomfortable moment in the visitors' goal and Arsenal came close again when Court drove wide. But the action dried up during a drab second half that saw Gould enter to cheers when he replaced Graham. It seemed that the tie would advance to White Hart Lane deadlocked. Then, two minutes from time, Wilson launched a long clearance and Spurs right-back Joe Kinnear headed towards his own goal, into the path of an unmarked and unforgiving Radford.

The big Yorkshireman, awarded his first England cap against Romania a few weeks earlier, was the subject of an early example of 'squad rotation' before the return leg. Mee knew that Radford was the one player he could not do without and, like Arsène Wenger resting Thierry Henry, he left him out of the Division One game at Burnley. Mee told his player to stay at home and not think about football for 48 hours. The decision was to be justified on two fronts. First, Radford's replacement, Jimmy Robertson, scored the only goal at Turf Moor, and then came a brutal second leg in which physical strength was the chief requirement, with Radford again the key Arsenal figure.

The Arsenal–Spurs rivalry may not be fuelled by religion in the manner of, say, Rangers–Celtic, nor driven by political and territorial considerations like Barcelona–Real Madrid, but as far as straightforward football feuds are concerned, where the simple concern is handing the enemy more beatings than they give you, the north London derby ranks right up there. Few meetings between the two clubs have better illustrated the bitterness of the dispute than the 1–1 draw at White Hart Lane that propelled Arsenal into their second Wembley final in two years. 'The Shame of London' was how more than one newspaper described it.

The first half was particularly vicious, full of nasty, niggly confrontations that did neither team credit. It was more like the kind of game that English teams complained about so bitterly when they encountered them in European football. By the final five minutes, the fans were mirroring what they had seen on the field. Police waded in to keep the fighting factions apart and one young fan was taken to hospital with a stab wound.

The game had barely started when England stamped on Wilson's toes and referee John Gow had to jump in to separate players bent on retribution. Terry Venables shot over the bar for the home team and Ure came close with a header before another battle broke out. This time it was Spurs centre-half Peter Collins who floored Wilson, prompting a flurry of Arsenal fists. When the attention returned to the ball, Radford was just wide, Gould forced a smothering save from Jennings and Bob McNab was denied by more brilliance from the Irish keeper. The referee's notebook finally came out after Radford sparked another incident by kicking the ball away at a free-kick. Knowles pushed out at the Arsenal man, who then connected with a punch. 'I could easily have been sent off,' Radford recalls. Instead, it was Knowles who was cautioned for aiming a blow of his own. England was booked minutes later for another assault on Wilson.

Armstrong missed a good chance to give Arsenal a half-time lead and the Gunners lost Bob McNab to injury before Tottenham went ahead after 69 minutes. A rare moment of fluent football resulted in Jimmy Pearce crossing for Greaves to bang in his 25th goal of the season. Two minutes later, Greaves almost gave his team an aggregate lead before further action in the Arsenal goalmouth ended with Alan Gilzean becoming the latest player to lash out at the victimised Wilson.

Once again, Radford struck late. Only four minutes remained when Armstrong swung a corner into the box and the Yorkshireman headed into the net. Once the scare of Collins bouncing a header off the crossbar had been survived, Arsenal were back at Wembley. That was all that mattered to Mee and his team, not the fact that the final part of their journey had been no carnival parade.

Speaking before an FA Cup third-round tie against Cardiff early in 1969, Mee outlined his hope of reaching two Wembley finals that year, but it was to be an unfulfilled wish. By the time the League Cup final came around, Arsenal had gone out in the fifth round of the FA Cup. After beating Cardiff and Charlton, the Gunners went down 1–0 at West Brom when Tony Brown drove in a loose ball after Jeff Astle had been beaten in the air by Ure, re-established in the team when Terry Neill was struck down by hepatitis. With dropped League points having left the Championship apparently out of reach, the League Cup remained the one realistic hope for that long-awaited trophy. And only Third Division Swindon stood in the way. The 'big sleep' of 16 years was about to come to an end . . .

Danny Williams, a former Yorkshire miner, had rebuilt the Swindon team after its two-year stay in Division Two ended in 1965. Taking over from Bert Head, he netted £70,000 from the sale of forwards Mike Summerbee to Manchester City and Ernie Hunt to Wolves, and used the money to buy ten new players.

Swindon had knocked West Ham out of the FA Cup in January 1967 and had begun gathering momentum in this particular League Cup campaign with hard-fought victories over Torquay, Bradford and Blackburn. That set up a tie against First Division Coventry, who were overwhelmed by three goals in a replay, and Second Division high-fliers Derby, who had knocked out Chelsea and Everton but were beaten by Don Rogers' fifth goal of the tournament in another replay.

Rogers, linked on more than one occasion with a possible move to Arsenal, had been quickly marked down as a future star after serving his apprenticeship with Swindon. He converted the promise of his debut season, 1962–63, into performances that had made him the town's biggest sporting celebrity even before the events that would propel him into football folklore. Dark-haired and solidly built at 5 ft 10 in., he had at this time yet to cultivate the thick, drooping moustache that gave him his distinctive bandit look in later years. Although he lined up at number 11, his manager knew that isolating him on the left wing was like loading only one barrel of a shotgun and he was given freedom to roam the field.

Semi-final opponents Burnley went into the tie on the back of eight wins and a draw in their previous nine games, but goals from skipper Stan Harland and Peter Noble saw Swindon return from Turf Moor with a 2–1 advantage. After conceding two early goals at home, a late strike by John Smith earned Swindon a replay at West Brom, where they had the staying power to win 3–2 by virtue of Noble's decider.

While Swindon counted their Wembley windfall, Arsenal reckoned they were making £52,000 from the tournament, which attracted a record total attendance of more than two million. But as Arsenal's players were figuring out how to spend the bonus money that would accrue to them in the event of victory, Swindon's men were forced to accept that the sight of the Twin Towers would have to be payment enough. So remote had their chances of advancement to Wembley seemed at the outset of the season that no one had written bonuses for reaching the final into their contracts, while Football League rules forbade the rewriting of contracts mid-season. Still, the Swindon players were so excited about Wembley that manager Williams arranged an advance trip to north-west London to get some of the anticipation out of their systems. 'It certainly shattered a few illusions,' said defender Frank Borrows.

Wembley had never looked worse, its once lush green surface a colourless swamp. During showjumping's week-long residency for the Horse of the Year show the previous autumn, the horses had packed down the turf so much that drainage through the soil was almost impossible. Heavy rain meant that the pitch had to be pumped free of hundreds of gallons of rainwater a few days before the League Cup final so that England's game against France could go ahead. After that, the only repair work the ground staff could undertake was to replace divots. The surface was too wet to be rolled.

When Arsenal visited the stadium on the eve of the game, they couldn't believe their eyes. The energy-draining mixture of mud, sand and water upon which the game would be played was clearly a potentially fatal combination for a team recovering from a virus that had swept through the club. The previous week, eight players had been struck down by a chest infection that created congestion of the lungs and made breathing difficult, sending sufferers to their beds. It had forced the postponement of the scheduled League game at Liverpool. Now, even one of the traditionally fittest teams in the country feared what could happen over the course of 90 testing minutes.

Jon Sammels recalls, 'I got out of my bed on Thursday and went to Wembley to look at the pitch on the Friday. The rain was torrential and there were planks all over the pitch. It was a bog.'

Ian Ure argues, 'The game should never have been played; the water was up over my shoes. I thought it was not playable, but because it was a final it went ahead.'

Trainer George Wright adds, 'On the morning of the game they had all these jet driers on the pitch. It was a right mess. The players took the field with tracksuit tops on and when I went to collect them I was up to my ankles in mud.'

Swindon's return trip to the famous old stadium began on the Friday before the game, when they arrived at their hotel in Gerrards Cross late in the afternoon. The following day, as the players sat down to watch previews of the game on *World of Sport* and *Grandstand*, they couldn't help but notice a greater number of correspondents swarming round the Arsenal hotel than there were at their own residence.

Reporter Brian Moore had been one of those spending as much time as possible around the Arsenal camp as he prepared for his first major final after switching from radio to front ITV's football output for the London region. The last stage of Moore's homework was his chats with players early on the day of the game. When he spoke to Bobby Gould, Moore noted that the player had secured a ticket for his father, who was blind, and his wife, who would be providing a running commentary.

The lack of attention given to Swindon did nothing to undermine the confidence of the underdogs. They saw omens everywhere, including a 3–2 victory by Third Division Queens Park Rangers over West Bromwich Albion in the competition's first Wembley final two years earlier.

So it was that on 15 March, a fateful date for no less a leader than Julius Caesar, Bertie Mee's hopes of taking a trophy back to Highbury were to be administered a deadly blow. The press pack had not contained a single soothsayer prescient enough to read the signs of a Swindon victory. Desmond Hackett had been typically over the top in announcing, 'This is like Arkle at his peerless best running against game selling-platers.'

Having completed the pre-game formalities with Princess Margaret, Arsenal, wearing yellow and blue, took the field with this line-up: Wilson, Storey, McNab, McLintock, Ure, Simpson, Radford, Sammels, Court, Gould, Armstrong. Sub: Graham. They started strongly but Peter Downsborough proved to be Swindon's Horatio, holding the bridge in the face of a fierce onslaught. 'Downsborough broke our hearts,' says Ure, the pain still obvious. 'He was stopping everything. He would be diving one way and the ball would hit his heel or something.'

The Swindon keeper had already made three top-class saves before Swindon took the lead. Ure wrote himself into Arsenal's hall of shame with an ill-judged attempt to get the ball back to Bob Wilson, allowing Roger Smart to score. Skipper Frank McLintock recalls, 'Bob was shouting for the ball and Ian kept on dribbling it back. He was probably a bit worried about the surface. All of a sudden he gave it to Bob from about five yards away and it bounced off him and they put it in the net.'

Downsborough proceeded to spend the second half as he had the first, denying the First Division team a goal. His most notable effort was a spectacular mid-air save from a thumping Sammels volley. After Gould launched two successive shoulder charges on Downsborough, both players ended up in the net, with referee Bill Handley warning the Arsenal man, 'Do that again and you'll be taking an early bath.' With four minutes to play, the Swindon keeper at last made a mistake. Bursting from his line, he booted the ball against Gould, who reacted quickly to head into an unguarded net. The man who had struggled to win back his Arsenal place raised his arms skywards and thought of his father being given the description of his goal. In the commentary box, Brian Moore was aware of the significance of the moment. 'When he scored I said he had tears in his eyes and that while he celebrated, his father would be told the news,' he revealed later. Gould would not forget the commentary and after Moore broadcast his final game in 1998, he sent his old friend a card, saying, 'I've got tears in my eyes – Bobby.'

Arsenal had been temporarily reprieved but Howe was fretting about his players' ability to last another half an hour. He pleaded with

Handley to abandon the game. The Swindon players were encouraged by what they saw, defender Joe Butler explaining, 'I remember seeing Don Howe going berserk. Obviously they were worried.'

McLintock, about to suffer his fourth defeat in a Wembley final after two FA Cup losses with Leicester, remembers, 'Up to 90 minutes I was still bombing forward on a pitch that was about a foot thick in mud. But as soon as 90 minutes were up, someone blew out my candle. I couldn't lift my legs.'

As the players took the field again, Rogers stood out as the freshest-looking, his mud-free kit indicative of the way in which he had skirted round the edges of the action. But he was about to make his mark. With half-time approaching in the extra half-hour, he forced the ball home following a corner. And, with only seconds of the game remaining, he raced clear from halfway, veering in from the right to deceive Wilson and score from an acute angle. 'And that is that,' announced Moore, a piece of commentary that, in the West Country, still resonates every bit as much as Kenneth Wolstenholme's 'It is now.'

As the manner of Rogers' decisive goal indicated, Arsenal had simply run out of energy. Secretary Bob Wall would later criticise Mee and Howe for urging the team to go for a win in extra time. 'That was a mistake,' he wrote. 'I should have advised them to close up the game and look for a replay. The virus left us physically weak and tactically vulnerable. In extra time we had players with lead in their legs.'

McLintock, overwhelmed by fatigue and disappointment, wandered in a daze among the uniformed men of the Royal Engineers band. 'I was knackered and shell shocked. It was a terrible experience. I said to myself, am I ever going to win anything? But maybe it was the start of us getting closer as a team.'

The press, like everyone else, were as stunned as the Arsenal skipper. Desmond Hackett apologised to 'one of the best teams seen at Wembley' and urged his readers to 'look with admiration at these heroic athletes from the Third Division who reduced the bold traditions of Arsenal to a miserable myth'. In the *Sunday Express*, Alan Hoby described Arsenal as 'slaves of their own system, methodical but utterly predictable'.

While the Swindon players went off to a reception in London's Mayfair, where guest speaker Bob Monkhouse quickly changed his routine to reflect the team's unexpected success, Mee was left to stress the progress made by his players. 'I do not intend to destroy everything we have built up over the last two or three years because of defeat in one match. We are not going to hold a massive inquest, nor are we going to shake up the team and start selling players. We are a better side than we were a year ago and we will be better a year from now. Our aim is to win a place in the Fairs Cup. We are professional enough and confident enough to do just that.'

With the season in its final throes, Mee and Howe decided to experiment with two significant, and not unrelated, positional changes. George Graham, his place in the front line relinquished, had been given a game in midfield in a 5–0 win at Sheffield Wednesday in place of the absent Frank McLintock a couple of weeks before the League Cup final. Appearing only as a substitute at Wembley, Graham was reintroduced to the team in the number 6 shirt and asked by Mee to 'play as an old-fashioned left-half'.

Graham says, 'Bertie and Don had an idea that I could play in midfield and come late in the box and maybe get a few goals. So I took on a new role and enjoyed it.' Mee was quickly singing the praises of Graham, saying, 'George has done a tremendous job for us since taking over a midfield role. He breaks well from behind and because of his very high skill he has given the side a better balance and extra striking power.'

Graham's switch meant that a new role beckoned for McLintock. But if the relaxed skill on the ball of Graham – the man they called 'Stroller' – made him an obvious choice for a midfield berth, few players were impressed at the suggestion of chief scout Gordon Clark that McLintock could be converted from a high-energy midfielder into a disciplined central defender. Mee, however, once again demonstrated enough faith in his staff to put Clark's theory to the test. McLintock concedes, 'It was a dangerous thing to do, but Don and Gordon said they thought I would extend my career and do better for the club if I didn't play as someone who was driving forward the whole time.'

McLintock turned for help to Bob McNab, who recalls, 'To say I was not enthusiastic about it would be an understatement. Frank had shown nothing to give any indication he would have the discipline to become a centre-back. But, once you know Frank, you know anything is possible. He became so comfortable.'

It would not be until midway through the 1969–70 season that the move was established permanently, but the eventual success of it – along with the signing of the big blond Welshman John Roberts from Northampton – meant that Mee would soon end the Highbury careers of Terry Neill and Ian Ure. And it was Ure who needlessly brought down Alun Evans for the penalty that allowed Liverpool to hold Arsenal to a point at Anfield on the last day of March, a result that left the Gunners seven points behind Leeds with only eight games to play.

By the time the League leaders arrived at Highbury a couple of weeks later, Mee's goal of European qualification had been secured. A comprehensive 3–1 win at Wolves, a game that saw Graham score one goal and make the other two, confirming his potential as a midfielder, meant that a goalless draw a day later at Leicester was enough to ensure Arsenal's position as London's leading club. With that pressure relieved, Mee chose the eve of the Leeds game to reveal the depth of his anguish at the Swindon defeat and deliver an assessment of his team's progress. He told reporters, 'I felt sure we could pick ourselves off the floor but at that moment I was talking to convince myself. When we got around to talking about that disaster we found the thing to do was to give ourselves another target. We pledged ourselves to trying to remain unbeaten until the end of the season. Leeds are probably two years ahead of us, or rather I can see in Arsenal what Leeds were two years ago.'

The Leeds game itself was the usual battle. After only five minutes, Gould and goalkeeper Gary Sprake tangled and Sprake laid out the Arsenal striker with a left hook. The result was a booking for both men. Leeds went on to win 2–1, with Ure's miserable run continuing with two mistakes contributing to goals. There were more ugly incidents in a defeat at Chelsea two days later when McLintock took the bold step of planting a head-butt on Ron 'Chopper' Harris. Houseman and Osgood exacted retribution and Court was booked for a follow-up foul on Osgood, before Robertson aimed a kick at Harris and was then booked for arguing. At the end of the game, a 2–1 Chelsea victory, Arsenal's players were reported to have confronted referee Norman Burtenshaw and been led away by Don Howe – a typical day in English football in the late '60s.

Mee would never outwardly condone such incidents. But Peter Storey, Arsenal's renowned hard man, who would snarl and swear at players as he went into tackles, believes Leeds had set a trend that other teams were forced to follow – especially if, like his own team, they were not blessed with outstanding individual talent. 'They started all the rough stuff when they got promoted and other teams thought, if we can't beat them, join them. It was a conscious effort to take them on at their own game. It was not right, but all the teams were doing it.'

On the final day of their campaign, Arsenal missed the opportunity to clinch third place in the table when a 1–0 defeat at Everton meant they finished below the Goodison Park side, who were destined to win the title 12 months later. Arsenal's tactics and approach may sometimes have been questioned, but fourth place and another Wembley appearance represented their best season for a decade. Even the most cynical of Arsenal fans settled down for a summer of Apollo 11-watching with the feeling that maybe their own team was ready to reach for the stars.

12

MASTER AND COMMANDER

Discipline is simply the art of making the soldiers
fear their officers more than their enemy.
– Claude-Adrien Helvétius,
French philosopher (1715–71)

ONE OFTEN HEARS A FOOTBALL TEAM'S LEADER BEING DESCRIBED
as a 'players' manager'. What exactly that term means is open to debate.
At its best, it can refer to a manager who inspires respect and trust,
someone who becomes a friend, father-figure or confidant. At its
worst, it can be a simple euphemism for a manager who wants to be
'one of the lads', someone who ends up being taken for a ride by players
who interpret his desire to buddy up to them as a sign of weakness and
simply take advantage. Bertie Mee suspected that more fell into the
latter category. It was a mistake he would never make. If the unseen
pulse of any team is the camaraderie between players, the banter and
the jokes that fill the changing-room, then Mee knew better than to
interfere with such a life force. As Fred Street recalls, 'Bertie used to
talk about being a part of, but apart from, the team.'

George Graham, Mee's most successful managerial student, earned
the nickname of 'Gaddafi' because of the way he ruled the Arsenal
dressing-room during his nine years as manager. 'I think the ability not

to worry about being popular goes with all successful managers,' he says. 'Getting results is the number-one priority and if you do that the players will follow you. Bertie got results, although he was never close to the players.

'Bertie was very businesslike, not like Tommy Docherty, whom I had worked with at Chelsea before I joined Arsenal. At Chelsea, it was all about having fun and going down the Kings Road, but Arsenal was like an army camp. It took me a good 18 months to get used to it. Tommy was wise-cracking with one-liners and loved a joke with the lads, while Bertie was a total professional, total business.'

Don Howe once said that he thought Mee's biggest fault was that he never put his arm round a player and said 'well done'. Mee's reasoning had been, 'Don, there has always got to be a gap between me and them. I can't afford to get too close to them. That would be a mistake.'

Jon Sammels adds, 'Aloof is not necessarily the right word, but Bertie was the manager and we were the players. I always found him very honest if you went to see him. He didn't try to flannel you, didn't pull the wool over your eyes. I liked him.'

The distance that Mee deliberately placed between himself and the players did, of course, leave him open to behind-the-back teasing. For the most part, it was good natured. Only on rare occasions were the comments seasoned with any real bitterness. One such time was after the final game of the 1968–69 season. Having lost out on third place following their defeat at Everton, the players were gathered together for a meal in a private room in an intimate country hotel on the outskirts of Liverpool. After achieving the club's best finishing position for ten years and reaching a Wembley final, the mood was light-hearted in spite of defeat, the future full of promise. Team captain Frank McLintock proposed a toast of thanks to Mee and Don Howe for the success of the season. But Mee's response quickly knocked the party spirit out of his players. He warned them that fourth place was not good enough for Arsenal. 'Some of you may fall by the wayside, but we are going to the top,' he told them in tones that scolded more than encouraged. Deep down, the players agreed with Mee's sentiment and ambition, but they thought his timing stank. Once their annoyance at Mee's outburst subsided, their manager's phrase retained a place in the vocabulary of the changing-room, used both to poke fun at their manager and to make light-hearted threats about each other's future at the club.

To a bunch of mostly working-class lads, Mee, with his correct and thoughtful use of the English language, smart suits, club tie and talk of 'The Arsenal', was, of course, an easy target for the jokers. Generally, it was tempered by the respect bestowed upon a man who clearly had the club heading in the right direction; a man who, according to Sammels, 'treated us like adults' – despite his dependence on discipline. It was that characteristic, born of his years in the services, that was his defining trait.

David Court, now one of Arsenal's youth coaches, explains, 'He was very strong on discipline. He knew that you could not allow the tail to wag the dog. Arsenal still have their rule book and a lot of our rules date back to Bertie. It is all about conducting yourself in a professional manner. We still tell our kids, "Remember who you are, what you are and who you represent." You are going to have major problems if you are not professional in the working environment. Sheer talent is not always going to see you through. Bertie got that message across, but it was not an authoritarian situation constantly. Once you knew what the parameters were, you acted accordingly and he trusted you to do so. Bertie was a strong person; he knew where he came from.'

That strength came from his conviction that the players believed in his management methods. And in the BBC's *Man Alive* documentary, he revelled in being asked if he was a disciplinarian:

> Very much so, yes. I don't think there is any doubt about that, as any of our players will tell you. But I prefer to manage with an enlightened discipline, not an authoritarian one. I will not tolerate any anti-social behaviour at all, in terms of practical jokes in hotels involving, say, bedrooms or in a dining room. This, I think, is intolerable and I won't tolerate this situation at all. I have got a good standard of behaviour from them from this point of view. They are high-spirited people and obviously one is tolerant from this angle but they have their responsibilities to the public and I think it is right and proper that they should behave sensibly when they are in public places. In relation to their own profession in terms of detail and training, once we are training we are applying ourselves and working hard and one is

getting over to them all the time this is their job. They are being well paid for their job and they must apply themselves all the way.

Mee, supreme at delegation when it came to his staff, believed in similar principles when it came to his players. The discipline and rigidity with which he ruled was designed to make it easy for them to fulfil their potential, breeding good habits that would produce obvious benefits for the team and ultimately instil in the players a desire to push themselves to the limit of their ability. Mee explained:

> We don't want a situation where the players will only work if they are supervised. I once saw a circus act practising on the slack wire. I later learned that one feat had taken two years to perfect before it was demonstrated publicly. This is the type of dedication that footballers must have if we are to keep pace with the demands of public entertainment. You cannot force men to apply themselves to their tasks; you can only encourage them to do so by stimulating their professional pride.

On another occasion, Mee spoke of his desire to breed among his players the kind of professionalism he had observed in individual sportsmen:

> I had been impressed by the difference between the professional footballer and the professional golfer. The golfer will always produce a highly competent performance no matter whether he has had a bad night's sleep or flown a thousand miles, or has to play on a strange course. He knows no one else is responsible for the figures he produces. Players are not so constant in football, where one can always excuse one's own failure by blaming it on others. To win the League you need a squad of footballers who will give you 45 top-class performances out of 50. Occasional brilliance is no good over a long season. That was what I set out to impress on my playing staff; that was the response I sought. We kept and recruited those who had that attitude. The others could go.

In his book, *Arsenal from the Heart*, club secretary Bob Wall said of Mee:

> He conveys a sense of quiet authority. He is not easily ruffled. He says he wants to get the players to express themselves as people both on and off the field. 'If I can help them, I believe they will help me,' is his philosophy. Bertie maintains that one of the basic principles of management is to encourage the development of responsibility individually and collectively.

Coach Don Howe explains, 'The discipline in the club was really on the ball under Bertie. The punctuality in the dressing-room improved and the general application of the players improved. He didn't go round shouting. He would take players into the office and tell them something and give them a chance. Then, if they didn't do the things he wanted, fines would start to take over.

'He used to love to take the players away for a break, often to Cleethorpes. We used to stay in this little hotel, nothing spectacular, but Bertie knew the people there. We more or less ran the hotel for ourselves – the players could go into the kitchen and make themselves a sandwich or something. The hotel had no customers in the winter, so it was a good situation for them. But the players knew not to mess about; they knew that the freedom they had within the hotel was there as long as they behaved.

'Bertie knew when to clamp down with the players. We had one or two who liked a good time, like Frank McLintock and George Graham. But Bertie made sure everyone knew that if they messed about, he would clamp down on them. The players respected him for that; they were happier knowing they could not get away with anything. Basically, he treated them like adults. In team talks, Bertie would say what he was thinking and would ask them to say what they felt. They had the floor and there was never anything they couldn't discuss. They had the freedom to come up with ideas and Bertie would always say that we should listen.'

David Court is another who remembers Mee's willingness to take his players' opinions seriously. 'He was a good enough manager that if you had a point of view, he would listen. If you were right, he would do things your way, but you had to be able to convince him.'

Bob Wilson adds, 'He was always enquiring about what you thought and why. With Bertie, you always had to have a reason why. He wouldn't just take what you said as gospel.'

Jon Sammels once wrote, 'When there is a dispute he wants to know what the other chap is thinking. There is none of that: "Shut up because I am the manager and you will do what I say." He will always listen to your point of view and not hold a grudge afterwards. When a row is over, it's really over.'

It was impossible for any player with experience of working under another manager not to notice that their new boss was cut from vastly different cloth. 'There was a distinct change in attitude immediately,' says Ian Ure of the transition from the genial leadership of Billy Wright. 'Suddenly there was discipline in the club. It began with things like timing; you had to be there on time. Most people admired Bertie for that and looked up to him.'

Goalkeeper Geoff Barnett was bought from Everton early in the 1969–70 season, after Bob Wilson broke his arm, and was impressed to find a more enlightened, less tense, manager. He explains, 'We called Harry Catterick "Boss" at Everton, but Bert was always "Bert". That was the big difference I found. You always felt that Harry had a lot of pressure on him from the Everton board but Bert was given the freedom to do the job the way he saw fit and the players benefited from that.'

England World Cup winner Alan Ball, who would become Mee's biggest signing when he followed the same route from Goodison Park to Highbury, used his column in *Shoot!* magazine to make a similar comparison. 'Mr Catterick is a very demanding manager – he kept on insisting that his players must work harder. Mr Mee, on the other hand, prefers to talk to his players, to coax the best out of them.'

Three decades on, Ball adds, 'I felt you could always go to Bertie and speak to him. He was always there for me and he knew there were times when I was frustrated at Arsenal. But you could sit with him and he was never afraid of being around the players. You could have a meal and a chat with him and he was good company. I liked the way he could talk to the players because he knew he had earned their respect.'

Ball also recalls that when Mee felt a player needed to be spoken to sternly, the conversation would take place away from the other players. There was no desire to make an example of one man for the benefit of the others. David Court backs that up by saying, 'Bertie would usually have a quiet word in your ear but he wasn't backward in telling you a few home truths, and nine times out of ten he was right. Bertie was a man you listened to. He never got involved much in team talks – the coaches did the football stuff – but if there were any disciplinary matters in terms of misbehaviour, he would deal with it.'

Sammels says, 'Bertie was not dictatorial in what we must do and must not do. He didn't mind you playing hard as long as you worked hard. And when you were training, it was hard. He would not take messing about. He didn't like you to step out of line, but he would not really lose his rag in the dressing-room in front of a group of players. He wasn't a cup-thrower.'

That did not mean that Mee couldn't lose his temper; rather that he knew the importance of composure in front of the players. Steve Burtenshaw says, 'Don Howe and myself would see him in moments when he was very intense. He has that image of being unflappable, but there were times when he would let rip. But he was very good at talking to a group of players and explaining why he felt like that. It was not a case of raising his voice and it would not be an undisciplined discussion. He would raise his voice, but it would not be a shouting match.

'If it was at half-time, there would be no discussion; that came later in the week. It was a case of one voice during half-time. What others thought might come later. He would correct things on Monday morning rather than discuss them irrationally after the game. He didn't allow any comebacks at the moment of intense heat. He tried to keep the pressure down and didn't want the players to feel it. Every now and again, there would be a group discussion, but most of the time everything that had happened would be allowed to calm down and private discussions would go ahead – maybe when you were just walking to and from the field at the training ground.'

Former club physiotherapist Fred Street says, 'I have seen Bertie giving a bollocking in the dressing-room for bad results, but he was aware that players know better than anyone if they have had a bad game so it didn't happen very often.'

John Radford says, 'He could recognise if people were giving everything. He would have a go there and then if he felt it was needed, but because he made such a big thing of discipline he didn't need to do it that often.'

Radford also confirms that being loved by the players was not a priority. 'He stayed away from the players, even on foreign trips. He would just read the riot act before we got going to ensure that nothing went off and there was nothing disruptive in the hotel and then we would never see him. Apart from training, he would disappear.'

Burtenshaw continues, 'Bertie wouldn't get close to the players. He expected the coaches to get close and to appreciate the problems the players had. He didn't want to be there first-hand. He wanted the coach and physio to handle most things and he would help if they needed it, or have discussions if needed. He was always close to his coach, and many, many times we went out for meals and discussed the players. He didn't have to be close to the players. As a manager, you just have to be seen to be doing your job to the best of your ability. Within any team there are players who like you and those who don't like you so much. And a lot depends on the individuals and how many you have to bollock. They respected Bertie because he brought them success. Whether you are a bullshitter or down to earth, if you get success, it is respected.'

Street believes that Mee's experience of life before he entered the football profession gave him an advantage when it came to his relationships with the players. 'He was not a bad psychologist. He had dealt with patients with dreadful disabilities, so I think he was not bad in doing that; handling people differently. In football, you work in a world of cosseted people but Bertie didn't share the view that football was everything. He knew there was a world beyond it. Bertie was as good as most at handling personalities and he was good at appointing people who could do it for him.'

Mee believed that the professional rapport between him and his squad once he had inherited the manager's position benefited from the trust that inevitably develops between players and their physiotherapist. In *Arsenal in the Blood*, he recalled two players approaching him while he was manager because they and their wives had been trying unsuccessfully for children for several years and were looking for referral to a fertility clinic:

> When a player comes to you with that sort of request, it is an important personal problem. The philosophy in which I had been brought up is what is called the holistic approach. You deal

with the person as a whole, not just his injury, or his sickness. That approach evolved within the club, and there was also the disciplinary side, which was very necessary.

Mee explained in another interview:

> I have been motivating people in one way or another all my life, whether they are troops, sick people or professional footballers. Basically, people are the same, whether they are footballers or factory workers.

Howe had the opportunity to observe Mee's man-management skills as closely as anybody. 'He knew the ones with the attitude problems and he knew how to deal with them,' he says. 'There would never be great long conversations. He would take a player to one side and say, "You are not doing it at the moment. It's only right that I warn you that you could lose your place in the team." Some players would later be left out but they could never come back and say that they had not been told their place was in danger. George Graham was a little bit erratic and Bert used to have George in quite often for talks. He knew he needed to be shaken up sometimes. Bertie could tell the players who weren't expressing themselves or maybe had a problem at home. He commanded great respect. In the Arsenal team there were probably six or seven leaders, real men's men. To handle them and earn their respect, you had to know your stuff.

'He was a man you always respected for his ideas and the way he conducted himself. He knew the players would moan about him sometimes, but they knew he was right. I think Bertie would have done very well at any time in football. He was a very intelligent man and he would handle players today exactly the same. He made a point and told them what he wanted for the future and then it was up to them. Nobody could ever say they didn't know where they stood with Bertie. He was very consistent.'

Mee understood that, although players' personalities meant they had to be handled differently, the same rules had to apply to all. Court continues, 'Bertie had the ability to get the best out of people without showing favour. He treated us all the same and was very fair across the board. I had a conversation with him in later years and he told me that, of course, he'd liked some players more than others, but he would not show it and would not let it colour his judgement. If one of his favourites needed to be dropped, he would be.'

Inevitably, Mee's domineering personality and disciplinarian streak did not meet with the approval of every player. 'Like many small men, Bertie could sometimes be too officious,' writes Terry Neill in his autobiography, *Revelations of a Football Manager*. 'He always gave the impression he was striving to be in control of his emotions. In football, that is not always possible.'

Fred Street says, 'There were players who didn't get on with Bertie – they saw him as a schoolmaster – but there was a sneaking admiration behind it. Frank McLintock had clashes with him but he respected Bertie as well.'

George Wright remembers 'a couple of up and downers' between Mee and McLintock, and not always over football. He alleges that Frank would even occasionally bring his suits and have them dry-cleaned at the hotel at the club's expense and that, eventually, Bertie would say to him, 'You are not taking that,' and throw his suit carrier on the floor.

Court says, 'Frank had his arguments with Bertie, but he was a good extension of Bertie and Don on the pitch. If people didn't want Bertie's sort of discipline, they were going to struggle. But, at the same time, if they were not of that ilk, Bertie would not have them in the team for long.'

McLintock acknowledges that his 'volatile' personality did lead to clashes with his manager. 'Bertie deliberately kept his distance from people. He didn't care whether you liked him or not. He was a wee bit bossy and could be annoying, but I still had a lot of time for him. He did not have an ego or try to take over everything.

'I would be strong and opinionated, whether I was right or wrong. I sometimes helped to change things and I would like to think Bertie and I had a respectful relationship. I would never take the piss. Sometimes some of the quieter players would ask me to go and say we want this or that. Sometimes it would be about something silly. I remember once when it was about tickets. I would say to them, "Fuck off, I don't agree with that." I would bring something up with him if I thought it was important or thought it was worth fighting for. Bertie would always listen, but would not necessarily agree and would make his own decisions. It was like going to see your bank manager.'

McLintock also recalls the bureaucratic atmosphere that Mee helped to spread throughout the club. 'I remember going to Tottenham once and seeing the players going into the offices to use the phones to call family and friends. You wouldn't do that at Arsenal. I was one of the few who could go into the office, but you would always get an icy stare. It felt a bit like something from Charles Dickens.'

In the treatment room, the players' occasional frustration at their manager found a voice, as Wright recounts. 'Players did let off steam sometimes but my job was to stick together with Bertie and the staff. It didn't matter what a player said to us individually; we would back each other up and support each other. Frank used to call Bertie "Wendy", but I never passed that back.'

Street recalls, 'Bertie was in charge of the dressing-room. He was a bit of a tyrant and everyone was on their toes. But George Graham was a bit of a con man and was clever at handling Bertie. I remember Bertie coming down to the treatment room and George was on the table. Bert and George had a chat and Bert gave him some instructions and George said, "Yes, boss, thanks," and gave me a wink behind his back. He was taking the piss really.'

Ironically, Graham is one of Mee's players who now most appreciates his methods, although it took a move away from Highbury and his subsequent entry into management to open his eyes. 'When I went into coaching and management, I realised what Bertie's assets were. He was tough, strong and authoritarian. I learnt a lot from Bertie about management, not necessarily about coaching but about handling people and groups of people. An important part of being a manager is an eye for detail. It is many, many little things that make you successful, like timekeeping for instance. There is no excuse for people being late. He believed in a dress code and I have always been a stickler for that, even though I know it has become unfashionable. Bertie was a great one for standards. That is the word that sums him up best. Everything was done with a bit of dignity.'

Wilson ponders the question of whether those priorities would make him a misfit in the modern game. 'I am not sure he could deal with the salary situation and he would be turning in his grave if he saw the dress code. When I used to walk up the steps into a ground with that gold badge on my chest and the team walked in as one, I felt great. It was like a military thing. Bertie would have to change a lot to suit the times.'

Alan Ball has memories of Mee as a very 'hands on' person when it came to dealing with his players, treating them as people rather than just numbers in a red-and-white shirt. 'He wanted you to understand that he was the boss. He loved football but he was a person who knew his strengths and worked to them. He worked within the regime he'd set up. He was very proud of Arsenal and what they stood for, and that was shown in the way he cared for the players. All you had to do was play football and everything else was looked after. You were never under any strain or stress in other areas. After I moved down to London, he made sure the club took care of everything for me, from schooling and housing to accountancy, solicitors and hospitals. I was treated like a king at Arsenal.'

Ball adopted a similar theme in his 1978 autobiography, *It's All About a Ball*, writing:

> Arsenal make their players feel important. The coach they travelled in had just about everything. There was waiter service and three-course meals. Anything you wanted was available: smoked salmon, beef salads, every drink you could think of, and cigars. It was luxury all the way down and that applied to foreign trips, where it was champagne service on the flight and only the best hotels. When I told the England players the sort of service we used to get at Arsenal, they wouldn't believe me.

Geoff Barnett recalls an incident when Arsenal arrived in Penang in Malaysia. 'We had been in Singapore, in a really nice place, and when we got from the airport to the hotel we could see this looked like a tough place. As we checked in at the hotel, Bert told us all to stay in the foyer and said to one of the hotel staff, "My man, can you get me a key." He went off for a while, came back down and looked straight at the tour organiser and said, "This is not the Arsenal. Get me a first-class hotel." Within an hour, we were in the best hotel in town.'

Mee did, however, harbour fears that the all-encompassing manner in which Arsenal looked after their players' every need and whim could ultimately prove counter-productive, as he explained to the *Man Alive* team:

We overprotect them in many ways and take away a lot of responsibility for them. And this doesn't add up with other situations where you want them to take responsibility. On the football field, you want them to take responsibility according to what is happening on the field, yet off the field we take away a lot of their responsibilities. We over-organise things for them. I know in many ways I have deliberately withdrawn some of their support from this point of view. I think perhaps we can go much further from this angle too.

Mee wasn't given the opportunity to explain in which areas he felt a reduction of support was desirable and it is a strange comment from the arch-organiser, but Mee was anything but a typical football manager.

Personal appearance was another pet subject for a man who was rarely seen without his club tie and white shirt. As well as instituting a dress code, he insisted on his players being clean-shaven. The Beatles may have been leading the way in promoting the growth of facial hair, but when four players showed up for pre-season training with a full set of whiskers, Mee warned them that no bearded player would be picked for Arsenal. The day before team selection was to be finalised, the players turned up without a bristle in sight.

At the completion of his first three years as Arsenal manager, Mee claimed that his methods were working. He had, he reported, yet to see the kind of behaviour from his players that would have led to serious disciplinary action. 'They are thoroughly committed to being professional footballers,' he said, 'and they know we wouldn't tolerate that sort of thing.'

Mee made it clear, to the younger players in particular, that there existed an acceptable code of conduct – not just as a professional footballer for Arsenal, but in life. 'It is no use a player negotiating a contract worth between £3,000 and £4,000 and then behaving like a hooligan,' he explained. He also liked to tell the story of the junior player who incurred his wrath by snapping his fingers at a waiter during lunch. In recounting the tale in the *Arsenal Football Book*, Mee stressed his determination to teach social skills to his players, as well as football skills:

This was in my early days at Highbury. I was horrified at the lad's table manners. It is all part of the educational process. We are trying to help youngsters mature and gain in confidence. The way they behave not only brings credit to the club but gives a player self-respect.

Street explains, 'Bertie was very much behind making sure the youngsters did their day at school. If it hadn't been for him, they probably wouldn't have. The year Arsenal won the Double, we also won the FA Youth Cup, but none of that team went on to make it at the club.'

In his interview for the *London Soccer Annual*, Mee explained his approach to working with the club's young professionals – an approach influenced by his own football background:

I had an elder brother who was a pro with Derby County and Blackpool, and another who spent a number of years on the verges of the pro game. I am the youngest. What I did appreciate early on was the insecurity of football and, therefore, I took the trouble to study something else at an age when everything was pushing me towards football as a teenager. This is something I have encouraged at Arsenal: all our youngsters get further education.

The Arsenal apprentice players are here to learn their job and you will not find them cleaning up the terraces and dressing-rooms. They are not training to be groundsmen but apprentice professional footballers and therefore spend five and a half days per week learning their profession. Fitness training, technique training, tactics, films, hygiene and diet are just some of the things they must work at and understand.

I think the most important thing is for the youngster to come into football without any illusions. Football is hard work, demanding complete dedication and today it is harder than ever before. The youngster must be prepared to give up many things – other pastimes or sources of entertainment – to reach ultimate success. To my mind, ability is useless without hard work and I would look for strength of character and dedication in a youngster as well as ability.

It may rarely have come to the surface, but Mee was not without his softer side. Under his direction, young apprentices were given frequent leave to return home to see their families, which often meant a trip to the other end of the country. Eddie Kelly, who journeyed from Glasgow to progress through the Arsenal ranks, recalls Mee as a caring, paternal figure. 'I know a lot of people were a little bit indifferent to him, and Charlie George hated him, but I liked wee Bert. He did all he could for the younger lads. I got married and I went to see him a couple of times for advice about getting a house and the club couldn't have looked after me any more than they did. And Bert was brilliant in the Double season when I was up before the FA after being sent off against Leeds. He stood up and said, "Eddie has just got into the first team and just got married. He is a fiery chap and he has got to curb it and he knows it." The good thing about Bert was that he would support you if he knew you were right.'

Given his background as a personal carer, Mee admitted on the *Man Alive* programme that the role of mentor and father figure was one of the most enjoyable aspects of his profession:

> This is something I enjoy. I have always worked with people and I have wanted to help people in the widest aspect. As long as it is appreciated what one does, and they in turn are helping themselves, then I accept this and I regard this very much as part of the job.

But, as any father will tell you, some children are born to be rebels, rewarding their parents with achievement, anguish and anxiety in equal measures.

13

BORN TO BE WILD

I wouldn't consider buying George Best because I don't think he would conform to the standards at Arsenal.

– Bertie Mee

WHEN BERTIE MEE LEFT THE NATIONAL HEALTH SERVICE IN 1960, the Britain he had played his own small part in shaping was still plodding away from the era of conflict and post-war reconstruction. The '50s had seen little relaxation of the nation's rigid social hierarchy. By the final year of the '60s, however, not much of the cultural structure of the country had remained untouched since Mee reported for duty at Highbury during the first summer of the decade. Advances in technology apart, it is doubtful that the former Sergeant Mee would have welcomed too many of those changes.

The rock and roll bad boys of the '50s had ultimately lacked longevity – even Elvis Presley was making dreadful mainstream musicals by the turn of the decade. It meant that in early '60s Britain, rebellious behaviour was largely the domain of the student classes, who rushed back from the university bars to watch David Frost's team deliver their anti-establishment humour in *That Was The Week That Was* while clutching their copy of the new satirists' bible, *Private Eye*.

In 1963, though, youth culture had found its new heroes in four engaging characters from Liverpool whose music had universal appeal across class groups and sexes. And, unlike the rock and roll era that had somehow phased itself out, there was no turning back after Britain's teenagers discovered The Beatles. Even when parents started tapping their feet and deciding that these loveable mop-tops were actually rather harmless, along came groups like The Rolling Stones and The Who. While the Stones wrecked hotel rooms and were arrested for possessing drugs and urinating in public, The Who were the adopted symbols of the Mods, who fought seaside battles with their '50s-throwback adversaries, the Rockers. Pretty soon, even The Beatles themselves were growing their hair, turning to illegal substances and provoking accusations of hidden Satanic meanings in their music.

London, meanwhile, was swinging, with icons like Mary Quant, Twiggy and David Bailey making it the centre of the fashion universe. And, as Britain's youth were exporting their music and fashion across the Atlantic, their American counterparts sent back the mood of protest that Vietnam and the ongoing civil-rights battles had instilled in them. Pretty soon, British youngsters were happily embracing the hippy ethos of making love, not war.

Nudity and violence became staples of the cinema screen and West End stage, while even the hitherto safe world of the TV sitcom was making heroes of the non-conforming youth. In the workplace it was Bob and Terry in *The Likely Lads*; in the classroom it was Eric Duffy, Frankie Abbott and the rest of Class 5c in *Please, Sir!* Youth culture had taken over and, as a major economic force in the country, could not be easily dismissed.

Soon it would be invading the often closeted world of football, and, therefore, the universe of Bertie Mee. The likes of Bob McNab and Frank McLintock might not have had to perform national service, but the years of their youth had been lived in an age of discipline, an era whose principles were applied by Mee at Highbury. But now there was an emerging group who knew only the new world of defiance and declining authority, players who would not have lasted long in the military world of the young Bertie Mee.

George Best, of course, had set the trend. But now more and more emerging professionals appeared to have spent as much time in their formative years watching *Top of the Pops* as *Match of the Day*. Fashion, and long hair, was no longer just for the girls. It is hard to imagine the likes of Charlie George agreeing to let their boss check whether their fingernails were clean. David Court ventures, 'I think it became increasingly difficult for Bertie to deal with the new breed of younger players coming through. There was an element that was a bit more difficult and who questioned him a bit more.'

Mee's daughter, Beverley, recalls that her father did not go out of his way to remain in touch with the cultural tastes of the younger generation. 'I can assure you that he never once watched *Top of the Pops*,' she laughs. 'I used to go upstairs to watch it.'

Charlie George was one of a pair of players introduced to the Arsenal team during 1969–70 who perfectly symbolised the pop-culture world of the modern youth. They attracted the kind of hero-worship of which Mee was deeply suspicious. George, the fearless, cheeky kid living the dream of every North Bank lad, was given his first-team debut on the opening day of the season. The fans idolised him, knowing he would have been standing right there with them but for his God-given ability with a football. Later in the season would come Peter Marinello, all flowing locks and vulnerable sex appeal. While the hard nuts of the North Bank might have waited to pass judgement on the winger bought from Hibernian for £100,000, a generation of star-struck teeny-boppers, most of whom had never been within a Tube ride of Arsenal, had a new hero. His picture would appear as often in girls' magazines like *Jackie* as it would in *Shoot!* Despite the common thread of the concerns they caused for their manager, the Arsenal stories of George and Marinello would be very different.

The relationship between Mee and George is infamous for its frostiness, with the animosity running deeper as time went by. As Frank McLintock says, 'Charlie couldn't stand Bertie. With Charlie you are either a diamond geezer or you're a cunt, no in-between. Charlie is very black and white and he will speak his mind. He never got on with Bertie and he never disguised it either. But at least there was no dishonesty. Bertie knew where he stood.'

Despite much prompting over the years, George has refused to bad-mouth his former manager in interviews. Pending a full explanation in his autobiography, it is left to others to speculate about their relationship. Peter Simpson ventures, 'Charlie didn't have much respect for Bertie because, football-wise, he thought he was limited. Bertie was a disciplinarian and Charlie is not the sort of person who takes to that very easily.'

The youngest of four children, and the only boy, George was brought up on the Holloway Road and was a lifelong Arsenal fan, which leads former teammate Geoff Barnett to suggest, 'Charlie was under tremendous pressure coming from north London, more than any other player. With his background, sometimes it was hard for him to take someone like Bert, who was well-spoken and strict. From Bert's point of view, the more talented players are always the toughest to train and to deal with. They have that little quirk in them; that is what makes them great players. You have got to be able to adjust to them and it is not always easy.'

Fred Street says simply, 'Bertie and Charlie were just chalk and cheese. Charlie was a rebel and if he hadn't been a player, he would have been on the terraces with his mates. To begin with, Bertie's view was, "We will teach him a lesson. We will make him do this and that."'

That kind of thinking may explain Mee's policy early in the 1969–70 season not to give George an extended run in the team. When Arsenal kicked off the campaign on a sunny Highbury afternoon against Everton, North Bank fans were thrilled to see the crop-haired number 8 who took the field. When the old enemy, Leeds, were the opponents a few days later, George was spared duty. Over the next few months, he would remain largely on the fringes of the action, starting only six First Division games before Christmas. It was not until the second half of the season, in the wake of a disappointing FA Cup defeat at Blackpool, that George became a fully utilised component of Mee's revamped team.

George's initial reaction to Arsenal's cautious policy was a diplomatic one – however unlikely it is that someone so possessed of self-confidence would have been happy on the sidelines. 'I'm in complete agreement with the way Mr Mee has treated me both off the field and on it,' he said in an interview that clearly bore the official club stamp. 'Hand-picking games might sound ludicrous, but it is very comforting for a player in my position. I admire Mr Mee for thinking along these lines.'

Every time George appeared in that first season, his hair got longer. Jon Sammels suggests that it was as much a reaction to Mee's preference for short-back-and-sides as it was a fashion statement. 'I remember Bertie telling me once to get my sideburns cut,' Sammels recounts. 'But although he knew you couldn't let Charlie do anything he wanted to, he realised he was a bit of an individual. Bertie knew that long hair was coming into fashion and he had to accept that it was Charlie's way.'

George would never have paid heed to Mee's orders to 'get your hair cut' in any case. In his book *Rebels for the Cause*, author Jon Spurling records George looking back three decades and saying, 'I'd rebel against almost anything. Even if he'd asked me to get it cut, I'd have ignored him.'

Perhaps that also explains George's choice of clothing when Mee allowed the players to adopt a 'smart casual' dress code for a summer tour. Bob McNab recalls, 'One player's interpretation of smart might not be another's and Charlie travelled in washed-out blue jeans with patches all over them and a couple of holes to add a little style. Bertie went ballistic and we never travelled casual again.'

George's contribution to the Highbury scene was immense. It was not just what he brought to the field: raking passes, flashing shots, strength of physique and lightness of touch. He was the one player who could add unpredictability and dash to what was basically a hard-working, technically superior and brilliantly prepared team. He had the swagger, the sulk and the star quality beloved by the tabloids. Thrown forward into the modern era, where the marketing world understands how better to connect such qualities with their customers, he could have made a fortune. The baffling 'E for B and Charlie George' egg advertisements hardly constituted a retirement fund. They did, however, along with the constant headlines, mark him down as a breed apart from any player his manager had previously worked with. 'It's impossible to keep him out of the spotlight,' Mee lamented.

Despite George's role in the Arsenal successes that lay not too far in the future, the pattern of his selection for the team was to remain largely as it was during his first season. Injuries, disciplinary problems and Mee's disinclination to persist for too long with a player who mixed inconsistency with brilliance meant George would never exceed the 28 First Division games in which he eventually appeared in 1969–70. In his second and third seasons in the first-team squad, he spent the first half of the campaign recovering from injury; the next year brought a pay dispute; the 1974–75 season, George's last at Highbury, degenerated into a series of squabbles and transfer demands.

As early as the end of 1971, Mee was dropping George and announcing that 'once he superimposes a higher work rate on his natural outstanding ability, he will be back in the first team'. Incidents such as V-signs at opposing fans, slapped wrists from the FA after writing that he would head-butt anyone who kicked him and a string of run-ins with match officials all exasperated Mee, especially as it wasn't just George who took the flak from the press over such incidents. There was implicit criticism of Mee in comments like those of journalist Ken Jones, who wrote:

> Arsenal seem to view this side of George's character with a mixture of misgiving and tolerance. They make no public show of admonishment when George is seen to step out of line and there is little indication of their true feelings beyond obvious respect for his talent.

Mee had always chosen to deal with incidents involving his players in the privacy of the dressing-room, and it must have disturbed the arch-disciplinarian that the media were now taking that as a sign of weakness.

There were times when Mee hoped that his young rebel was maturing, like November 1973 when he restored George to the team once more and said, 'He has lost a little of his sparkle in recent matches through biting his lip to stay out of trouble. This is an attitude which has become part of his self-conscious. I'm sure we'll soon see all the potential he has shown blossom totally. He had to create a new image and he is well on the way to it.'

But little changed and the frustrations of the relationship were felt equally by George. Back on the transfer list for the final time by the mid-point of the 1974–75 season, he would tell the *News of the World*, 'Bert and I rarely speak to each other now and we'd both be better off if he sold me. I just don't understand why he is not playing me regularly. It just has to be something he has against me but I honestly don't know what it is. I admit that a couple of years ago I was hard to handle and gave Bert problems. He did me some favours in those days and I'm grateful, but I'm completely different now. I'm wasting away and I'm only 24.'

Don Howe says, 'I don't know what it was between Charlie and Bertie, but Bertie was the boss, the disciplinarian, and that is never easy. Charlie became a star before he was ready to become a star. There was a lot of adoration from the press and different people. Bertie thought he was a very good player but that he was getting publicity he didn't deserve. It happens. It has been happening with Wayne Rooney. They become classed as good players before they have done anything. It creates a difficult situation.

'Bertie used to try to keep Charlie's feet on the ground. He got him in to talk to him, or he would use Frank McLintock or one of the other senior players to have a word. But Charlie was so confident in his own ability. Everyone was overdoing the praise and publicity and Bertie felt he had to deal with that if he was going to stay a good player.'

Bob Wilson got to know George as well as anyone at Highbury, having first encountered the swaggering schoolboy while spending his afternoons teaching at Holloway School. 'Charlie was Jack the lad, but he had that desire to play for Arsenal. He still loves the club, loves to wear the club suit when he is working around the museum. He's an absolute loveable rascal, but he was everything that Bertie wasn't. There was just one free spirit in our successful teams and that was Charlie, but we accepted him because he was so talented. I don't think there was a problem between Charlie and Bertie initially. It was only success that created that problem. Charlie fell out of love with Bertie when he became a big star. Then there had to be a clash.'

Speaking in 1972, Mee acknowledged that the pressures on successful young players made it harder for them to conform to the game's code of conduct:

> You must remember that young players have to perform in a highly charged atmosphere of high rewards. Some of them find it difficult to control themselves when they are on their own in these circumstances. The press and television do great damage by aggravating the problem. They shower the adulation on young players who are not mature enough to absorb it and this creates a great problem for the manager.

This was where Mee faced his biggest dilemma. He had experienced enough of the human psyche to know that players, like anyone else, had their individual personalities and problems. He acknowledged that players like George faced unique challenges. He knew that, in trying to get everyone to conform to his vision of the way players should conduct themselves, not everyone responded in exactly the same way – some had to be cajoled and encouraged, some bullied and barked at. Yet there was still enough of the army in him to discount any flexibility when it came to the application of the platoon regulations. Patting someone on the head instead of bawling them out was one thing; creating a different set of rules was different entirely. To do that would have meant turning away from his beliefs and, as friend Graham Perry says, that was impossible. 'Bertie always struck me as a person of some moral rectitude, something which gave him quite clear standards. He could not act in a way that went against his nature.'

To some, Mee's rigidity showed strength of character; to others, it demonstrated a bloody-mindedness that could only harm the team. Wilson, who sits more in the second of those camps, says, 'It was a sign that Bertie did not really accept that sometimes you have got to just allow someone to do his own thing. You have got to be able to accept that you have to treat some players differently and I don't think Bertie was capable of doing that.'

Bob McNab, one of George's biggest fans, believes Mee learned from his experiences and, in later years, adopted a different approach in handling the next prodigious young talent to emerge from the Gunners' youth team, Liam 'Chippy' Brady. But he does not necessarily agree with Mee's compromise. 'After I was injured, I was running up the stands one day with Chippy. I remembered how demanding Bertie had been with us in years past but we did about a third of what we would normally do because he was obviously going easy on Chippy. I saw it as a real weakness, but maybe he was remembering the problems he'd had with Charlie.'

McNab also speculates that the arrival of Alan Ball at the club at the end of 1971 did not foster harmony between George and his manager. 'I always felt Charlie's problems increased when he and Ballie banged heads. Ballie and the new coach, Bobby Campbell, seemed connected at the hip. Football managers will put up with a lot from a player if he produces on Saturday afternoon but maybe Bertie was persuaded that Charlie was not doing enough for the team and that we could not afford Ballie and Charlie in the same team.'

George's six seasons in the first-team squad would be punctuated by transfer-listings, sulks, public admonishments from his manager and the authorities for ill-advised behaviour on the field and, most memorably, moments of sublime skill and high drama. David Court adds, 'Given his time again, Charlie might have done things differently. But there was an element of the rebellious youth in him that made him the player he was.' And, acknowledging that today's game contains many more players of George's character than three decades earlier, Court ventures, 'I am not sure how Bertie might have adapted to the modern players. They have many more quirks than they used to.'

George might have been a terrace hero but, having progressed through the Arsenal system rather than exploding into the London scene via a transfer, there was – early on, at least – none of the baggage that accompanied Peter Marinello following his £100,000 move from Hibernian in January 1970.

Marinello was more of a pop star than the artist at number one in the charts at the time – Rolf Harris with his 'Two Little Boys' – and, once the deal was concluded, the young man hailed as the South's answer to George Best worked the press into frenzy by scoring a brilliant individual goal on his debut at, of all places, Old Trafford. Within weeks, Marinello was reportedly earning £100 a time for putting his name to a ghost-written *Daily Express* column, to which his manager had surprisingly given his blessing. He was making advertisements for the Milk Marketing Board, being featured in pop magazines and appearing on the bedroom walls of every self-respecting young teenage girl in the London area. When he married his 19-year-old girlfriend Joyce Murray in the summer of 1970, a supposedly secret ceremony in Edinburgh was besieged by weeping adolescents.

It was a phenomenon for which Mee was unprepared. After all, Arsenal, with its outwardly stuffy traditions, lack of success and absence of 'sexy' football, had not exactly seen the pop press beating a path to its door. John Radford says, 'Peter had so much going on, with all the modelling and the magazines and all the other stuff. In later years, a team would protect their young players from all of that – like Alex Ferguson did at Manchester United with Ryan Giggs. Arsenal were probably at fault for not protecting Peter better, saying, "No, you can't do this or that, you need to concentrate on your football and your training," but that kind of thing had never really happened before so it was understandable that they weren't ready for it.'

On the field, Marinello never lived up to his stunning debut, eventually losing out to the stubbornly consistent George Armstrong in the battle to fill the wide berth in Mee's line-up. A frail figure, he struggled with the physical demands of the First Division, despite the weight-training programme to which he was subjected. He does, however, retain his fans among his former teammates. 'I thought Peter was a great signing,' says Eddie Kelly. 'He could beat men better than George and was more flamboyant and I suppose Bertie thought at the time that we needed that. Peter gave you an extra dimension and George was certainly put under pressure by him. But George was so consistent and would get every cross in, whereas Peter could go past two or three players, but his crossing wasn't always great.'

By the end of his first season at Highbury, Marinello may not have succeeded in dislodging Armstrong, but with time on his side he still appeared to have a role to play in Mee's long-term plans. He was certainly not ready to criticise his manager. Instead, he said of Mee, 'He seemed like a person you could trust and that is the way it has turned out. Some people say he is remote, but that's not a fault in my book. He has a tremendous dignity and carries a tremendous responsibility, with pressures coming from all sides. The boss was very good to me when I arrived. I admired him a lot for publicly stating that I would need time to settle in the side and that he didn't expect the best from me until my first full season. He could have put me under terrible pressure to be an instant success. He gave me time and I'll never forget that.'

In the end, however, not even the patience of his manager or hours in the gymnasium would be enough to help Marinello become an Arsenal regular. Almost three decades later, Mee admitted in *Arsenal in the Blood*:

> Marinello was a mistake on two counts. He had outstanding ability – there was no doubt about that – and I thought that in our environment at the club he would be disciplined by the rest of the players, and that was the first mistake I made. But there was a more fundamental mistake I made with Marinello.

Immediately he'd signed, he came to me the next day and said, 'Look, boss, my uncle is a feature writer at the *Express*, and I'm committed to write articles for him.'

I said, 'Don't let that happen again. If you're committed and you've given your word, then OK, but you will not commit yourself to anything outside of this club without my permission.' So I think I made a mistake there. It was a learning experience. He had a lot of ability but he didn't have the necessary get up and go. He got better, tougher, but not enough.

Marinello would occasionally earn brief favour before leaving Arsenal for Portsmouth in 1973. Most notably, he had a run of games early in 1972–73 when Mee experimented with a more fluent style of football. But the superior form of the rival for his position and the harsh physical realities of the First Division meant that the off-field distractions that marked the early months of the Scot's Highbury career naturally ceased to be a factor. Bertie remained in love with George Armstrong and the teenage girls transferred their affections to David Cassidy.

14

THE SOUR AND THE GLORY

We want to be hated again on every ground we visit, as we were in the 1930s, because that will mean we are back among the game's prizewinners.
— Foreword, *Arsenal Football Book*, 1969

THE FIRST EDITION OF THE *ARSENAL FOOTBALL BOOK* WAS prepared for publication at the beginning of the 1969–70 season, opening with the mission statement above. Hated on every ground? A few weeks into the season it seemed that no one despised Arsenal as much as their own crowd at Highbury. By the middle of October, the team's performances had been so disappointing that Bertie Mee's position as manager appeared under serious threat for the first time. At one match, a dreary goalless draw against Sheffield Wednesday, many fans had pointedly left the game early; those who stayed did so to join in the slow handclaps that made funereal progress around the ground. How different to the scenes that the stadium would witness at the end of the season.

After three years of steady, if unspectacular, progress and a pair of Wembley appearances, the stakes were clearly higher for Mee and his team. Now they not only had to deal with the demands created by past achievements, they'd also generated genuine expectation that this team

169

could return the club to football's highest order. Mee, however, chose not to identify specific goals for his players. Jon Sammels explains, 'Bertie didn't set targets. You were always made aware that there was a certain standard to be maintained but he never put pressure on the players by setting targets. He made you aware that you were good enough to win this and go for that.'

Defeat at home to Everton on the first day of the season was followed by a 0–0 draw at Leeds that had the home fans chanting, 'We want football!' Those sentiments had been adopted by their own crowd by the time the Gunners were held by Sheffield Wednesday, Arsenal having won only two of eight League games.

It was already apparent that Mee intended to follow through on his warning that certain players would not be around to see the team reach its potential. Defender Ian Ure was gone after the first handful of games and Bobby Gould was put up for sale shortly thereafter. Ure had been in and out of the side since the Swindon disaster, missing the final four games of 1968–69 after severe criticism for a late-season performance against Leeds.

He believes, though, that his days under Mee had been numbered for the whole of the previous season. 'By that time, my knee was shot and Arsenal knew I was finished,' he remembers. 'I was taking pills like sweeties to get on the field. My cartilage had first gone not long after I went to Arsenal and then it went again in the same place.'

The matter came to a head during the summer of 1968 when Ure told Mee he did not want to go on the club's trip to the Far East. 'I advised Bertie to take one of the young lads. I told him, "I need to get back to Scotland and drink beer for two months and give the knee a rest."' Mee's hard line took Ure by surprise. 'He said, "We must take the best team." But I refused to go. In some ways that was the final nail in the coffin.'

Given the extent of his injury and the fact that Stoke appeared his most likely destination, Ure was taken aback, four games into the new season, when he found Sir Matt Busby, newly elevated to general manager at Old Trafford, waiting to offer him a move to Manchester United. The deal was completed for £80,000 and Ure recalls that neither he nor Mee could believe their good fortune. 'They were buying a pup. You didn't advertise it if you weren't right, but Arsenal must have known and they kept quiet.'

The comparisons offered by Ure between United and Arsenal reveal much about life under Mee. Initially, Ure claimed that United offered 'professionalism without the strain I felt constantly at Highbury'. He explained, 'There is a different approach at Old Trafford. There is more freedom. Their pre-match planning is not nearly so intensive and players are not restricted so much in the way they play.'

Nowadays, Ure looks back at the less pressurised atmosphere at Old Trafford – where George Best was just beginning his series of walkabouts – as evidence of two clubs headed in the opposite direction as the harsh world of football in the '70s approached. 'United were dying. They were old dogs who had been over the course and were on their way down. But they stuck with the old dogs and didn't make a stand on George Best. If he had been at Arsenal, Bertie would have made him the first one out of the door. He would not have got away with it.'

Southampton's aerial master Ron Davies and West Bromwich centre-forward Jeff Astle were identified as the men on whom Mee would like to spend the proceeds of the Ure deal. The scenes at the Wednesday game demonstrated the fans' frustration at his failure to do so. A 1–0 win against Burnley did little to lift the spirits, coming as it did with the high price of goalkeeper Bob Wilson's broken arm, leaving teenager Malcolm Webster as the senior healthy keeper. As a result, Everton's experienced reserve Geoff Barnett turned out to be Mee's first signing of the season, for a £35,000 fee.

After Burnley, the Gunners failed to win any of eleven games in three competitions, including a League Cup exit in a replay at Everton. Mee complained about the excess of fixtures – twice they were forced to fulfil League Cup replays only two days after playing earlier during the same midweek – while the fans complained about the shortage of new players and signs of improvement. Only 21,000 attended the game against West Brom, when John Radford scored Arsenal's first goal for almost eight hours, while Stoke manager Tony Waddington claimed that Arsenal's defensive tactics at the Victoria Ground could have been carried out by 'ten navvies'. Arsenal's campaign in the Fairs Cup had progressed only as far as disposing of the Irish part-timers Glentoran, which didn't provide Mee with much evidence of achievement to present before the court of public opinion on Monday, 27 October 1969.

Several hundred of the most committed Arsenal supporters arrived at the club's annual meeting of shareholders determined to subject the manager to the toughest of cross-examinations. The morning newspapers outlined the fans' case that Arsenal had spent too much on paying the existing players, but not enough on the acquisition of additional strength. Exhibit A was the statement of club accounts, which showed that while income from the gate had risen by £76,000 to £400,000 in 1968–69, more than £45,000 of that increase had gone straight to the players in bonuses. Meanwhile, a potential transfer fund of £290,000 sat untouched in the bank. One shareholder told the press, 'Last year we spent nearly £160,000 on wages and bonuses. Does it look like we are getting value for money? We would have been better off paying them less and putting that money towards new players.'

Club secretary Bob Wall explained patiently, 'Our system here is to pay by results. It was the players' performances that brought in record gate money so it was right that they should share it.'

Mee, whose military background meant that he was not one to back down from a battle, appeared to relish the prospect of confrontation. 'I appreciate people will have a go at me,' he said. 'I am going to tell them the facts. Then they can see for themselves how unfair these criticisms are.'

And that is exactly what he did. The next day's newspapers would carry colourful reports that portrayed Mee as an evangelical figure, turning back the angry mob with his honesty, optimism and passion. Mee, so the reports went, 'turned jeers to cheers'. Brandishing two pieces of typed paper that supposedly contained the name of every player about whom he made inquiries, he challenged the audience to 'name a player of quality whose name is not on that list'.

Mee reeled off names like Francis Lee, Allan Clarke, Colin Stein, Mick Jones, Alan Birchenall, Derek Dougan and Hugh Curran. Then he explained why deals had not materialised, citing everything from players' reluctance to travel south and cautionary tales from previous managers to last-minute changes of heart by individuals and the excessive demands of the vendors. 'That one? I have bid for him twice this season and you can imagine why.' 'Yes, we could have had this one – if we had been prepared to let our own best player go in exchange. That wouldn't have helped.' 'That deal was set up even before the player came onto the market.'

As he continued through his roll-call of near misses, Mee added, 'We had no illusion that the side needed strengthening, but do you really think it is easy? We have watched these 76 players and I have made more than 30 direct offers. We mentioned figures of £150,000 and £160,000 and the clubs know these were opening offers. In addition, I and the club scouts have watched more than 560 League matches and more than 350 schools games. Nobody who could be the slightest use to us has been left out.'

Turning to his current squad, Mee stressed, 'I will not allow anyone to criticise my players for what they have tried to do. They have never lacked effort. They need my support and they have got it all along the line. We did well last year and we can do so again but we need confidence and conviction in the side.'

Future generations of more enlightened and cynical fans may not have been appeased so easily at what could appear to amount to no more than a list of excuses, yet, at the time, Mee's performance was intoxicating to fans unused to seeing managers dignifying their grievances in such a way. The fact that he remained chatting to members of the audience for an hour after the meeting won him more admirers.

Mee was aware that Arsenal, known as 'The Bank of England Club' in the '30s, had more recently acquired a reputation for being slow to become active in the transfer market. In the second *Arsenal Football Book*, published at the end of the season, he further discussed the club's approach to acquiring new players:

> There are factors involved in transfers which, in certain instances, cannot be disclosed. Backroom politics, undesirability, indeed a dozen reasons for not going for a player. Our supporters at times must have been surprised when it seemed we were going for a player and then discontinued negotiations just when they expected us to complete the transfer. In our defence I would say that we had our reasons. We did, of course, go for Peter Marinello and signed him last season. But even in his case the impatience of our critics and supporters for success has put him under tremendous pressure.
>
> I expect the first £200,000 transfer any day. Leeds, Manchester United and Everton are all capable of paying this

sort of money. In many ways it is a good thing. It shows the professional management and big thinking of clubs. But you can only have a limited number of these massive deals. It could lead to economic suicide. While certain clubs will continue to engage in this high financial game, it will remain a luxury event. Even they will have to have first-class arrangements for rearing their own talent. The finding of young talent will always be of prime importance.

The biggest crisis of Mee's managerial career had been averted, at least partly. But now came what was shaping up as one of the most important games of the season. The day after the shareholders' meeting, Arsenal flew to Portugal's capital city to face that country's top team, Sporting Lisbon, in the second round of the Fairs Cup. Several of the Arsenal players noticed a few signs of shell shock in their boss as they boarded the plane. Some speculated that, in spite of his winning performance in front of the fans, an Arsenal loss in this tie could mean the sack for their manager.

Mee's untypically negative comments on arrival in Portugal hinted at such pressure. 'We wanted mud, lots of mud,' he said, firing a disapproving look in the direction of clear blue skies. 'I wonder how much the bone-dry autumn in England has contributed to Arsenal's problems. We are a good side on heavy going.'

Hardly the most confidence-inspiring speech from the manager, who also drew comparison with the situation Newcastle United had found themselves in a year earlier. 'They were struggling like mad when they started out in the Fairs Cup last season and look what happened to them. Not only did they go on to win the trophy, they gained fantastic confidence and became a fine side again in England.'

Ken Friar states that he and his fellow Arsenal directors were at no time influenced by media speculation over Mee's suitability to continue in his position, neither in 1969 nor in the later, less successful years of his reign. 'Bertie was never subjected to that kind of pressure from within,' he says. 'Arsenal have always been loyal to their managers and we don't appoint somebody for ten minutes. Newspapers know they can sell a lot more newspapers by being critical.'

Any nerves that were taken onto the pitch in Lisbon were more apparent in the performance of the home team than in Mee's squad.

George Graham and David Court had already come close before Sporting finally began to exert second-half pressure and won a 72nd-minute penalty when Peter Simpson fouled Marinho, who made his way behind the goal for treatment. Peres struck the kick to Barnett's right, but the Gunners' stand-in keeper stretched to make probably the most important save of his Arsenal career. 'After I pushed it away, the guy who was off the field came back on and went after the ball and kicked me,' the hero of the hour recalls. 'It was hilarious, although I had to go straight to hospital for an X-ray.'

Arsenal played out the remaining minutes for a valuable draw and, while the Lisbon fans threw seat cushions at the local police force, Mee, according to one player, 'was walking around like we had won the cup'.

As the Gunners returned to London, Mee's performance before the shareholders and the team's display against one of Europe's better teams seemed to have ended any discussion about his suitability to continue in charge. The existence of such pressure in Mee's profession had been the subject of discussion during the *Man Alive* programme aired earlier in the year, referencing the sacking of Alec Stock as Queens Park Rangers manager a few months after he had led the club to Division One. Speaking thoughtfully and eloquently, Mee had readily acknowledged this reality of his job:

> It would be very wrong of me to say I don't worry about this situation because I have responsibilities family-wise. I think there are two aspects: one is that I am with a first-class club with an understanding board, a tolerant board, and they are not demanding ultimate success every week or every season. I think the other point is that I am reasonably well equipped in terms of other qualifications to take a job in other walks of life, therefore I have other alternatives. I think this gives me some sense of security and probably helps me.
>
> [Stock's dismissal] seems very disturbing to me. I am very worried about the game; I am worried about where it is going. I am worried about the standard of ethics and behaviour at all levels – from director level, which may be responsible for the situation you have just posed to me; some of my colleagues, manager colleagues; and indeed the behaviour of players, too. I

think there needs to be some fundamental thinking done, some good discussion at all levels, otherwise the game could well deteriorate over the next ten years.

Arsenal looked like a team reborn in their first League game after Lisbon. Showing the fluency that had been missing all season, they thumped Crystal Palace 5–1 at Selhurst Park, where Radford's hat-trick was overshadowed by a Graham volley that would earn him the 'Golden Goal' award on ITV's *The Big Match*. A week later they were emphatic 4–0 winners against a Derby team on their way to a fourth-place finish in their first season after promotion. European progress was then assured with a 3–0 victory over Sporting as a patient Arsenal were rewarded by goals from Radford and Graham, who struck twice.

A famous visitor to Highbury at the end of the year was struck by the chemistry he sniffed at the club. Henry Cooper, in the process of bidding to regain his British and European heavyweight championships, had undergone surgery to rectify a cartilage problem in his right knee. A renowned Arsenal fan who had fought Muhammad Ali for the world title in their stadium three years earlier, Cooper was invited by Mee to train at Arsenal five days a week to regain his fitness. 'I was impressed with the togetherness there,' he wrote in his autobiography. 'Everybody was Arsenal. Even the office cleaner and the guy who looked after the boots and equipment would get the chance of a trip abroad to one of Arsenal's European matches.'

Not everyone was happy, though. The forgotten man, Bobby Gould, accused Mee of having ignored him since dispatching him from the first-team squad, although he did not let his feelings get in the way of his football, scoring 30 goals in 23 enthusiastically approached reserve games.

The team's new buoyancy could not survive the ebbing tides of the domestic season. Another run of ten games without a win ensured they finished no higher than twelfth in the League, while the FA Cup brought the disappointment of a 3–2 replay defeat at Blackpool after taking a two-goal lead.

That it was European football that kept the season afloat was somewhat ironic, given that before the team had been able to think about grabbing their passports, they had encountered obstacles from within their own organisation. The Fairs Cup was littered with stories of brawls between English teams and their Continental counterparts and in January 1968 the situation had been of sufficient concern for Arsenal chairman Denis Hill-Wood to say that the directors would have to think seriously about whether to accept any subsequent invitation to compete in the competition. But a couple of years later, Bob Wall, in tones of surprisingly reluctant acceptance, said, 'We cannot look a gift horse in the mouth.'

Perhaps if the club had realised the springboard that the tournament would provide for the team, it would have been approached with a little more enthusiasm. A simple aggregate victory over Glentoran in the first round – 3–0 at home followed by a 1–0 loss in the second leg – was memorable mostly for the sending off of Charlie George in Ireland after swearing at the linesman. The manager's comments reveal his acceptance of the often vulgar new world in which he was operating, and his desire to shield his young protégé. Explaining that there would be no appeal against the dismissal, Mee stated, 'We were tempted to fight it on a point of principle. Swearing is now part and parcel of the game. Whether you like it or not – and I personally do not – you have got to comes to terms with it. But we don't want to expose our player to any further pressure. I have spoken to the boy and he realised the gravity of the situation and what it could have meant to us to lose a player in a more difficult match. He must learn to control himself.'

Having then disposed of Sporting Lisbon, Arsenal made heavy weather of a moderate French side, Rouen. Mee was absent from the trip to France because of sickness, but he didn't miss much – a goalless draw in which the Arsenal players showed laudable restraint. The second leg was equally hard going. Rouen scarcely had a shot all night and George was lucky not to be punished once more when he swung a punch at an opponent. It was not until the final minute that George headed on for Jon Sammels to score from close range.

Some of Arsenal's best moments had been born of the inventive play of new signing Peter Marinello, building on the instant reputation he had established with his debut goal three days earlier. It would not last, but in his first two games the Scottish teenager was justifying Mee's unexpected foray into the transfer market only weeks after his lengthy rationalisation of why he could not sign the players he sought. 'The transfer market is so difficult at the rarefied height at which Arsenal operate that when a player of this quality becomes available you must try to sign him,' Mee had said. 'He's similar to George Best in the way he takes on players and has flair and initiative, qualities we have been lacking.' Mee also added, 'There's no question of us asking him to have his hair cut.'

Marinello's transfer, incidentally, had caused Mee some public embarrassment after denying reports late in December that the player was heading to Highbury. He later explained that it had been Hibernian's wish not to make any statement about transfer developments, but, having been found guilty of telling white lies, he admitted, 'I am conscious that the image of Arsenal does not stand up very well to the events.'

John Goodbody, who was at that time a reporter for the Exchange Telegraph sports agency, was the one who uncovered Mee's deception. 'We fell out slightly over it,' he recalls. 'I lived in Islington close to Highbury and I was told that Peter Marinello was being transferred. I encamped in the marble hall but there was no evidence of anything and Bertie came out and ordered us to leave. He said, "There is no story here; this has been made up." My girlfriend picked me up and, as we drove away in her Mini, a car shot out of the ground with Marinello in the back. We followed him all the way to Barnet, where he went to look at the club's house, and then to Heathrow. We caught up with him there – me and one other writer, Michael McDonnell.

'Bertie came out and apologised and said he'd had to do it for all sorts of reasons, but I was very disappointed. I felt unhappy that someone who had displayed such integrity, which was a rare thing in football, should have done something like that.'

The signing of Marinello was part of a mid-season evaluation that led Mee to make some important decisions by the time Arsenal boarded their flight to Romania to face Dinamo Bacau. David Court and Jimmy Robertson were excluded from the travelling party. Instead, the likes of Eddie Kelly, Ray Kennedy and, of course, George and Marinello had been designated as the future of the team. Asked about the missing men, Mee's response was brutally honest. 'There is no possibility of them being needed and I regard them as virtually departed from the club. And there are others who will follow them later. I want to use the players we have earmarked for next season. What would be the point of bringing back experienced players we have decided we can do without? We know that what they can do is not enough.'

Looking back at the season in the next edition of the *Arsenal Football Book*, Mee would discuss his disappointment at certain members of his squad.

> Could anybody argue that we have established the tightest of defences? But unfortunately, and I'm talking about last season, our goal scoring failed miserably. This placed a terrific strain on the players. The ones who should be doing a job and aren't get further in a rut and those who are doing well get frustrated at the lack of reward and *they* become stale. This was only too evident last season when even our fine defence began to show signs of strain. It was when this deterioration was setting in that I dropped various players and replaced them with our own home-bred youngsters. The time had come when these lads had to go out and prove themselves.

David Court bears no bitterness over the decision that would precipitate his departure from Highbury for Luton Town. 'Bertie did it up front,' he says. 'He didn't shilly-shally about; he was not a politician in that respect. He obviously showed a certain amount of care and, to be honest, most players know whether their career is going forward. But I always felt he put a great deal of thought into all of those decisions.'

The trip reinforced the players' preconceived notions of the bleak existence beyond the Iron Curtain. Few had seen such poverty at close quarters and they soon understood why Mee had insisted on the club packing their own food in the plane's hold. The arrival of an emblem of Westernism like the Arsenal Football Club sent the locals into a frenzy, with thousands lining the team's route from the airport at Bucharest to the hotel. The day of the game had been declared a national holiday and more than 20,000 crammed in to watch.

The first half was uneventful, save for some eccentric interpretation of the rules by the Hungarian referee, and Arsenal went ahead after 57 minutes when Jon Sammels was in the right place after George's effort banged against the bar. Kelly, mature and confident in midfield, instigated a move that resulted in Radford heading a second goal ten minutes from time. The return leg was a formality, but Arsenal made it a memorable night by scoring seven goals, including two each by George, Radford and Sammels.

The semi-final and, fingers crossed, the final would be played during four successive weeks in April, following the early completion of the Football League season to allow extended preparation for England's Mexico-bound World Cup party. The draw for the last four paired Arsenal with Ajax of Amsterdam, beaten finalists in the previous season's European Cup and possessors of one of Europe's most gifted young players, Johan Cruyff. Belgian team Anderlecht would contest the other tie with Inter Milan. 'I feel more comfortable facing Ajax than either Anderlecht or Inter Milan,' said Mee. 'Their football is familiar, not foreign. I'm supremely confident we can play in the final.'

If there is one game that gave the first real hint of what this Arsenal team had the potential to achieve, it is their 3–0 victory over Ajax in the first leg at Highbury. This was not a bunch of Irish part-timers or a below-average French side. Here was a team that had already gone close to the summit of European football and would plant their flag there for the next three years. Mee's team tore into them from the kick-off, with Bob McNab, informed earlier of a late elevation to England's 28-strong preliminary World Cup squad, threatening twice and George testing the Ajax defenders on several occasions. Only 17 minutes had been played when George executed a ferocious shot that barely left the ground as it went in a blur past Bals, the Dutch goalkeeper.

Arsenal withstood Ajax's best period of the game, with Frank McLintock called upon to clear off the line from Cruyff, who was largely being subdued by the typically fierce marking of Peter Storey. But the Gunners desperately needed to score again and Mee made what proved a significant move when George Armstrong was sent on to evict Marinello from the wing position in which he had been squatting for the previous three months. The dependable Geordie played out of his skin, more or less relegating Marinello to the sidelines for the rest of his Arsenal career. With only ten minutes to go, Armstrong set up Sammels to force home a vital second goal and, four minutes later, Graham was pulled down in the box. The importance of the penalty kick barely registered with the cocksure George. 'All right, give it here, son,' he said to McNab before placing the ball on the spot and firing his team closer to the final.

Events elsewhere in the world, and beyond, became woven into Arsenal's trip to Amsterdam. Only the most committed of fans managed to turn away for too long from that week's morbidly gripping drama of the Apollo 13 crew battling for survival in a stricken spacecraft. When they did turn to the sports pages, they read that Olympic Stadium in Amsterdam was under police guard after threatening letters to Ajax directors, staff and players from an Arab terrorist organisation. One note to the club, which had strong Jewish connections, warned, 'One day we will destroy your stadium. Will it be while you are playing Arsenal?'

When the second leg kicked off it became clear that Arsenal could not afford distractions. Bob Wilson saved early on from Cruyff, and Peter Simpson, a monumental figure throughout the game, blocked from the same player. Once Arnold Muhren scored after 18 minutes, the Gunners' resolve stiffened further and the home team's attacks became more infrequent and less menacing. Arsenal were in a major final for the third year running. 'I was very worried,' Mee admitted. 'But after we had the chance to talk to the players at half-time, they calmed down and produced a fine defensive performance.'

Belgian football may not exactly be renowned for its passion – fans of teams like Standard Liège and FC Bruges will never be granted the mythic status of the *tifosi* of Milan or the *cules* of Barcelona – yet the atmosphere in the Parc Astrid stadium, home of Anderlecht, semi-final conquerors of Inter Milan, on the night of Wednesday, 22 April slapped the Arsenal players in the face with all the force of a jilted lover.

More than 30,000 fans created a claustrophobic, intimidating environment. Mee had warned his players that 'this will be like playing an FA Cup tie at Queens Park Rangers' – but only if horns, sirens and firecrackers had been sold along Loftus Road. Arsenal had an allocation of only 1,500 tickets.

Mee sent out the men who had clearly established themselves as his favoured starting line-up: Wilson, Storey, McNab, Kelly, McLintock, Simpson, Armstrong, Sammels, Radford, George, Graham. But after matching their opponents early in the game, they collapsed inexplicably midway through the first half. Simpson's failure to clear allowed Devrindt to score under the diving body of Wilson and six minutes later Devrindt created space to cut the ball back for Dutch striker Jan Mulder to score with a brilliantly executed half-volley. Frank McLintock recalls, 'They just knocked the ball about and were very patient. But all of a sudden it's, boom, a goal. You're thinking, "lucky bastards". They go back to the same tempo again, probing, probing, probing. It lulls you into a false sense of security. Suddenly, another goal, 2–0 down, and you feel as though you have been doing well.'

Anderlecht pressed patiently for the third and were rewarded when Mulder shot past Wilson after linking with Devrindt. It was time for another significant substitution. Don Howe recalls, 'There were not as many substitutions in those days and it was one area where Bertie and I would perhaps not always agree. You never had long to discuss things and we would sometimes have a difference of opinion.'

On this occasion, the Arsenal management were in accord. The big, powerful 18-year-old Ray Kennedy would enable them to be more direct in their search for a goal. George, limping from an injury, departed. Twelve minutes to play. Within five, Kennedy had, not for the last time, written himself into Arsenal lore. Armstrong crossed, the teenager rose and his header reduced the Anderlecht lead to 3–1, giving the Gunners a valuable away goal in the event of a draw after two legs. Mee told the travelling English reporters, 'Now we have something to fight for. I just hope our crowd can give us the kind of support the Belgians gave their team tonight.'

In the Arsenal dressing-room, McLintock, beaten in four previous finals with Leicester and Arsenal, emerged from the showers to urge his team towards victory in six days' time. 'He was like Mel Gibson in *Braveheart*,' says Wilson. 'By the time we left to go back to the hotel, we were all convinced we could win.'

However, the surge of confidence on which Arsenal travelled back to London soon began to dissipate. Arsenal, it was claimed, had agreed to suspend the recently introduced rule of away goals counting double when European ties ended level on aggregate and had accepted that a third game would be played at Highbury. The club protested vigorously that no such deal had been struck. Unless the situation could be resolved, Mee's team would be left needing two goals to force a replay, not to win outright.

Arsenal's protest would not be heard until midday on the day of the game, when the Fairs Cup committee would meet at a London hotel under the chairmanship of FIFA President Sir Stanley Rous. The club would have no representation and Sir Stanley seemed already to have made it clear which side of the fence he occupied. 'The clubs arranged to play a third match in the event of a draw,' he said. 'It is obvious that the rules regarding away goals and tosses of a coin are enforced only if needed to avoid an extra fixture. Arsenal seem to be changing their minds.'

Usually reticent with the media, Mee turned this time to them for support. He told Jeff Powell of the *Daily Mail*, 'They must not change the rules in the middle of a tie. Our tactics in Belgium were shaped by that rule and without it we would never have gone there to attack. Our problem now is how to make that protest heard. Our only hope of putting our case is if they read the *Daily Mail* in the morning. We understood there would be a play-off only if it was necessary to avoid the trophy being decided on the toss of a coin if we were level on away goals as well as aggregate.'

Whether or not the committee paid heed to the newspapers, one can only speculate, but Sir Stanley emerged from the meeting to announce a ruling in favour of Arsenal. The initial skirmish had been won; now Mee had to send his troops out into the real battle theatre.

It was a historic couple of nights for English football. Tuesday night would see Arsenal bidding to become the third English team in succession, following Leeds and Newcastle, to win the Fairs Cup. The following evening, virtually unnoticed, Manchester City would be getting drenched in front of a sparse crowd in Vienna's Prater Stadium as they beat the Polish side Gornik Zabrze in the final of the European Cup Winners' Cup. Meanwhile, a record combined audience of more than 30 million would sit down for BBC and ITV's simultaneous broadcast of the FA Cup final replay between Chelsea and Leeds. They were to witness a triumph for Mee's original right-hand man, Dave Sexton, and his enterprising Chelsea charges. But Sexton's former boss had beaten him to the first managerial success of their respective careers by 24 hours.

Mee's unchanged team, including a fit-again Charlie George, were welcomed onto the glossy Highbury pitch by the kind of atmosphere that had been absent from the club for 17 years. A lung-restricting mixture of anticipation and excitement squeezed out of the 51,612 present, rising into the night to be met by a cascade of rain before returning to earth as a covering of pure adrenalin. Those not already drenched by the downpour come kick-off time were bathing in the stress of the occasion.

The Arsenal players appeared to be as badly affected as the crowd, although, showing the fierce discipline instilled in them by Mee, they refused to allow anxiety to launch them into wayward attacks. Instead, they proceeded with calm restraint, repelling early pressure and then producing a pair of headers from Graham that forced saves out of the visiting goalkeeper, Trappeniers. After 26 minutes came the goal that produced one of the biggest outpourings of relief Highbury can ever have experienced. Radford won a corner, Armstrong delivered the ball into the area, McLintock touched it back and Kelly, the teenager who had barely been born when Arsenal last won anything, took a couple of steps and smashed the ball in from 20 yards.

Surely, now, it was simply a question of when the next goal would come. The Gunners washed over the visitors in a tide of pressure and Trappeniers saved at the toes of George. Anderlecht found some respite early in the second half with Wilson having to deny Devrindt and Mulder, but then the waves of Arsenal attack returned. With 19 minutes remaining, they brought with them the goal that, thanks to the Fairs Cup committee, effectively put the Gunners in front. McNab slung in a high ball from the left and Radford, arms spread wide, punched an unstoppable header beyond the keeper's reach. It was appropriate that one of the men brought up with the ridicule and bad times had put Arsenal on the brink of redemption. Two minutes later, Sammels, a man who had experienced personal trauma as well as sharing in the collective suffering of the club, wrapped it up, racing onto George's pass to fire in the third goal. One score from the visitors could still have forced extra time but it was never a serious threat. Demoralised at becoming the first team in the history of European finals to squander a three-goal advantage, they had little left. The whistle sounded on Arsenal's triumph, the fans clambered deliriously over or through the moat surrounding the pitch and Bertie Mee claimed his place as the first Arsenal manager since Tom Whittaker to bring a trophy back to Highbury. The 'big sleep' was over.

Having helped skipper McLintock to collect their prize, the Arsenal players returned to the pandemonium of a dressing-room over which even Mee had no control. Windows were yanked open and shirts, shorts, socks and shinpads were tossed into the mass of humanity that surged along Avenell Road. Champagne soaked everything and everyone, washing away the expectation and underachievement that had tainted the club for so many years.

McLintock recalls, 'On the night, as a team, individually and collectively, we couldn't have played any better. Everyone was on fire and the crowd was really behind us. Winning that cup was so important – the first trophy in 17 years. We were becoming a good team and now we had the confidence to go with it.'

In the Highbury boardroom, where the celebrations were a little more sedate, one of the players approached chairman Denis Hill-Wood and barked, only half in jest, 'Now you know what you can do with your bloody Alex James.' Secretary Bob Wall, who observed the incident, remarked, 'To me and, I daresay, our chairman it was music to the ears. I honestly can't overestimate the stifling effect our past success had had on our players. More than anything else, that great win over Anderlecht sets them free.'

If it seems like that final point has been laboured here, it is only to stress what may well be the greatest achievement of Bertie Mee's managerial career: to simultaneously ignore and uphold the traditions of 'The Arsenal'. Under his leadership, the spectre of past glories had been removed from the dressing-room without compromising the heritage, the standards, the expected mode of behaviour of anyone connected with the club.

This Arsenal team had earned the right to have their own photographs hanging on the walls inside Highbury; had stepped out of the shadow cast by James and Mercer. Bertie Mee could now smile knowingly at the bust of Herbert Chapman when he arrived for work.

15

THE DOUBLE

What I want to see resting in the trophy room is the European Cup. That would mean we had won the League title the previous season. It is that high success the club are striving for.

    – Bertie Mee before the 1970–71 season

ON ONE MEMORABLE EVENING IN THE FOURTH MONTH OF THE new decade, the misery of the '60s at Highbury had been wiped out. As the first full season of the '70s approached, Bertie Mee outlined Arsenal's ambitions for the forthcoming ten years in the second edition of the *Arsenal Football Book* – in an article published after, but penned before, the Fairs Cup victory:

> Success, success and success again. That's what I and everybody connected with this great club want in the '70s. The decade ahead I expect to be the most exciting in the history of the game and we have no intention of being left behind. I honestly believe the foundations for the return of the club to the highest spheres of domestic and international football have been laid. When I took over as manager I gave myself a four-year plan. That four years ended at the close of last season. The success

they produced as far as honours was limited. We did get into the final of the League Cup twice, had an exhilarating League run the season before last and we returned to the European front in the Fairs Cup. But is that good enough for Arsenal? Of course not.

Anticipation for the new English season was higher than at any time since Mee's debut campaign as Arsenal manager in the wake of England's triumph of 1966. This time it was another World Cup that had captivated football fans. Pelé and his Brazilian colleagues had flashed across British screens twice a week – in colour, if you were lucky enough – playing football that at times bore only a passing resemblance to the comparatively laboured efforts of the teams of Alf Ramsey, Don Revie and, it must be said, Bertie Mee. The somewhat grainy quality of the pictures that arrived 'via satellite' just served to give their football a greater feeling of otherworldliness.

Don Howe hinted that Highbury had caught the mood of Mexico '70 when he said in pre-season, 'We will be looking towards the young players to give us more flair.' But before getting too carried away he remembered that the Baseball Ground in February was rather different to the sunshine of Guadalajara. 'We all admired the Brazilians, but the game must be adapted to suit your conditions. There is more physical contact in our game and that hinders individual flair. Most managers will continue to do what will bring success.'

For most of the previous decade, any match Arsenal managed to win had qualified for Pelé's 'beautiful game' description in their fans' eyes. The question now was whether they were good enough to win as many as their European triumph suggested was possible, or whether their erratic League form was a more accurate reflection of their ability. One thing, of course, was hugely different as Arsenal travelled to face the new champions, Everton, on the opening day of the season – they went with the swagger of trophy winners, their belief in their management team absolute.

'The Fairs Cup win gave the players the confidence that what Bertie and Don Howe were doing must be right,' George Graham explains. 'When you are teaching people to absorb what you are putting across and you have success with it, they think, "I like this teacher. I am going to work even more."'

Bob Wilson adds, 'Don Howe did things in such a simple way. He would put things on the board and you would say, "Christ, I see what you mean." Things like playing into space, the value of getting in behind defences. He was a really good teacher with a teaching plan.'

On a practical level, the money earned through the European run paid for a new under-soil heating system at Highbury, although secretary Bob Wall correctly predicted that Bertie Mee would not be investing in the transfer market. 'Bertie has virtually told our youngsters that they are being given every chance to establish themselves,' he said.

Mee quickly had the opportunity to demonstrate the accuracy of Wall's statement. Injuries suffered during a pre-season trip to Denmark sidelined Jon Sammels with a cracked bone in his right ankle and Peter Simpson, who needed a cartilage operation. Then, in scoring one of the goals that earned Arsenal a 2–2 draw at Goodison Park in the opening League game, Charlie George broke his ankle in a collision with Everton goalkeeper Gordon West.

There had been no major signings to replace the players who had departed in the previous few months: Terry Neill, who took the player–manager's position at Hull City; Bobby Gould, sold to Wolves for £55,000; and Jimmy Robertson and David Court, who departed for Ipswich and Luton respectively. Instead, Mee took the opportunity to further test the strength of Steve Burtenshaw's reserve squad, which had successfully graduated George and Eddie Kelly to the first team the previous season. Taking George's place up front was Ray Kennedy, rejected as a teenager by Port Vale manager Sir Stanley Matthews and now rewarded for his contribution to the Fairs Cup win. Peter Storey was pushed into midfield to replace Sammels, allowing the young Belfast boy, Pat Rice, to begin a decade in the number 2 shirt. The 40,000 miles that Mee estimated he drove each year looking at potential young Arsenal recruits was proving to be a road worth travelling. The sturdy Welshman John Roberts, signed early the previous season from Northampton, took Simpson's place alongside Frank McLintock.

Mee, who prided himself on knowing his youth team as well as the first team, had organised the club's feeder system to prepare for times like this. 'The reserves played in the same way as the first team, and the youth team,' says Burtenshaw. 'All the teams at the club played the same way so that everybody could step up without worrying about if they could slot in.'

Bob McNab praises the role Burtenshaw played within Mee's structure, saying, 'I think a great deal of thanks should go to Steve for coaching this group of youngsters and preparing them for the first team.'

By the middle of January 1971, Arsenal had lost only two out of twenty-four League games and occupied second place in the table behind Leeds. It may not exactly have been like watching Brazil, but four-goal victories at Highbury against Manchester United, Nottingham Forest and Everton, a six-goal romp against West Brom and a pre-holiday thumping of United at Old Trafford had been pleasing on the eye. The partnership of two big men up front – John Radford and Ray Kennedy – had clicked sufficiently to silence those who felt that they would simply get in each other's way. They had scored 15 and 17 goals respectively in all competitions.

'It worked right away,' says Radford, 'even though I had hardly ever played with Ray or had the chance to train with him. We used to come back and work in the afternoons. Don Howe would come and do a lot of work with us, showing us the kind of movement he wanted. It was all in and outs – one player going for the ball and the other making a run in behind him. We also did a lot of coming towards the ball and spinning off. We used to work endless hours at that.'

During an eventful first half of the season, certain games had proved even more significant than facile victories over fading former champions and relegation battlers. As always, the first clash of the season against Leeds, in early September, had been eagerly anticipated. It certainly added to the clubs' growing catalogue of ugly, controversial contests.

By the late summer of 1970, Leeds had begun to shed some of the reputation for on-field warmongering that had marked their rise to the top of English football. They could still be as sly and cynical as ever, but since winning the First Division title in 1969 had felt sufficiently liberated to allow the delicious talents of Eddie Gray, Johnny Giles and others to reveal themselves more frequently. They had even attracted public sympathy when, in the chaotic latter weeks of a truncated 1969–70 season, their gallant challenge for European Cup, FA Cup and League Championship had ended in disappointment on all fronts.

However, it was the old Leeds who showed up at Highbury on this occasion. Billy Bremner went unpunished for clattering into Kelly and it was the Arsenal man who was sent off, after only 28 minutes, when he exacted swift revenge. With the crowd baying at referee Iowerth Jones, who would need a police escort at full-time, Arsenal's ten men dug deep and battled to a 0–0 draw. They had stood face-to-face with the school bully and not given an inch. Typically, the fact that the newspapers decried the game as an affront to football mattered little to Mee, who said, 'It was the best performance I have seen by an Arsenal team against a side of the calibre of Leeds. If my youngsters can live through a game like that, they can live through anything.'

Little did Mee know that an even greater test of their manhood was awaiting them two weeks later in Rome. Arsenal had been given only a last-minute entry into the season's Fairs Cup competition when the rules were changed to allow the holders an automatic berth, along the lines of the European Cup and Cup Winners' Cup. Mee believed that Arsenal's good record of behaviour in an often violent competition had helped their cause, but now that resolve was to receive a stern test. Even before they landed in Rome, they had reason to expect the worst. Lazio, their first-round opponents, had been involved in a brawl with their Wolves opponents during the summer's Anglo-Italian Cup, a competition that appeared to have been devised more to foster ill will between the nations than offer the chance of European glory to the likes of Blackpool and Swindon. Meanwhile, Lazio's coach, Juan Carlos Lorenzo, had a bit of history of his own. He had been in charge of Argentina's 1966 World Cup squad, the team labelled 'animals' by Alf Ramsey.

These were the days, of course, before the cross-pollination of football styles that has occurred since the advent of the Premiership. A handful of England players had been tempted by the Italian lira before the abolition of the Football League's maximum wage, but the borders were still strictly defined and styles of play vastly different. Italians thought the British players were clodhoppers, for whom the tackle from behind was a thing of beauty. The Brits, meanwhile, saw the Italians as deceitful con men who would spit at you and then collapse like a Shakespearian tragic actor in the hope of getting you sent off. Mee knew that provocation was on its way. 'You must smile and walk away,' he told his players.

It wasn't easy. While fireworks exploded around the ground, Bob Wilson recalls, 'They were treading on us and elbowing, and they would spit in your face at a corner. And they went up to the younger players and pulled their hair to provoke them. It really was horrible stuff.'

At the end of a bad-tempered game, in which Arsenal were pegged back to a 2–2 draw – one of the Lazio goals a disputed penalty – the teams attended a banquet. These were also the days before the visiting team would jump on the first available flight and get the hell out of town. Arsenal had to hang around to listen to local dignitaries and to be presented, much to their amusement, with leather handbags that were considered fashionable by the Italians but effeminate by a bunch of English lads. The bags quickly became missiles.

When Ray Kennedy went out of the small, stuffy restaurant for air, a Lazio defender and two companions made a comment to which he took exception. Sammy Nelson, the full-back from Belfast who had gone outside with Kennedy, recalls, 'The guy who had been playing against Ray tried to knee him as he was passing. Ray just went "Smack!" and splattered him. I couldn't believe it. The others lads were coming out and there was shouting and screaming. It was like a comedy film, with people being thrown over Fiat 500s. People were opening their shutter windows and looking out and shouting, and then the police arrived.'

Word of the fight quickly penetrated the restaurant, out of which players of both sides poured. Various accounts have Bob McNab pinned against an iron grille by six assailants and almost pushed through a window; George Armstrong slammed against the side of the team bus; Peter Marinello hurled over a car; Frank McLintock throwing punches with an Italian hanging from his shoulders. Several minutes passed before the sight of police guns appeared to restore some kind of order, by which time Mee had appeared on the scene. 'Their manager picked up Bertie Mee by the lapels and stuck him on the team bus,' says McLintock.

Mee's hopes of trying to keep the incident out of the newspapers lasted about as long as the bus ride back to the hotel. When Arsenal landed in London, the press pack were waiting to get their eye-witness accounts. Mee may have been a disciplinarian, but his fierce sense of right and wrong told him that Arsenal, on this occasion, were innocent victims. 'I am proud to be the manager of these players,' he announced. 'They withstood terrible provocation during the match. It was asking too much of any group of men to then resist defending themselves when they were provoked again and more seriously after the match. I cannot condone fighting but the players all have my sympathy.'

Several Arsenal players cite the importance of the incident in the growth of the togetherness and team spirit that would distinguish Mee's squad from most of their contemporaries. They had stood and fought shoulder-to-shoulder on a foreign street; they could certainly rely on each other in a scrap at Anfield or Elland Road.

Whether or not it was a delayed reaction to the events in Rome, four days after despatching Lazio in an uneventful second leg at Highbury came a defeat that is remembered almost as much as any of the triumphs of the season that lay ahead. Stoke City were building a useful team, one that would play an important part in the Bertie Mee story over the next couple of years, and had already beaten Leeds 3–0 in the League. They were to do even better against an Arsenal team that looked like they had barely been introduced to each other, let alone shed blood for one another in Italy. The Victoria Ground witnessed a mixture of casual, ill-advised defending, goalkeeping errors and inspired shooting, all of which produced a 5–0 victory for Tony Waddington's team.

The players slouched back to the dressing-room to await the verdict of their manager. In such moments of disappointment can a season be made or broken. Aware of the mental strain his men had suffered in the aftermath of Rome and the build-up to the return game, Mee knew that it was no time for histrionics. 'You have just had a great run of seven games unbeaten,' he told his shell shocked players. 'Now you are going to start another run.'

Instead of dissecting every goal and every slip, Arsenal's management team decided that the mature way of responding in the days that followed was to let the players figure out for themselves what had gone wrong. Eddie Kelly recalls, 'I think Bertie and Don felt we might be fed up with listening to them and thought it would be better for the lads to have a chance to say how they felt. Frank McLintock led the meeting and he insulted a few of us. One or two had a go back. It was a vicious meeting but it was really good, much better than if the manager or coach had taken it.'

Howe adds, 'We used to have regular team meetings if things were not right. We had a little room halfway down the tunnel at Highbury, on the way out to the pitch. We used to have real up and downers in there. We'd had a real beating but the players responded the right way. It really was a slating match but it was a man's way of dealing with it.'

Mee could have harked on about the game and risked making it bigger in the players' minds than it was. Instead, he had enough faith in the maturity of his squad and the leadership within it to allow the players to have a good old squabble among themselves – and then it was history. Apart, that is, from the haranguing Mee gave goalkeeper Bob Wilson a week later when, on his regular slot on *Grandstand*, Wilson talked the BBC viewers through the five goals. 'Bertie went apeshit,' Wilson recalls. 'He thought it was unprofessional to be talking about our own team like that.'

Arsenal's response could not have been more emphatic: a 14-game unbeaten run that kept them on Leeds's tail. An unexpected loss in a League Cup replay against Crystal Palace did little to diminish increasing anticipation among Arsenal fans that this could finally be the year their team seriously contended for the title. But defeats at Huddersfield, courtesy of a controversial penalty, and Liverpool persuaded Mee that it was time to inject new life into their Championship challenge.

While Simpson and Sammels had been reintroduced to the team – Simpson at the expense of Roberts and Sammels in place of, first, George Graham and, subsequently, Eddie Kelly – the recovery of Charlie George had taken a little longer. With a handful of reserve games behind him, however, plus an FA Cup appearance against Portsmouth, his talents were ready to be unleashed on the First Division once more. The Gunners' midfield had displayed more method than magic in the previous months. Few could deny that the ploy of sitting Peter Storey in front of the back four had been a success. Never mind that Storey himself disliked his designated role as a destroyer, a task that kept his own not inconsiderable ball skills well hidden. But while George Armstrong was consistency and perpetual motion on the wing, Kelly had struggled to maintain his early season form and Sammels was still feeling his way back to full fitness. Graham, meanwhile, was as maddeningly inconsistent as ever, despite scoring some cracking headed goals from late runs into the box and banging in a stunning volley as a substitute in a home game against Liverpool. It left room for improvement in the middle of the park and Mee had even made a £125,000 bid for West Bromwich Albion's Scottish international Bobby Hope. Now, with Kennedy and Radford established as the pairing up front, the answer to the search for more creativity in midfield lay within Mee's own squad in the shape of a fully fit George. On his return to First Division action, Charlie showed Highbury his full range of passing and ball control in a 1–0 win against Manchester City. However, another defeat, 2–0 at Derby late in February, left Arsenal seven points behind Leeds.

The FA Cup, therefore, appeared to offer the best chance of a second trophy under Mee. Having already made light work of non-League Yeovil in the third round and heavy weather of Second Division Portsmouth – who were finally beaten 3–2 in a Highbury replay – the fifth round had thrown Manchester City in the Gunners' path once more. And, again, it was George who shoved them aside with an inspired individual performance in the Maine Road mud. Spurred on by Frank McLintock, who made a point of telling George that the City coach, Malcolm Allison, had been rubbishing him in the newspapers, the Gunners forward won the game with two cracking goals. In the first half he stepped up to drive in a free-kick from outside the box and after the interval he raced from the halfway line, defenders trailing in the wake of his flowing locks, to stroke the ball past City keeper Joe Corrigan. Charlie at his best.

As well as reaching the last eight of the FA Cup, Mee's team had progressed to the same stage in defence of the Fairs Cup. And it was in the aftermath of the Maine Road victory that Mee made one of his most memorable speeches to his players. Not noted for chest-thumping rhetoric, Mee gathered his players in the Highbury changing-room, his trembling hands belying the calm of his delivery. 'Look, you have a chance here to put your names into the history book for always,' he started. 'But to do so, you have got to make football the priority of your life, at the expense of your family, your wife and everything else. You have got to try to explain to them that this is your chance for glory.'

It was not an instruction given lightly by a man who valued time with his own loved ones, who had seen enough of life to realise that football was of secondary importance to what happened within the walls of domesticity and family. He later explained, 'I told them, "This is the time to be really ambitious and to aim for the success which may never be possible for you as players again in your lifetimes." The point was expressed that all three trophies should be aimed for.'

Bob Wilson says, 'The timing of that meeting was fantastic. Just at the time where we knew Leeds had to slip up in the League and we had to keep winning. And that is exactly what happened.'

John Radford adds, 'I think we were maybe just getting to the point where we were thinking we would just coast along in second in the League and go for the cups. We needed that lift. Bertie made sure that our ambition matched his.'

As it happened, the Fairs Cup quickly slipped out of Arsenal's grasp, an away-goals defeat to the German team FC Cologne leaving Mee red-faced with rage. Following a 2–1 win at Highbury, Arsenal went down by a single goal in the second leg after Romanian referee Konstantin Petres awarded a penalty against an aghast McNab. The official further incurred the Gunners' wrath with a series of mystifying bookings. Mee was never one to rush into criticism of officials – for one thing, as would be the case later in the season, he was sensible enough not to antagonise someone who could be in charge of your next big game – but Mee had been angry enough to complain to the watching UEFA dignitaries during the game and was moved to describe the Romanian's performance as 'the worst display of refereeing Arsenal have ever met during their Fairs Cup history'. Despite George having to be manhandled away from the referee at the final whistle, Mee praised the self-control of his frustrated players.

With only domestic competition to concern them, Arsenal's League campaign gathered pace. After losing to Derby, they reeled off nine wins, maintaining clean sheets in eight of them. Such was the discipline and determination of the team that, once they went ahead, there was little likelihood of a lapse in concentration. George Graham admits, 'People said we were like a machine. Well, when you get a successful team you are like a machine. Everybody knows your style of play but they can't beat it.'

Looking back on the 1970–71 season in the third edition of the *Arsenal Football Book*, Mee outlined the ingredients of his team's achievements:

Our success last season was built on 100 per cent efficiency and endeavour . . . and that will keep us at the top for several years. Success results from a combination of hard work and a determination to figure in Arsenal's return to greatness. I think our greatest qualities are confidence and character, the two vital ingredients that every side with ambition must boast.

It has been my job to create the elusive qualities by the organisation of the staff . . . I wanted no stirrers in the backroom jobs that could cause discontent in the club. I worked on the same principle when I looked at the playing staff. There was no room for players with low morale who were not prepared to fight to the last for the club. Everyone was set the task of breaking the mythical barrier of the past.

Even when they didn't score the first goal, Bertie's boys simply refused to be beaten. After another vital George effort – this one a header – had seen Arsenal beat Leicester City in the quarter-finals of the FA Cup, Stoke awaited the Gunners at Hillsborough in the last four. And the club from the Potteries, one of the finest footballing teams of the early '70s, found themselves leading 2–0 at half-time. The first goal had been a lucky ricochet off their centre-half, Denis Smith; the second, a gift from George, who laid an intended back pass into the path of centre-forward John Ritchie. The possibility of the Double was quickly disappearing, although not in the minds of the players. 'We had this fire about us,' says McLintock. 'It was a matter of, "Come on, let's get back in it. We shouldn't be 2–0 down against this lot. We are better than them."'

If Welsh midfielder John Mahoney had been able to beat Wilson when he was through on goal early in the second half, one of the most memorable comebacks in Arsenal history might never have happened. Instead, Storey volleyed in from the edge of the Stoke penalty area with 40 minutes still to play. Jimmy Greenhoff then fluffed a chance to kill Arsenal's hopes and, in this season of dramatic deeds, the score remained at 2–1 until referee Pat Partridge allowed the game to advance into injury time.

Over the protests of England keeper Gordon Banks, who claimed he had been fouled during a scramble in front of the goal, Partridge awarded Arsenal a corner. McLintock met Armstrong's delivery with a header towards the keeper's right-hand post and Mahoney dived to turn the ball away with his hand. Storey stepped up to confront Banks from the penalty spot. Banks jumped and jerked on his line, but Storey refused to be intimidated. 'He kept moving about a lot, which was probably to put me off, but I didn't let it,' Storey recalls. 'I hit it to his left but not as far as I meant to.' It was far enough. Banks shifted his weight onto his right foot and the ball rolled in. Four days later, Graham and Kennedy scored in a 2–0 replay victory at Villa Park and Arsenal's fourth major final in four successive years awaited them.

As Mee's team kept winning, so title rivals Leeds, often accused in previous years of cracking at moments of high pressure, began to drop points. Few expected Don Revie's team to falter, however, when West Brom visited Elland Road in the middle of April, even though Leeds had won only two of their previous six matches and Albion boasted the season's leading Division One scorer in Tony 'Bomber' Brown. But with the visitors already holding a one-goal lead, Leeds were outraged when referee Ray Tinkler allowed Jeff Astle to score the most controversial of second goals. Tinkler ruled that Albion midfielder Colin Suggett, although clearly in an offside position, had not been interfering with play when the ball bypassed him as Brown broke into the home team's half. The apoplectic Leeds players screamed injustice in the face of the official, while manager Don Revie joined them on the field in protest and several fans advanced threateningly on the pitch. When the furore had abated, Leeds had lost the game 2–1, Elland Road would be closed by the FA for the start of the following season and Arsenal, thanks to Charlie George's stunning strike late in a tense Highbury contest against Newcastle, were top of the League on goal average.

As the excitement of the season built towards tumult, Mee had been forced to perform one unhappy duty. As usual, he didn't flinch.

Midfielder Jon Sammels had been under increasing fire from some sections of the Highbury crowd. A sensitive player with a deep-rooted love of the club, Sammels found that the harder he tried to please, the worse his game became. After substituting him midway through the home leg against Cologne, Mee broke the news to his player that he could no longer use him in home games. Odd afternoons on the bench away from Highbury were all that remained of Sammels's ten-year Arsenal career.

Sammels has long since accepted Mee's decision and acknowledges the humanity he displayed in carrying it out. 'I would have done the same thing,' he says. 'You couldn't afford to have somebody out there playing in the home games who, for whatever reason, was going to do something that would affect the team. Bertie was sympathetic but you can't worry too much about one player who is unhappy. As a manager, you have got to think about the whole team and keep the main goal in mind. I accepted that and I didn't really expect him to come across and feel sorry for me. But he always made sure he involved me in everything we did and offered to try to get an extra medal for me after I missed the FA Cup final.'

Meanwhile, the differing fortunes of Arsenal and Leeds meant that when the Gunners travelled to Elland Road on the final Monday in April, they knew that victory would give them their first League Championship for eighteen years, with two games still to play. Even a draw would make it a virtual formality. That is why Arsenal were so incensed when Jack Charlton was ruled onside as he scored Leeds's winner in injury time after a game that had been predictably combative and which neither team had dominated. Bremner had pulled back a cross from the byline and, after Giles saw his shot blocked, Clarke fed the loose ball through to Charlton, who scored at the second attempt. Bob Wilson and Frank McLintock were the first players to confront referee Norman Burtenshaw. Screaming for offside, they were joined by several teammates, including Charlie George, who hoofed the ball into the stand and was booked. It was all becoming so ugly that Mee felt compelled to urge his players to call off their protest. In the end, it took five minutes for the game to restart, a little longer on the team bus away from the ground before a penitent Bob McNab confessed that he might have played Charlton onside after trying to block Bremner's original cross.

In contrast to the earlier disappointment in Germany, Mee took the diplomatic approach when asked about the pivotal decision. 'Never was a defeat less deserved,' he said, declining to point the finger at Burtenshaw – sensibly, considering the official's appointment as FA Cup final referee. But he did speak up for his players, explaining his sideline intervention and refusing to condemn the unseemly scenes that followed the Leeds goal. 'I had certain responsibilities,' he said, 'to my club, to the players and to myself. I had to ensure that the game got under way again because the dignity of the club was involved. Nevertheless, I know how the players felt and I defend them.'

The evening offered another example of Mee's impressive self-control. When the Arsenal team arrived back at the Queen's Hotel in Leeds, Graham Perry – later to become a good friend – was among the throng of people waiting in the lobby. He recalls, 'In walked Bertie, looking as neat as always. It was mayhem. There were microphones being pressed up against him and everyone wanted him to comment about the goal. He just said, "My first duty is to my team and I am going to take care of their needs, to make sure they get their food. I will speak to you later." Boy, that was authority. He could have used the moment for grabbing headlines. Here was a man under stress, yet completely in control.'

The pressure grew on a tense final Saturday of the League season. Leeds beat Nottingham Forest, while Eddie Kelly, sent on as a second-half substitute for an injured Storey, snatched the only goal at Highbury against Stoke. In a finale that could not have been dreamt up by *Shoot!*, Arsenal were left one point behind Leeds, but with an additional game to play – two days later at White Hart Lane against Tottenham. A win would give Arsenal 65 points, one more than Leeds's final tally; a draw would leave the teams locked together on 64 points. And while a 0–0 scoreline would maintain Arsenal's goal average at a fraction above the Yorkshire side's, any scoring draw would hand the title to Leeds. Spurs, of course, would be in no mood to make life easy for Arsenal. They'd rather enjoyed the privilege of calling themselves the only team in the twentieth century to win both League and FA Cup in the same season.

Mee and Howe decided that there was no way to play for a goalless draw. They would approach the game like any other. The defence, after all, had already kept 24 clean sheets in the First Division, so the odds were in their favour. 'You send your team out with tactical ideas and motivation,' Howe explains. 'You just try to get the team right, every individual player right and the shape right.'

Mee had informed Kelly earlier in the day that he would be playing only his second full game since November, Storey's ankle injury having responded slowly to treatment. Kelly recalls, 'The club tried to keep Peter's situation low key. They didn't want to say he was out because he was the key man in the team in that midfield position. But the players knew he wouldn't make it.'

The most specific instruction given by the Arsenal management was to John Radford, who was told to drag Tottenham centre-half Peter Collins into wide positions in order to exploit their preference for man-to-man marking. On the day of the game, there was no time for any last-minute strategic rethink. Tens of thousands of fans locked outside White Hart Lane formed a barricade of humanity, forcing Arsenal's players to abandon their becalmed bus and leg it into the stadium half an hour before kick-off, barely in time to get changed and warmed up. Unless you were one of the 51,992 who made it inside the ground, there was no way to follow the action live – no radio commentary, no television highlights later that evening.

The lucky ones crammed into White Hart Lane saw some early flashes of brilliance from George give way to the physical combat that was typical of recent games between the two teams. Tottenham, third in the League and winners of the League Cup, were certainly not handing the title to Arsenal, no matter what manner of paranoia may have inhabited the mind of the watching Don Revie. Martin Peters threatened either side of half-time and Alan Gilzean came close to rounding off the best move of the game after an hour. Pat Rice cleared off the line from another Peters effort and McLintock was denied a shooting chance by the unfortunate positioning of referee Kevin Howley. With four minutes to play it was still 0–0.

It looked likely to remain that way when a harmless long ball was gathered by Spurs winger Jimmy Neighbour. Yet he put full-back Cyril Knowles under pressure with an ill-judged pass and George was able to send in a cross that was scrambled out to the relative safety of the Arsenal left wing. There, Armstrong gained control and delivered a perfectly placed cross to Kennedy, whose header from ten yards out squeezed between the crossbar and Knowles. Arsenal were ahead but, having been cruising towards a title-clinching goalless draw, they had riled their opponents into a vicious counter-attack. A Spurs goal in the remaining time, which included an additional four minutes for stoppages, would give the title to Leeds. As Wilson recalls, 'For the eight minutes after the goal, all hell broke loose. They came piling back and the atmosphere was extraordinary.'

As were the scenes when the referee blew for full-time; just as one year earlier at Highbury, the Gunners players were engulfed by their fans. Arsenal were the champions of England for the eighth time.

'Doing it at Tottenham was incredible,' says Frank McLintock. 'That night in the Fairs Cup at Highbury and winning the Championship at Tottenham were the two greatest nights of my life. The Championship was the hardest thing of all to win. The emotion that night and the feeling I got were everything I had always dreamed of.'

As the players finally made it back to the dressing-room, many of them robbed of their shirts by souvenir-grabbing fans, they were greeted by a shirt-sleeved and beaming Mee, who, in the mayhem of champagne corks and back-slapping, received a telephone call. It was the Liverpool manager Bill Shankly congratulating Bertie on his achievement and looking ahead to the FA Cup final. 'You may even give us a game,' he said.

Even during the dramatic closing stages of the Division One season, in the weeks since Arsenal had edged past Stoke in the FA Cup semi-finals and Liverpool had overcome Everton, Bertie Mee had found time in his busy schedule to turn his thoughts towards Wembley – towards creating a mini-Wembley, in fact, in the confines of Arsenal's training ground at London Colney. Mee had literally, if not metaphorically, allowed the grass to grow under his feet. When the Arsenal players reported back to duty after 24-hours' celebratory leave – Mee's own Championship party had consisted of a quiet drink at home with Elli Baram and a couple of other friends – they found a wide pitch with a lush green surface waiting for them.

One of the few moments of discord during the build-up to the game came about when Mee managed to inadvertently upset Peter Storey during a meeting about ticket allocations. Storey recalls, 'Bertie came in and said, "You will be sitting with us," pointing at me. Don Howe said to him, "You can't say that, he might be fit." It wasn't until the Friday the ankle suddenly felt better and I had a fitness test.'

It was the second time in the space of a few weeks that Howe had intervened between Mee and Storey, the first having been when the player's successful season won him an England call-up. Arsenal were due to be playing Burnley in the League the night before England met Greece in a European Championship qualifier and Mee summoned Storey and Bob McNab, also selected, to ask them to withdraw from the squad. According to Storey, Howe snapped, 'You can't ask them to drop out of the England side.' Mee, caught up in the intensity of the

Championship challenge, relented. Storey says, 'If Don hadn't spoken up, I might have had to pull out and I don't think I would ever have got picked again.'

The Wembley line-up read: Wilson, Rice, McNab, Storey, McLintock, Simpson, Armstrong, Graham, Radford, Kennedy, George, with Kelly's return to the bench being the one change from the team that played against Tottenham.

The blazing sunshine Mee had anticipated presented itself above Wembley and, having kept Liverpool sweating in the tunnel before leading his yellow and blue-clad team out from the dressing-room at the last possible moment to join them, Mee must have felt he had won another small victory when he glanced at the heavy long-sleeved shirts worn by the Anfield team. With regard to the Arsenal kit, Ron Goodman recalls, 'Bertie was always very particular about what he wanted. It was mainly cotton shirts in those days. Nylon was around but pro-clubs didn't want to use it. When they played Liverpool in the FA Cup, Bertie opted for the Airtex kind of material England had used in the Mexico World Cup. He was very pleased about that; Bill Shankly had not known about it.'

The Liverpool team was going through a transition from the Championship-winning side of the '60s to the squad that would dominate the '70s. Their strength was a defence that matched Arsenal's for solidity, which meant that few observers were expecting a classic of footballing skills. So it proved, with Charlie George's rising shot after forty minutes and two saves in quick succession by Bob Wilson belatedly enlivening a tense first half. Kennedy missed a simple chance after being fed by Radford early in the second half and he was wide with a more accomplished effort after 74 minutes.

George Graham had been moving elegantly around the Wembley field as if to the manner born, the slower pace of football in a heatwave suiting his languid, thoughtful style of play. He came close to scoring twice within a minute, heading against the bar and then onto the grateful boot of Liverpool left-back Alec Lindsay on the goal line. Nevertheless, the game, Arsenal's 64th of a tortuous season, was extended by a further 30 minutes. Mee went round to each player in turn, offering a final encouraging word, but most were too exhausted to take in anything he said.

It was Liverpool who struck first, within two minutes of the restart.

Steve Heighway, the long-legged winger with the university degree, bounded down the left and, seeing Wilson move to cover yet another of his crosses, drove the ball in at the near post, where the keeper had left the smallest of openings. It was more or less Wilson's first mistake of an immaculate season and he partly made amends shortly thereafter with a reflex save from Brian Hall, the other graduate in Liverpool's ranks. And with four minutes left in the first period of extra time, Arsenal were level. Radford hooked the ball over his shoulder into the penalty area and Kelly, a second-half substitute for the struggling Storey, made contact with his swinging right leg. Graham also flicked out at the ball as it rolled lazily past Liverpool keeper Ray Clemence, although highlights on *The Big Match* the next day proved he had not made contact.

Arsenal's winning goal, after the teams had changed ends, was as emphatic as the equaliser had been scrappy. Graham headed forward to Radford, who nodded the ball back to George. Radford received it back from his colleague, squared it again to George and then, along with everyone else in the stadium, watched in awe as the former North Bank kid teed up a shot that exploded past Clemence's right arm from 20 yards. In celebration, George lay down on his back, arms upstretched, one of the most enduring images in the history of the club for whom he was born to play. When Norman Burtenshaw's whistle blew for the last time some nine minutes later, Bertie Mee and his players had become only the fourth team to achieve the Double.

The duopoly of Arsenal and Manchester United may have made it a more commonplace feature of English football in recent years, but almost three and a half decades after Bertie Mee's finest hour, football is still waiting to see another English-born manager emulate his achievement. 'It is the supreme culmination of five years spent clearing away the cobwebs of a glorious past that was hindering the development of the club,' he said. 'Football success moves in circles and ours has been long overdue.'

Even as the final whistle sounded on his great achievement, one that would add Manager of the Year to his résumé, Mee remained, outwardly at least, a picture of calm and composure. There was no racing across the field in the manner of Sunderland manager Bob Stokoe two years later. Instead he waited until Charlie George had almost reached the touchline before going forward to greet his match-winner with a hug. And even in the kind of heat that would have seen the members at Lord's down to their shirtsleeves, Mee's two-piece grey suit remained correctly in place. He had not even allowed himself the comfort of loosening his club tie. But as Frank McLintock brought the Cup back down the steps from Wembley's Royal box, Mee threw his arms round each member of his team. Bob Wilson recalls, 'Bertie had lost the plot; he was so excited. For him, it was extraordinary behaviour. It was hardly in his nature to say, "well done". He was hugging and kissing everybody.'

Mee claimed he'd believed all along that, with the Championship success having eased the pressure on his players, the Cup would be resting at Highbury. And he dedicated the day to skipper McLintock, a four-time Wembley loser with whom, he revealed, he had discussed winning the FA Cup several months earlier.

But he also had every right to enjoy this moment, his day in the sun, if you like, for himself. From the monumental decisions of appointing Don Howe as his right-hand man and instigating a professional, even military, attitude and organisation within the club, even down to the smaller detail of the training pitch at London Colney, Mee had constructed the Double out of the debris of disappointment and underachievement that had been his inheritance as Arsenal manager. Even Emlyn Hughes's claim that Liverpool's choice of shirts cost them the final does not seem so ridiculous given the thought that Mee put into selecting Arsenal's attire for the game. In the next edition of the *Arsenal Football Book*, Mee would comment:

> As soon as I was appointed, I set up a routine that brought new discipline and efficiency to the club. My aim had been simply to establish and then to maintain a stable environment in which a club can flourish. All must be well ordered and controlled. So, although I had my doubts at first, I am now satisfied to have seen my ideas put into operation and carried out so successfully by the players.
>
> This is unquestionably one of the great Arsenal teams of all time. Our Championship was not a freak. It was based on the consistency of a long-distance runner, which lasted from October, when we moved into second place, to the end. In winning the Cup, we showed the qualities of a sprinter. I always

felt we had the ability to win the Championship, particularly at Highbury, where we dropped only three points all season and conceded just six goals. But our indifferent early-season away form was to create many problems later on, although we showed our fighting spirit by recovering from that humiliation at Stoke to take nine out of ten away points. In the final analysis, our magnificent defence, which did not concede a goal in the last six home matches, gave us the stability we needed when the real pressure mounted towards the end.

Mee's players had achieved the history with which he had challenged them earlier in the season. But nothing stands still for long in football and new, even greater, challenges lay ahead. 'I wanted the Championship for our chairman, Denis Hill-Wood, and the Cup for Frank McLintock,' he said. 'I wouldn't mind the European Cup next season for myself.'

16

FAR FROM THE MADDING CROWD

Winning the Cup and the League will amplify his confidence as experience altered a tendency to involve himself in pedantic phrases when dealing with even the most harmless interrogator. There are times when the set of his face and heaviness of his words seem to capture all the pressures of big-time football. When he learns to accept people as individuals instead of pigeon-holing them by profession, he will have completed the making of an outstanding manager.

– Ken Jones, writing about Bertie Mee in *Goal*

THE ABOVE ASSESSMENT OF BERTIE MEE BY ONE OF THE country's leading football journalists came at the end of an article that was, for the most part, in praise of the accomplishments of the man voted Manager of the Year. Mee's history of less than idyllic press relations over the years was not allowed to pass unmentioned, but the writer at least mitigated his comments by acknowledging that it was the demands of the job that created Mee's long-standing reticence with the media.

Mee was, indeed, guarded in much of his behaviour – you would never see him pumping his fists or embracing Don Howe when an Arsenal goal went in and rare were the occasions when he would allow the passion or pressure of the moment to break through the cordon of self-restraint that surrounded his public statements. No Malcolm Allison was he. No outrageous boasts, fedoras, cigars or baths with naked porn stars for Mee of the Arsenal.

Questioned about his impassive veneer by the BBC's *Man Alive* crew in 1969, he said:

> I have to work at it, certainly. Basically, I am not demonstrative and theatrical, if you like. Nevertheless, there are occasions when I have to take a hold of myself and remain controlled. I enjoy it when we play well, when we win, certainly. I don't mind losing providing we play reasonably well and are happy that there is some future and things are going to get better, and there are things that happen on the field that you can work at to improve. I think if the team plays badly and you see no future, then this is a different cup of tea entirely. This produces a lot of worries.

Bertie's wife, Doris, was asked in the same documentary whether her husband felt the pressures of his profession. 'He must, of course,' she replied, 'because it is, I should imagine, the most tension-making job of any. But he doesn't show it. I do notice when I am sitting fairly close to him at a game a little muscle twitching in his cheek. Being a non-smoker and a non-chewer and a non-anything, he does show his tension this way. And then I get slightly worried, thinking, "Goodness, he's worrying about something." But other than that, no, he is very quiet, very reserved about it all. It is almost a refusal, a point-blank refusal, to open any kind of discussion.'

Mee felt it was important to minimise the emotional ups and downs that invade any club during a season and believed that his example could help to keep his players on an even keel. Those close to him, however, knew when the stress of guiding Arsenal Football Club was at its most burdensome. Former Gunners coach Steve Burtenshaw says, 'You could tell if he was under pressure. He was always restrained, but you could tell if things were bugging him. You knew the little telltale signs. He would be more uptight.'

Ex-Arsenal physiotherapist George Wright remembers Mee being 'a bit snappy' on the day of a big game, while Bob McNab recalls Mee's private method of calming himself before kick-off. 'If you left the changing-room behind him, say you were a little bit late, having that last pee or something, you might see Bertie having a quick swig of brandy to calm himself. He hid the stress very well because it is a huge pressure to be manager of a club like Arsenal.'

Mee's daughters, Beverley and Allyson, separated by two years, explain that even though they had to get used to their father's frequent absences during the football season, the problems of his profession were left at the front door when he arrived home; never were they allowed to impinge on quality time with his family. Such moments included driving his daughters to school when his schedule allowed, even on Beverley's first day back after Arsenal had won the Double. 'I didn't really appreciate the magnitude of it all,' she says, 'but when we got to school, to my utter embarrassment, all the boys were outside shouting and carrying on. When Daddy drove off, they followed him down the road cheering and waving their scarves.'

Mee's sense of fun and devotion to his family made for a happy home life. Allyson recalls, 'Mummy used to tell him how much she loved him and how glad she was she married him. Daddy was her true gentle man. They had the perfect marriage, a perfect partnership.'

As a father, Mee found time in the hectic schedule of a football manager to act as guide and mentor to Allyson and Beverley throughout their school years and on into their careers in later life. Fond childhood memories include being taught to swim by their dad and his entertaining version of O'Grady Says, which delighted their friends at birthday parties.

Allyson adds, 'I remember him coming to support me at a school hockey match. It poured with rain, but Mummy and Daddy stayed to the bitter end and were completely drenched. Daddy ruined his sheepskin coat. I was the envy of all the girls because my parents stayed to support us.'

Family life helped Mee to maintain a sense of equilibrium, a balance he strove to enhance further by setting aside time for things beyond his football club. He told the *London Soccer Annual*:

> I try to develop a sense of priorities. I have been kicked around
> in other situations outside football: this was a good experience

and you develop a certain resilience. I think this was responsible for what I hope is my present balanced attitude. You can get caught up in the tramlines, so to speak, too wrapped up in the football, the club. I try to take an interest in other things and so approach my work fresher, but I may be kidding myself here.

I am fond of gardening and I realise I have a certain obligation to my wife and two children. I have a small circle of friends outside football and generally I regard Thursday as my night off, when we go out for a meal and talk about other things. Again, I am trying to widen those tramlines. There are also calls on one's time to address functions or to watch other games, all the time it is a question of assessing the relative importance of the various demands.

In an interview published in August 1971, however, Doris revealed the increasing difficulty her husband encountered in devoting the time he desired to life away from Highbury. She gracefully accepted that her husband was 'totally claimed by football', no longer able to indulge his interests of gardening, ballroom dancing and visits to the ballet. She explained, 'He seems to have been fearfully busy the last five years and we hardly get any time now. It is almost as if he is married to the job. He is a tremendous stickler for punctuality. He hates to be late for anything and his life is geared to his timetable. The family really see very little of him. I remember that when Allyson was about to be born he was chief trainer at Arsenal. That was the only time I was absolutely firm. Bertie was going to the stadium as usual when I said to him, "Oh no you don't. You are taking me to the hospital." Well, he drove me to the hospital and then went to the stadium. All there is for the wife of a football manager is, mostly, a lot of loneliness. I do, of course, gladly accept this. I am his greatest fan.'

Bob Wilson witnessed Doris's devotion to Bertie and believes that it added a sharper edge to his own career goals. 'I think the real inspiration for Bertie was Doris,' he says. 'She was the one who gave him ambition. He had this incredible record as a physio – he was the best in the country by a mile. I think he would have been happy with that, but when the opportunity came to manage Arsenal, I think it was Doris saying, "Bertie, you can achieve, my darling." She was this lovely little gentle lady who wanted him to succeed. The full circle of that is that when she became very ill in later life, his dedication to her was extraordinary.'

Throughout Mee's career, Doris stood loyally alongside her husband, taking pride in his successes and charming everyone along the way. Graham Taylor says, 'I have never met a person like Doris. It didn't matter what you said, I have never heard Doris say anything bad about another human being. You might think at times she was naive, but I just don't think Doris has a nasty bone in her. We all loved her.'

Doris would accompany her husband to games whenever possible, as daughter Beverley explains. 'She had a complete love of football and would go to every game she could. It helped them to be a social couple. She would be the hostess.' In their early years, Beverley and Allyson would complete the Mee contingent at the stadium. Allyson – named after her father's favourite film star, June Allyson – remembers, 'We used to take our drawing books with us. We would sit in the front of the directors' box in the first half and by the time the second half started we were sitting with our books in the ladies' lounge eating chocolate gateau.'

Sunday was the one dedicated family day of the week. The morning was spent doing the usual weekend chores of car cleaning and gardening, as well as taking calls from reporters, while the traditional roast lunch would be followed by *The Big Match*. And the importance of the day remained throughout Bertie's life, even when the children had grown and Beverley had married Gianni Miserotti, an avid Arsenal fan. The whole family, which grew to include granddaughters Daniella and Jianna, would gather for afternoon tea. Bertie would enjoy discussing football with Gianni – 'the son he never had,' says Beverley – or would sit good-humouredly as the young girls clambered on his lap styling, rearranging and putting bows into what was left of his thinning hair!

'He loved the family times we shared together, especially with our extended Italian family,' says Allyson. 'An Italian Christmas was very special, always ending with a birthday cake for Daddy.'

Now in their late teens, Bertie's granddaughters maintain special memories of such occasions. 'I would see Granddad every weekend,' says Daniella. 'I used to enjoy his visits on Saturday mornings for coffee and doughnuts. He would always take an interest in our schoolwork and our friends, and he would discuss football with my dad. Whenever my sister or I were ill, we would go over to Nanny and Granddad's house and he would tend to our every need. He would constantly check that we were OK and would play games with us or perform magic tricks with cards to cheer us up.'

Jianna adds, 'Granddad was a wonderful person, whom I knew as my "Guardian Angel". When he walked into a room the atmosphere would change from sad or ordinary to happy and full of laughter. You could say he had a contagious smile. He has been a great influence on me and my sister throughout our lives and will continue to be so. He gave us the determination to achieve our dreams. From the minute I was born, he influenced my thoughts and the decisions that I have made in life.

'My sister would love to work with children but also link this with something in the medical profession. I would love to become a lawyer and Granddad has given me the strength to reach for the stars. I want to make it as a lawyer so that he will be proud of me, because he always had the confidence that I would achieve this.'

Mee's appreciation of the family unit extended beyond his own loved ones to his players and even to strangers, as two stories illustrate. Goalkeeper Geoff Barnett explains, 'One Christmas, Frank McLintock had said that it would perhaps be nice if we did something for our families. Bertie said to leave it to him and a few days later we got all the wives and kids to the stadium and went up to the gymnasium. I was dressed up as Santa Claus and Bertie had bought presents for all the children. Then he led us through to the boardroom and he had arranged a full spread there. Nobody had asked for all of that – he just did it.'

And Jeanette Kliger, an Arsenal fan from Gothenburg, Sweden, recalls, 'My father, Paul Pollak, first took me to Highbury in 1957, when I was 11 years old. In September 1971, my father became ill and was slowly deteriorating in hospital. I was so desperate to lift his spirits that I wrote to Bertie Mee at Arsenal to ask the team to visit him. My father unfortunately died shortly thereafter and on the following Saturday we were called by Arsenal to say that they were coming. When they heard that he had died, they invited my mother, brother and me to come to Highbury and meet them. We met the whole of the Double team, together with Bertie, and it was a very sad and wonderful occasion. I shall always be grateful to Bertie Mee and

Arsenal for their kindness. If my love of the team was not enough, the kindness of Bertie Mee has welded me and my family to Arsenal for ever.'

At home, as at work, Mee was a stickler for routine. 'Daddy was a very organised, methodical person,' says Allyson. 'Punctuality was very important and we were always early, never late. Harry and Paula Hopker tell the story about their holidays at their home in France. Daddy and Mummy would drive there and if Daddy said he would be there at three o'clock, they would arrive exactly at three o'clock.'

But along with the discipline, the insistence on good manners and the instilling of 'values' that his daughters remember as components of home life and part of their father's character, there was the humour and sense of fun that few beyond Mee's close circle of friends and family ever got to see. The distance he deliberately placed between himself and his players meant that many probably didn't believe in the existence of such a trait.

Those who did witness it, though, remember it well. Don Howe says, 'Bertie had a good sense of humour. When we went away to Cleethorpes, he used to give them one or two nights out, telling them they did not have to be in until midnight. On those nights, he would say, "Come on, Don, we are going to see my brother in Blackpool," and we would all go out. I don't think Bertie ever laughed so much in all his life as on those nights with his brother, George, who had been on the fringes of the entertainment business. He was a little pudgier but you could hardly tell him and Bertie apart. It was not so much that Bertie was a changed character on those nights, but you saw how much he loved a laugh and a joke and a drink. He used to really enjoy himself.'

Howe also remembers coaching seminars run by the FA, where Mee and others 'would put on this little concert thing. It was hilarious. He could really get us all rolling around with laughter'.

Steve Burtenshaw remembers that Mee 'liked a glass of wine and knew a lot about it'. He adds, 'I travelled with Bertie to many games scouting and looking at teams we were playing. He drove there so he could have a drink in the directors' room if he wanted and I would drive back. On the way, we always had a varied discussion about all kinds of things and on the way back it would be about the game we had seen and the club, and football in general. In all honesty, Bertie was one to hide his true feelings at times under an austere appearance, but he could be very friendly and enjoyed a laugh.'

Very few players saw the boss let his hair down, although, in *Revelations of a Football Manager*, Terry Neill recalled:

> Bertie was a good dancer. On one of the club's close-season trips, we stopped off at Kuala Lumpur in Malaysia. Hostesses in gold lamé dresses looked after us and after a few drinks inevitably some of them ended up in the pool. Bertie took the floor and we did our best to mess up his efforts to make an impression as a ballroom dancer by constantly changing the record.

And Frank McLintock adds, 'Bertie told us a story once about when he was in the army in the desert. He was on a horse and bursting for a piss. He got down and did one and then he couldn't get on the horse again. He was only a little bloke and every time he tried to take a run up and jump, he couldn't make it. He even tried to build a sandcastle next to the horse to stand on that. He ended up walking the horse five miles through heavy sand back to the barracks. I was pissing myself while Bertie was telling the story. I had not heard him tell a story like that against himself before.' The animal, in fact, came to occupy a special place in Bertie's affection and for many years a photograph of him mounted on the horse sat in his wallet alongside a picture of Doris.

Mee was at his most relaxed when he was away from the football environment, but, even then, his friend Ron Goodman says that 'in a way, he was prim and proper'. He continues, 'It took a couple of whiskies to relax him. We met Bertie and Doris in Portugal one year and it was the only time I have seen him completely relaxed. We spent one day at our hotel and one at theirs. We brought an inflatable dinghy, which we put in the pool, and it was amusing to see Bertie pulling the kids about in the boat. He did not seem to relax that easily – even with his own family.'

Goodman also recalls Mee putting his organisational skills to good use on what was supposed to be a relaxing visit to the 1974 World Cup finals. 'I had fixed up a trip with Adidas for English managers to watch the World Cup. There was Bobby Campbell, Dave Sexton, Bobby

Robson, Jimmy Sirrell, Freddie Goodwin, Willie Bell, Mike Kelly, Gordon Milne and Tommy Casey. Bertie was in his element. He kept them all in order for me. They loved it too. They never quarrelled about anything. I wouldn't have been able to keep them on time for buses like Bertie did. He was a lovely dictator. It needed someone at their own level to organise them.'

Fred Street is another who saw Mee's desire for order on social occasions. 'We used to go out once a month when I was at Arsenal. There would be me and my wife, Jane, Bertie and Doris, Ron Goodman, maybe one or two others. We would take it in turns to pay. One month it is Ron's turn, so he decides where we are going and we are all having a nice time. It gets to ten o'clock and Bertie, says, "Right, gentlemen. We are all finished. Time to go." But my wife says, "Hang on, Bertie. We are all having a nice time. You go, if you want to." That was Bertie. Very much in charge, even off duty.'

Friends recall that football was not one of Mee's favourite subjects in a social setting. Goodman says, 'He would never talk about the club off duty. I sense that he always appreciated that I would never ask him. I have seen him get angry with friends who asked him about events at Arsenal. Maybe we stayed friends so long because I understood that.

'Bertie was always such pleasant company. I never saw him get very annoyed in social settings. He was always very comfortable. He and Doris used to have quite a few parties where John Crane, the Arsenal doctor, and his wife, Penny, and ourselves and maybe Fred Street were the only football people there. Most of his other friends were not involved in the game. He used to like that. I remember he had a friend who played a banjo or guitar or something. Bertie used to get involved and sing along. He did enjoy those parties. The only player he seemed to have at parties was George Armstrong. He used to like him.' Those parties, often held on a Thursday night, became the stuff of legend among Mee's friends, often featuring Bertie showing his prowess at playing the spoons and one time ending with the pots and pans being brought from the kitchen to form a complete percussion section.

Harry Hopker saw as much of Mee at play as anyone, witnessing his enjoyment of a good night out, especially if it included a few glasses of wine. 'My wife is French and we had a holiday house in France for years. Bertie would come there with Doris and other friends. He used to love travelling and he was always very thrilled by the surroundings.

I remember him sitting there many times while someone would be cooking an evening meal. While we ate, Doris would do most of the talking and the pair of them would creep out of the house at three o'clock in the morning, by which time the table was laden with bottles. Bertie loved wine and through Arsenal he had access to some very good wine. We had wonderful wine when we went to his place.'

Bob Wilson witnessed at first hand how his manager prepared wine. 'I was one of the few players who ever got invited to his house. I remember asking Bertie how he got his red wine so perfectly warm. "Well, it is a very difficult skill," he said. Then he went to get another bottle and he had three of them lying on the radiator. They were nearly boiling.'

Hopker also remembers Mee's ability in the garden and his favoured method of relaxation. 'He was a very keen gardener. He never had much opportunity after he went into football because he was very busy, but their little suburban back garden was impeccable. They had a swing for the children on the lawn and it had to be shifted continually otherwise it left marks. He used to cultivate sweet peas as well. They were beautiful. He was so meticulous in arranging them. He could have become a very good gardener.

'He told me once that wherever he was he always managed to get a half-hour kip after lunch. I have one particular holiday snap and, sure enough, there are a couple of us poring over a map and there is Bertie having a sleep.'

Eddie Plumley, who was to work with Mee in later years at Watford, recounts, 'We had an awful lot of fun together. I remember Watford touring China in 1984 and Bertie, who had been there before, was explaining to a player in Shanghai how the table worked, with its centrepiece that moved the food around. The players had never seen anything like it. "When you want food from that side of the table, you swing it around like this," he said. As he did so, it went so fast that food and crockery went everywhere. Poor old Bertie was a bit taken aback.'

The phrase 'taken aback' didn't begin to describe the shock Mee received on his return from the summer break following Arsenal's Double. Don Howe, the man who had shared the stresses of management and helped his boss reach the summit of the profession, was leaving Highbury.

17

NEW CHALLENGES

I do not like to repeat successes. I like to go on to other things.

– Walt Disney

EN ROUTE TO WINNING THE FAIRS CUP IN 1970, ARSENAL HAD outplayed Ajax of Amsterdam, now champions of the Continent after their Wembley victory against the Greek underdogs Panathinaikos. As manager of England's new champions, Bertie Mee was relishing the prospect of sitting down with his brilliant coach Don Howe to plot the downfall of teams like Inter Milan, Benfica and the Dutch masters themselves. He saw no reason why his Arsenal team could not emulate Manchester United, England's only previous European Cup winner.

United's own fortunes had plummeted since their triumph of 1968. After Frank O'Farrell, who had led Leicester to promotion, was hired to take the manager's position at Old Trafford, it was Howe who was touted as the leading candidate to move into the vacant slot at Filbert Street. Howe publicly rejected the opportunity, saying, 'My future lies at Highbury – as far as I can tell you at the moment anyway.'

Perhaps Mee should have noticed a warning in that statement. Five days later, Alan Ashman was sacked by West Bromwich Albion and Howe accepted the chance to return to his former club as manager.

The loss that Arsenal were suffering in the departure of Howe was evidenced by the comments Mee had just contributed to the third *Arsenal Football Book*, in which he described Howe as 'the best coach in the business and an ideal right-hand man'.

Mee soon discovered that Howe was taking trainer George Wright, who would become Albion's assistant manager, and youth-team coach Brian Whitehouse, who had just led the club's juniors to victory in the FA Youth Cup. While Arsenal chairman Denis Hill-Wood huffed that 'loyalty is a dirty word these days', Howe insisted that he had placed Wright and Whitehouse under no pressure. 'When they learned I was leaving Arsenal, they asked to come with me. Arsenal's reaction is difficult to understand.'

For Mee, a manager whose biggest strength was the ability to construct an effective framework and place the right people within it, the damage to his precious infrastructure was made all the worse for having been without warning. Howe admits that his departure was not discussed in advance, nor did he hear from Mee in the aftermath of his announcement. 'I really don't know what Bertie's reaction was because we never talked about it. I had a chance to go back to my old club as manager and I went. Bertie didn't ring me up to talk about it and I didn't call him. Bertie used to accept things, so I am sure he just got on with things without me.'

The lack of communication is, however, a strange state of affairs for two men who had worked so closely together. And it rather undermines Mee's subsequent public comment that, 'I will miss him from a personal friendship point of view.'

Many remain surprised at how little resistance to Howe's departure Mee and Arsenal offered, and how easily Howe left the man who had given him his big break. 'Bertie and I had a good working relationship,' says Howe, 'but he was a bloke that I worked with; he wasn't a bloke I went out to dinner with. I have always been grateful to him for giving me the chance to work with Arsenal and giving me the chance as first-team coach. But this was a great opportunity for me.'

Howe acknowledged some years later that the promise of eventually succeeding Mee as Arsenal manager could have tempted him to stay, 'but nobody said that', he commented. Howe would return to Highbury in 1977 as first-team coach under Terry Neill and would later be promoted to manager. He eventually arrived back at Highbury for a third time to work with the youth team under Arsène Wenger. But he explains that he had little contact with Mee following the break-up of their partnership. Similarly, George Wright reports that his decision to join Howe effectively ended his relationship with a man with whom he had shared a house two decades earlier. As Bob Wilson points out, 'Loyalty was the great basis of Bertie Mee. Loyalty to his players, his workmates – right back to his old clinics.'

Mee apparently interpreted the West Brom exodus as disloyalty. Wright says, 'It didn't go down well. But I was going to get promotion and an increase in salary. Bertie offered me the same money to stay but I told him I was going because I was getting promotion. He said, "Don't be ridiculous. It is only West Brom." I don't think he ever forgave me. We met on other occasions, but there was a bit of coldness there. We had both moved on. We never swapped Christmas cards.'

Mee's friend Ron Goodman believes that it was Wright's move that bothered him most. 'When Don left, it hurt Bertie that George went with him. He was very sad. He didn't understand why George went or why Don had made him assistant manager; he was not cut out for it. Bertie felt George could have come and spoken to him about it. Instead, he was on holiday and came back to it.'

Ever the realist, however, Mee wasted little time in putting together a new team. Once more, he looked to the reserves for a new first-team coach. Steve Burtenshaw recalls, 'I had just gone to visit family in Brighton. I got a telegram from Bertie saying to phone him immediately. He told me Don was leaving for West Brom and he wanted me to take over. He acted quickly because he'd heard that Brighton were going to offer me the manager's job that week.'

David Smith, former chief coach at Newcastle and Burtenshaw's ex-teammate at Brighton, was named as the new reserve-team coach, while former Scotland Under-23 international Ian Crawford was put in charge of the youth side. Meanwhile, it was time for Bertie to intervene in Fred Street's career once again. Having seen Mee chart his course into the health service, Street had been working, again in no small part due to Bertie's influence, for three years as physiotherapist at Stoke City. 'I had been working in Australia and had come back and taken Bert's old job at Camden Road,' says Street. 'He rings me up one day and says, "Stoke City want someone and they are in London tomorrow."'

That was how Street had ended up on the opposition bench during the epic FA Cup semi-final a few months earlier. But now he was to swap sides. 'I was at a seminar at Loughborough and news broke that George had gone with Don to West Brom. I think George had probably had enough of Bertie, who could still be aloof. Friends you might be, but he could still be difficult. There are 150 delegates around and there is an announcement: "Phone call for Fred Street." Everyone is joking and shouting, "It's the Arsenal." And it was. It was Bertie saying he wanted me to join them.

'I said I had to talk to the Stoke chairman. I wouldn't have left them to go to Manchester United, but this was a chance to go back to London. I said I'd let him know the next day. I told the chairman that Bertie had offered me the job and said, "If you say I can't go, I will stay. No strings." The chairman said we would work something out. Bertie rang me that evening and said, "You start tomorrow. We have paid five thousand for you." That was Bertie organising my life again!'

The early weeks of the 1971–72 season were memorable for the sudden clampdown by referees on foul play and the stunning march of newly promoted Sheffield United to the top of the First Division. Arsenal fell victim to both phenomena.

With their triumph in League and FA Cup having thrown the traditional FA Charity Shield match-up into disarray (Cup runners-up Liverpool ended up taking on Division Two champions Leicester), Arsenal's first competitive match was a 3–0 walloping of Chelsea on a sun-drenched Highbury afternoon; a perfect setting for the parade of the previous season's silverware. They had, however, already shown impressive form in beating Benfica, Eusebio and all, in two challenge matches, including a 6–2 win at home.

The opening shots of the season were soon forgotten, though, after Football League referees received a memorandum in the post on the morning of Monday, 16 August. It was the beginning of what the press would dub 'the Refs' Revolution'. The document clarified the way in which various laws were to be interpreted. Offside, offences against the goalkeeper, time-wasting and attitudes towards match officials were among the topics covered, along with sections on handball, obstruction, tripping and tackling. Under the last of those headings, it was made clear that the tackle from behind was no longer permissible and noted that it was virtually impossible to make such a tackle without making contact with the opponent first.

The clampdown had been hinted at in the weekend's newspapers, with Frank McLintock saying, 'Even as a defender, I'd like to see this tackle outlawed. I think forwards would play with more confidence.'

Even so, no one expected the events of the first Tuesday of the season, when 32 players were cautioned in 15 games – an insignificant number by modern card-happy standards, but enough to cause ripples across 1971's stream of complacency about foul play. At Portman Road, six men, a phenomenal number for one game, were cautioned by Tonbridge official Ron Challis in Ipswich's game against Coventry. The following night, seven players were booked as Tottenham and Newcastle fought out a 0–0 draw, after which Newcastle captain Bobby Moncur commented, 'The referees are turning it into a game for sissies.' Elsewhere that night, three players were sent off, including George Best at Chelsea, and thirty-eight more booked. By mid-December, cautions would reach the 1,000 landmark and when referee Brian Daniels failed to book anyone in a game between Fulham and QPR he was sent a 'Get Well' card by a fan.

Mayhem ruled, the newspapers had a field day and, of course, the referees couldn't win. Leicester official Gordon Hill, one who was reluctant to go to his notebook, was accused of letting Arsenal's game at Southampton get out of hand. One newspaper described the game, which degenerated after Saints midfielder Hugh Fisher had his leg broken in an accidental collision with Bob Wilson, as 'a return to the Dark Ages'.

Players argued that early-season bookings should not count because they had not been warned of the new hard line, while referees threatened to strike if disciplinary committees overturned their decisions. Finally, a summit meeting of all interested parties early in October seemed to quell the storm with referees, managers and players agreeing to form a working committee to look into all of the issues.

Once the shouting had abated, few doubted over the forthcoming months that the so-called revolution had a positive effect. It certainly contributed to one of the most exciting First Division title races for many years, won by an elegant Derby County on the final day of the season after a four-way battle involving Manchester City, Liverpool and Leeds. Even the dainty George Eastham, five years after Arsenal decided he was losing his effectiveness in the modern game, would return from a spell in South Africa to lead Stoke to the first trophy in the club's history. His winning goal in the League Cup final against Chelsea completed one of the season's most romantic tales.

It is not unfair to suggest that Arsenal, as a team that relied on solidity and organisation more than flair, were among those teams to benefit least from the new directive. They might not actually have been hampered, and John Radford's calves might have been spared a few bruises, but the new laws were designed less to help Bertie Mee's team than the likes of Chelsea, Derby, Stoke and Manchester City. McLintock suggested, 'I feel we were affected in those early matches by the referees' crackdown. It probably made us less challenging.'

After winning their first two games, Arsenal slumped to three consecutive defeats. The second saw their first League defeat at Highbury for nineteen months: 1–0 at the hands of a Sheffield United team on their way to taking eighteen points from their first ten games to lead the First Division. Six wins from seven games then saw Arsenal reproduce something of their previous season's consistency, only for November to bring a three-game losing streak that culminated in a 5–1 hammering at Wolves. The same month brought an end to the Gunners' League Cup campaign, the impressive Sheffield United inflicting further damage upon Arsenal's season.

With key men like Charlie George, Bob McNab, Peter Simpson and John Radford all missing a significant number of games through injury, loss of form or suspension, Arsenal lacked the cohesion of the previous season. There were bad runs, like three consecutive goalless defeats in March, and good spells, including unbeaten sequences of twelve and nine games. It all added up to fifth place, although they were never more than outsiders in the title race.

Looking back on the season in the fourth edition of the *Arsenal Football Book*, Mee would excuse his players for the failure of the defence of their title:

> I can have nothing but admiration for the way in which the Arsenal players stood up to the demands of the 1971–72 season. Unfortunately there had to be some sort of reaction to the Double. I felt it myself on a personal level; I had a tremendous feeling of let-down and all the symptoms that go with it. Inevitably, the players could not go on and on from

where they left off. Our performances had to sag a little and I felt that one or two early reverses in the League meant that we would have an almost impossible job in retaining the Championship. As it happened, after these early setbacks we played with a reasonable consistency.

As well as witnessing the players' mental struggles, Mee, an expert in physiology, believed his squad's bodies had suffered from the effects of the previous season, in which they had played 64 games. Speaking at a Sportswriters' Association lunch in March 1972, he said, 'It could be that we have reached the point where we cannot fairly ask any more,' he said. 'I believe that from the physical aspect we have reached the maximum. I am thinking in terms of wear and tear, and what we can ask the body to do.'

The First Division might have quickly proved beyond Arsenal's ambitions, but the second half of the season still harboured hopes for the European and FA cups, particularly with Mee having strengthened his squad with the biggest signing of his career.

Alan Ball had already been the subject of one major transfer when, with his tireless, bare-legged running in England's 1966 World Cup final still fresh in the nation's minds, he moved from Blackpool to Everton. At Goodison Park, he formed, with Colin Harvey and Howard Kendall, one of English football's most effective midfield combinations. Fiercely competitive, possessed of a sharp football brain and the loveliest of touches on the ball, he had driven a stylish Everton team to the First Division title in 1970. By the December of 1971, at only 26 years old, he had set a new trend by wearing white boots, remained anchored in the England team and was writing a weekly column in *Shoot!* magazine. In short, he had attained the star status that no Arsenal player had enjoyed since Joe Baker and George Eastham. Mee had never before signed a player of such renown.

The transfer took most people by surprise; there had been no protracted speculation in the newspapers. Everton manager Harry Catterick simply summoned Ball to his office in the days after a disappointing home defeat against Derby, told his player that he would be dropped and that the club were prepared to release him. Arsenal had already expressed a firm interest. Ball felt that Catterick had not taken into account that his wife had given birth to their second daughter the night before the game in question and by the time he met Mee there was not much persuasion needed. 'I'd already decided that I would never play for Everton again,' Ball said later. 'I'd given everything to the club, but my pride had been hurt, my faith destroyed. Arsenal were willing to pay a record fee for me, yet I wasn't good enough for Everton.'

Mee had agreed a British record sum of £220,000 and, three days before Christmas, Ball arrived in London. He was taken to the White House Hotel in Regent's Park, where a verbal agreement was reached over personal terms. Ball then underwent a medical check-up and met the press at Highbury, where he said, 'I am sure I will fit in quickly at Arsenal. They are a workmanlike side who play for each other, and that will suit me fine.'

After the disappointment of the Peter Marinello deal two years earlier, Arsenal fans had wondered when, or if, Mee would again make a bold move into the transfer market. They were as relieved as they were excited about the unexpected turn of events.

Having won the FA Cup in 1971 after being drawn away in every round, it was with a feeling of resignation that Arsenal waited for the balls to come out of the velvet bag when the defence of their trophy began. Once again, they would be on the road – the M4, in fact – as they travelled to Swindon. Their opponents' name still sent chills through the club, but the past was partly exorcised with a comfortable 2–0 win in which Ball scored his first goal for his new club. Pat Rice was the unlikely scorer of the winner in a 2–1 win at Reading – the M4 again – before the fifth-round draw sent Arsenal to the Baseball Ground to face Derby.

Charlie George, recovered from his early-season cartilage operation and replacing the injured Radford, scored twice in a 2–2 draw before a goalless replay at Highbury. That game remains memorable only because it was played on a midweek afternoon due to the ban on floodlit games during the power workers' industrial dispute. Kennedy decided the second replay at Leicester and, five days later, it was Ball who got the single goal that beat Second Division Orient in the quarter-finals at Brisbane Road.

By this time, several months after an emphatic entry into the European Cup, Arsenal's ambitions of becoming champions of the Continent were hanging in the balance.

Confident of making a strong challenge for club football's biggest prize, Arsenal had taken only 90 seconds during their debut in the competition to register their first goal. The Norwegian club Strøemsgodset of Drammen were no match for the Football League champions, going down 3–1 on their own ground, with Marinello – benefiting from the absence of George and Armstrong – scoring one of the goals. A 4–0 Gunners victory in the second leg was highlighted by two goals by Radford. Arsenal's second-round tie against Grasshoppers of Zurich was also effectively over before reaching Highbury, goals by Kennedy and Radford giving Mee's team a comfortable cushion. The advantage was extended to five goals in the home leg.

Four games was all it took to reach the last eight of the tournament back in pre-Champions League days and the tournament went into winter hibernation with Arsenal knowing that the holders, Ajax, were lying in wait when the action resumed.

Unlike the teams' contest two years earlier, the first leg was played in Amsterdam, where, thanks to resilience, determination and the excellence of Bob Wilson, Arsenal escaped with a 2–1 defeat. They were clearly no match for the skill of the home team, for whom Johan Cruyff was predictably outstanding, coming close to scoring twice inside the opening few minutes. It was Arsenal who scored a surprising first goal when Ray Kennedy pounced on a defensive mistake and it needed a deflected 25-yard shot from Muhren to level the score. A disputed second-half penalty, converted by Muhren, secured Ajax's lead but Mee declared himself happy with the result and singled out George's performance for praise.

Two weeks later, despite the absence of the suspended Radford, the ineligible Ball and the injured McNab and Kelly, Highbury greeted Arsenal with high expectations of a place in the last four. Those hopes rose even higher within the first minute when Marinello, in his first game for six months, picked up a misplaced pass and bore down on goal. He struck his shot straight at the keeper's legs. Within 15 minutes, further disaster had struck. Ruud Krol crossed the ball and, as Wilson began advancing towards it, Graham stretched and glanced a header beyond him into his own goal.

For the rest of the game, Arsenal appeared weary and bereft of ideas. The tie was already beyond redemption by the time George hit the post with a minute remaining. Ajax coach Stefan Kovacs delivered what would prove to be a significant condemnation of the English champions. 'I was a little surprised that Arsenal seemed to have so few ideas. All they did was concentrate on the long ball down the middle.' Mee would take such criticism to heart.

Bob Wilson recalls the growing excitement about the Dutch style of play but believes a little luck could have seen Arsenal progress. 'We were disappointed because we knew we were capable of winning in Europe, but we knew we were playing a team that was becoming a force there. Everyone was talking about the Dutch and "Total Football", which basically meant that you could find yourself in any position and feel comfortable. Ajax had found these lads who were technically gifted at a young age and kept them together. But we survived really well out there and it was a dubious penalty that beat us.

'For the goal at Highbury, we were shouting at George to leave the ball but it was noisy and George never heard it. The disappointment was tempered as time went by because we realised how close we came to beating a great team even though we were under strength.'

Mee admitted Arsenal's inferiority but offered an explanation. 'Some of the Ajax technique was much greater than ours. This is because Ajax play one game a week and the opposition is inferior, enabling them to develop their skills. We don't get that opportunity. At Highbury, we no longer train but just play two games a week. We don't have time to develop our individual skills.'

The FA Cup remained to be won again, however. And not only had the tournament sent Arsenal on their travels in every round for the second straight year, but Stoke City, the new League Cup holders, were once more their semi-final opponents. Villa Park was the venue and this time it was the Gunners' rivals who came from behind. Armstrong had taken Arsenal into the lead from the edge of the penalty area but an injury to goalkeeper Bob Wilson, capped by Scotland earlier in the season, changed the course of the game. With 20 minutes remaining, Wilson leapt to deal with a high free-kick but, in twisting, stretching and landing, he badly damaged his knee. During the five minutes he remained on the field after suffering his injury – which Wilson describes as 'a poor decision' on the part of himself, Street and Mee – Stoke equalised. Arsenal's defence had looked nervous around their immobile goalkeeper and when Simpson had gone to intercept a ball he would normally have left to Wilson, he succeeded only in diverting it into his own goal. Mee had seen enough and Wilson was taken off, the big-hearted Radford taking his place between the posts for the final 15 minutes. But there were no more goals and, for the second year running, Stoke must have felt they had blown their best chance of winning the tie.

In the replay at Goodison Park, Geoff Barnett, playing his first game for more than two years, found himself beaten by a Jimmy Greenhoff penalty. Charlie George equalised, also from the spot, and delighted in reminding Gordon Banks of the previous year's events as he did so. Banks and his team, aggrieved at the penalty that rescued Arsenal a year earlier, this time debated the Gunners' winning goal, scored by Radford after George had appeared to be offside in the build-up.

The final, the fifth in five years for the club, brought Arsenal into combat yet again with Leeds. This time there was the added bite that Don Revie's team would, if they won at Wembley and then drew at Wolves two days later, emulate the Gunners' hard-earned Double. When such high stakes were added to the memory of the awful League Cup final between the teams four years earlier, few expected the day to produce much spectacle beyond the pre-game celebration of the tournament's centenary. Quite who BBC commentator David Coleman was referring to when he said during the second half, 'There were some people who expected this game to produce a lot of goals,' is anyone's guess. Even the skies above Wembley were suitably grey for the occasion. Mee slipped a brown raincoat over his club suit to lead out this Arsenal team: Barnett, Rice, McNab, Storey, McLintock, Simpson, Armstrong, Ball, George, Radford, Graham. Sub: Kennedy.

The action lasted for all of three seconds before being halted by the first free-kick of the game after Allan Clarke fouled Ball inside the centre-circle. Determined not to be outdone, Bob McNab lunged at Peter Lorimer on the touchline and had his name taken. And still only 45 seconds played. The tone had been well and truly set. Norman Hunter was booked for a hack at Ball late in the first half and when Leeds won a free-kick just outside the Arsenal box, Clarke could be seen reaching out his right arm while standing in the Gunners' wall and jerking back George's head by his hair. George, in turn, talked his way into the book early in the second half but survived further punishment after a nasty-looking challenge on Clarke. Then Ball, frustrated by Bremner's successful shielding of the ball, hacked through the back of the Leeds captain's legs before further endearing himself to his opponents by trying to haul the apparently stricken Bremner from the grass.

It might not have plumbed the depths of the teams' previous Wembley encounter, but it was hardly entertainment fit for the Queen, who watched patiently from the Royal box. No wonder that, when the prospect of another Arsenal–Leeds final loomed one year later, Eric Nicholl would write in *Goal*, 'I think I'll go to the pictures. Anything must be better than that.'

In between the stoppages, there was some football. Not a lot, and most of it – at least in the early stages – played by Leeds, who came closest to a first-half breakthrough when a Lorimer shot was turned away unconvincingly by Barnett. The goal that earned Leeds the Cup for the first time in their history eventually arrived after 54 minutes. A half-slip by McNab as he challenged Mick Jones gave the Leeds forward enough room to pull back a cross for Clarke to guide a diving header beyond Barnett's flailing left hand.

The nearest Arsenal came to equalising was midway through the second half when a patient build-up ended with Ball shooting low from outside the box. His effort ricocheted off a defender and George, sporting red boots, hooked a first-time shot from 15 yards over keeper David Harvey, only to see it slap against the bar. If the rebound had fallen to a more reliable goalscorer than Simpson, Arsenal could still have been rewarded. With 17 minutes left, Mee sent on Kennedy for Radford, which did little to change the pattern of play. Eddie Gray cut in from the left to force a save from Barnett and could have made the game safe if he had passed to Clarke instead of trying to score. In the end, an increasingly tired and ragged Arsenal were unable to equalise and Mee was the first to congratulate Don Revie when the final whistle signalled the end of his team's reign as Cup holders.

The Arsenal manager was left to find silver linings in the clouds of Arsenal's first season without a major trophy for three years. 'Losing to Ajax was a blow and there is no point pretending otherwise,' he said. 'But you have to admire the way Frank McLintock led the boys back to the final of the FA Cup.' It was the European defeat that was to have a more lasting effect on Mee than the loss to Leeds, who missed out on the Double when they were beaten at Wolves. The start of the following season would see a brand-new Arsenal.

18

GOING DUTCH

There is more to football than hitting high balls into
a crowded goalmouth.

— Johan Cruyff

WHEN AJAX WON AT HIGHBURY IN MARCH 1972, THEY DID MORE
than end Bertie Mee's ambition of bringing the European Cup back to
Arsenal. Watching the Dutch close up and seeing them progress to a
second successive European Cup triumph, Mee had been enchanted by
Johan Cruyff and his team's 'Total Football', the flexible, fluent style
that would win Ajax a third European title and would propel Holland's
national team to consecutive World Cup finals. The West German side
that was steered towards the European Championship in the summer
of '72 by the commanding play of blond midfielder Gunther Netzer
and the graceful versatility of Franz Beckenbauer made no less an
impression. The influence of such teams was even greater given the
Arsenal boss's increasing sensitivity to criticism of what many saw as
the bleak, methodical manner of his own team.

Mee was uncomfortable with the derogatory comments of Ajax's
coach and star player after their European Cup visit to Highbury. Not
much time had passed since *Goal* editor Alan Hughes had described
Arsenal's Wembley contest against Liverpool as 'without doubt the

worst for years' and had continued, 'Many more like that and the distribution of Cup final tickets shouldn't be a problem. Only the fans of the two teams will want to go.' And that was before he had seen the Leeds final.

In the throes of rebuilding his club, Mee had been realistic enough to recognise that his players were never going to dance a Brazilian-style samba around their opponents. But here was a man who was constantly telling his players to 'remember who you are and what you represent'. He felt a responsibility to send out a team that would add to the club's repute, not provoke rebuke. Arsenal had already been supporting the game's adoption of more attacking measures as a way of countering the criticism of the 1970–71 season, in which only 1,089 First Division goals – 635 fewer than a decade earlier – had been scored. Club secretary Bob Wall had even advocated bonus points for goals scored. Mee, however, was not prepared to wait for football's legislators. He felt that a club of international standing should act unilaterally.

So, with the confidence that came with silverware and the bruises caused by the brickbats, Mee decided that his team was ready to march to the beat of the Dutch drum. 'A wind of change is blowing through the game,' he said. 'Ajax and West Germany have proved you can entertain and get results.'

The change in Arsenal's style at the start of 1972–73 was significant not just for its impact on the pitch, but also in the way that Mee pulled rank over his coach to achieve the realisation of his vision. In the past, he had been guided by his lieutenants on major battlefield policy; this time, Mee went to Steve Burtenshaw and told him that he wanted to radically alter Arsenal's tactics.

Already battling to fill the shoes of his predecessor, Burtenshaw now had to implement a new method of football, over which he was at odds with his manager. 'Bertie wanted a more Total Football type of team because he was very impressed with Ajax,' Burtenshaw explains. 'I was not 100 per cent in agreement. Bertie wanted to think about building for three or four years ahead, but I was more interested in the next few games. He felt that Arsenal should be innovative. More Arsenal performances were praised for their hard work than for silky skills.

'He thought that we'd done well with what we had, but now he wanted a more attractive style. To do that, we had to change our philosophy and change players. I warned him it would not come quickly or easily. I said we needed to show restraint. I tried to give back a phrase to him that he used a lot: that it was not gambles we needed, but calculated risks. I felt it was a gamble. If Bob McNab's studs had not got stuck at Wembley, he would have blocked the cross that led to the Leeds goal in the 1972 FA Cup final and we could have won. But Bertie felt after the Double that there was a need to start changing the image a bit.'

For the first few games, Arsenal exhibited a pronounced distaste for their previously successful methods, flitting around the field like a dance troupe. They put five goals past Wolves in their first home game and made it three wins out of three by beating Stoke 2–0, prompting Peter Batt to write in *The Sun*, 'I saw enough here to convince me that these new-style Gunners really can lead English soccer out of the dark age.'

One player in particular was thriving. Alan Ball cut a happier, more confident figure in the Arsenal midfield now that more of the play was being directed through him. McLintock recalls, 'Things weren't working out for Alan Ball at the start after we signed him. We were used to hitting good balls from back to front and Ballie liked it played to his feet. He was very frustrated and thought it was making him look bad. I said to him, "Look, we have been doing this for seven years. You will have to be patient."'

Ball himself adds, 'When I signed, I was in a team that had been successful playing a certain way and quite understandably they weren't going to change right away. It was hard for me because at other teams everything had been played through me. Arsenal were a terrific side and there were times early on when I scratched my head as to why they bought me.'

The Arsenal fans were delighted, if a little surprised, at events unfolding before them. A letter from Islington resident L.P. Ruse to the Arsenal programme said, 'I would like to praise Bertie Mee and Steve Burtenshaw for the courage they have shown in introducing more attacking football into Arsenal's play. The times I have heard people accusing Arsenal of being too predictable; now no one outside the team knows what Arsenal will do next.'

By the end of August, Arsenal had won four and drawn two of six games and Mee was named Manager of the Month – justification, for now at least, of his insistence on the team's makeover. Burtenshaw believes that, even before facing Ajax, Mee had been contemplating change and was tempted to offer freedom to his players in the way that Don Revie had liberated his team after they began winning trophies. That is why he had been keen to bring in Ball, one of the best touch-footballers in the country. 'You have got to start somewhere and it began with Alan Ball. One way to change is to work with the players you have. But if they have been successful with a different system, you have to try to change slowly – not overnight. Or you can change players. That was going to take time as well. Bertie appreciated that, but at the same time Arsenal needed to continue to be successful.'

Bob McNab adds, 'It was apparent that Bertie wanted to appease some of our critics who had been describing us as predictable. Well, our greatest quality was that we were predictable to one another. Our two central strikers were the best in the business, so why would you not play that way? The season after the Double, teams did start sitting central midfield players in front of Raddy and Ray, which killed the space in front of these two and prevented long early balls into feet. Now we needed to develop attacks through the midfield, so in came Ballie.'

But, as Burtenshaw recalls, it needed more than just Ball to effect the changes Mee was seeking. 'Getting the players Bertie wanted took longer than he hoped, so what do you do? He had specific players in mind but it was difficult to get them. The type of money that those players would cost may have been in his budget but not in his mind. I often heard him say, "I am not paying that." He wasn't worried about paying it for Alan Ball but there were others for whom he would not pay that money. Also, I remember sitting in a hotel waiting for an Alan Ball-status player to turn up to sign, but we got a message from the other team's directors saying that the deal would not happen. That happened about three times. It stops you progressing as quickly and you start thinking about whether to settle for lesser players.'

In the fourth edition of the *Arsenal Football Book*, published early in the 1972–73 season, Mee commented:

> I have never believed Arsenal should sign ordinary First Division players. I'm on the lookout for people who will bring the League Championship trophy back to Highbury. At the start of the [1971–72] season I could have named four or five

231

players of this calibre who obviously would have improved our squad. Alan Ball was one of them. When he became available, I didn't have to think twice.

Without the new players that Burtenshaw felt were needed to carry Mee's vision beyond the first few games of the season, the Gunners showed signs of faltering. Ball alone couldn't carry the burden of creative play and Arsenal had to wait until the final week of September to win a Division One game that month. Mee's short-term solution was to offer a run of games to Peter Marinello and to bring back Charlie George, out of favour for the early games because of a pay dispute. Ray Kennedy, struggling with his form and weight, and George Armstrong were the men to make way.

In defence, Mee added a new face; his second £200,000 signing within a year. Jeff Blockley had spent 18 months at Highbury as a teenager before being released, but his performances as skipper of Coventry City had persuaded Mee to spend a small fortune to recapture his services. Blockley had also caught the eye of Sir Alf Ramsey and earned an England cap during his first few days as an Arsenal player – before he'd made his debut for his new team. A big stopper whose dark, wavy hair gave him the look of a cabaret singer, he would, however, do little in the next couple of years to persuade the North Bank that much had changed since the club had originally labelled him as 'too casual'. In his first Arsenal game, at Sheffield United, it was his uncertainty that gave the home team their winner.

Arsenal's form continued to be patchy, until, at the end of November, came two results that forced Mee to admit that his team simply weren't the new Ajax. First, Norwich knocked the Gunners out of the League Cup by three goals at Highbury. Four days later, at Derby's Baseball Ground, the deficit was five goals. When Leeds came to London a week later, Marinello and George were out, Armstrong was back and the Radford–Kennedy partnership was restored, along with the more direct approach that had served Mee so well in the Double season. Arsenal won 2–1.

Writing in *Goal*, Ken Jones noted, 'So ended Arsenal's four-month flirtation with a more flowing style. It had not been entirely unconvincing. But something had gone from Arsenal's game. The remedy did not exactly dishearten the team. Appealing football has little credibility unless it is seen to be successful.'

Geoff Barnett, who began the season as Arsenal's keeper while Bob Wilson continued to recover from his knee injury, recalls, 'You could see from the players Bertie added to the team that he wanted to change away from the old style. Ballie wasn't a stopper in midfield. He loved to get forward. But we had such a good back four and we always seemed to have most success when Geordie Armstrong played and supported them. Peter Marinello just didn't have the same ability tracking back. Trying to get away from our old style of play was tough because that was the stuff we played so well.'

McNab also contends that Arsenal's attempt to play a ground-based passing game was hampered by a change in the under-soil heating system that left the Highbury pitch in less than pristine condition. 'We ended up with a field with rises and falls every six to ten yards. You could almost get seasick running down the wings.'

Mee was ready to put up with more criticism if it meant a return to grinding out victories. Beginning with the Leeds game, in fact, the Gunners would remain unbeaten for fifteen matches, pushing themselves into a two-horse Championship race with Liverpool and advancing to the quarter-finals of the FA Cup. In only one of those games did they score more than two goals.

As well as the brave new world Mee was attempting to create, it was the old chestnut of players' wages that had created headlines out of Highbury early in the season. And the storyline had the most compelling of leading men in North Bank hero Charlie George.

During his reign as Arsenal manager, Mee had been forced to deal with transfer requests from Frank McLintock, Jon Sammels, Ian Ure, George Armstrong and Bob McNab. It was McNab's threat to leave Highbury early in the 1970–71 season that had revealed many players' distrust of a salary structure weighted disproportionately in favour of the more experienced players. And it was this that led George, along with fellow former youth-teamer Eddie Kelly, to put in a written transfer request to an Arsenal board meeting in August 1972.

Arsenal announced that the players were up for sale, with club secretary Bob Wall stating, 'Arsenal will never be held to ransom by two young players.' The tabloids, focusing more on the higher-profile

George, put the story on the front pages. The club did attach the rider that no transfers would take place until suitable replacements could be found. But if Mee had conducted a poll on the North Bank, he would have found that George was irreplaceable – even if Derby were, as reported, considering coming up with £300,000 to sign him.

Mee himself had recommended to the board that they accept the players' transfer requests. His unyielding response to this most public of challenges from the young renegade George appeared to strip away the last vestige of a relationship between the two. Mee announced, 'There were other personal factors I had to consider besides the contractual disputes.'

The previous 12 months had seen George getting into more and more scrapes with officials. He was criticised for an incident when he poked fun at the Chelsea winger Charlie Cooke, could easily have been sent off in a League Cup game against Sheffield United and caused outrage by sticking two fingers up at Derby fans after scoring in the FA Cup at the Baseball Ground.

For George, however, this was not a personal matter. It was not about his distaste for Mee's brand of discipline, nor his refusal to take part in psychological studies at the request of his manager. It was about money and principle. Even after their achievements under Mee, Arsenal's players were far from being the best paid in the First Division. During the Double season, the top basic weekly wage had been £90, with their pay packets being topped up by win bonuses and the controversial 'loyalty bonus'. That was a system by which players received an additional 12.5 per cent of their bonus money for every completed year at Highbury. It meant that £1,000 worth of win bonuses produced an additional £250 for a player with two years' service and could lead to the situation where a long-serving fringe player earned more than a younger first-team regular. McNab recalls, 'It was a very irritating situation. It was a good idea, but it didn't work. It is a good idea to reward loyalty but when players who are basically reserves are getting more than someone who is in England squads and is playing every game, there must be something wrong. I thought it was fundamentally unfair.'

George took the same view, even threatening to take the club to court to fight the system. 'We feel there is an unfair gap between us and the older players when it comes to money,' he said. 'We are all in the same team and it can't be right that we should be so far behind them because we are younger.'

Bob Wilson, who spent four decades at Highbury as player and goalkeeping coach, believes that the dispute was symptomatic of the club's long-standing approach to rewarding its staff. 'Arsenal have always been like that when it comes to money. They believe you should feel privileged to be connected with them. They are still like that with some of the coaching staff and the people who work in the offices. They can sometimes take advantage.'

The situation had been further complicated by the signing of Alan Ball, reportedly earning at least £10,000 a year and, as other players assumed, not subject to the vagaries of the loyalty-based salary structure. So now even some of the senior players, who had been relatively well rewarded because of the loyalty bonus, were becoming as disgruntled as their younger colleagues. Geoff Barnett recalls, 'It soon got through to us that Ballie was getting paid more money. My big buddy John Radford resisted him because of that. His attitude was, "Who is this guy coming in and being paid all this money?" In the end, we had a players' meeting about it. It was not unusual. One of the things Bertie always did was to let us sort things out ourselves. We met in the room down the tunnel and had a right old ding-dong. Ballie said, "Don't blame me." He told us what he was earning and said, "It is there for you guys to attain."'

Players who had achieved increased status within the game, thanks to honours won under Mee, were no longer willing to accept what they saw as inadequate rewards. And even if it was not the manager who was held responsible for that situation, it was he who was left with the problems that arose from such discontent. Radford argues, 'Bringing in Ballie caused a lot of aggro. I remember going in to see Bertie for a rise and was told there was no more money. I said, "Well, what about Alan Ball?" I was told, "He is a superstar." Players who were being signed were getting signing-on fees. Niggly things like that don't help when you are trying to win trophies. Once you start getting older and start finding out what other players are being paid, you fight your corner. As a youngster, I would have played football for nothing, but when you get older and wiser you want a little more of what others are getting.'

The dispute with George ended quietly on Friday, 22 September, when he agreed to sign a new contract and asked to be removed from the transfer list once he had won back his first-team place, which took only a few days. 'I've proved a point to myself by holding out for six weeks,' he said. But the bigger point had probably been made by the club.

Barely had Mee seen the George–Kelly pay dispute settled before he had another unhappy camper to contend with: the man whose jaw-jutting clenched-fist passion had personified the team spirit and bloody-mindedness of Mee's Double winners.

The apparently expendable gifts of George and Marinello were not the only victims of Arsenal's deteriorating results. With Blockley representing a significant investment and Peter Simpson recovered from his early season injuries, Mee decided that it was the captain, Frank McLintock, who would be the odd man out when he made his defensive permutations.

Three decades later, McLintock believes Mee handled the situation with a lack of understanding and feels that his demotion was the result of a misconception about events after the defeat against Norwich. 'Apart from Alan Ball, our team was the same players that won the Double and I felt we were starting to lag behind. I felt as though a lot of players were resting on their laurels. Steve Burtenshaw was different to Don Howe and wouldn't kick you up the arse in the same way. I decided to get the players together for a meeting and I really ripped into them. I'd asked Bertie and Steve not to come in and it didn't go down very well. I think they thought I was slagging them off and thought I was plotting. I felt they thought I wanted to be the coach, but nothing could have been further from the truth. I just wanted to play for another four years.

'Then Bertie dropped me and that was when I fell out with him. Bertie felt we needed kicking up the arse. He took me all the way up to Birmingham and said, "I am leaving you out tonight." He made me feel like a 17-year-old kid. I punched the wall and smashed an oak panel next to his head. I took it badly. But I was that type of person, very volatile. The chairman saw me later and asked why I wasn't getting ready. I said, "Ask that so-and-so over there." I was broken-hearted.'

For the remainder of the season, McLintock would play only in the event of an injury to either Simpson or Blockley, which meant he still got a good share of the action. But the fact that he was no longer a regular sat badly, not only with him, but some of those who had fought alongside him over the years. McNab confirms McLintock's memory of him pleading with Mee to reinstate his battle partner. McLintock says, 'Bert said I had done this and that and burned my bridges. Bob said to him, "He has fought and died for you and now you expect him to take it lying down. You know Frank better than that." Bertie thought I was a spent force. I remember him saying that Don Revie bought four centre-halves because he wanted to be ahead of the game when Jack Charlton was gone. I couldn't stand the thought of Jeff Blockley or anyone coming in who I didn't think was a good player or an Arsenal type of player. Jeff was trying to find his feet and we lost our shape at the back.'

By April 1973, with Arsenal out of the hunt for honours, McLintock agreed to a £25,000 move to Queens Park Rangers. Sadly, in light of the contribution he had made to Arsenal's revival under Mee, it was to be an acrimonious parting. 'I told Bertie I couldn't play in the reserves,' he remembers. 'I had tried to help the young players, but then I said, "I can't handle this. I am too good to play in reserve-team football for anyone." Maybe that forced the issue for Bertie and prevented him having to make the decision. Bertie said he would let me go and I asked whether I could have a testimonial game. He said he would put it before the board but when I went back to see him he said that I could only have one after ten years, and I had only been there nine years and six months. I was furious and I said, "If I ever become a manager, I hope I never turn into a manager like you." I think he handled it badly, even though the League rules said I could not have a testimonial. I felt I deserved better. They could have offered me one when I retired, which they were allowed to do.'

Bob McNab says of McLintock's departure, 'I think Bertie did a very poor job in this case. He should have known how Frank would react after nine years. He was not ready to be put out to grass. I was in no doubt that Frank could have been persuaded to stay. I recall saying to Bertie that he was asking Frank to lay down dead, which was completely against his nature. But Bertie seemed entrenched in his position.'

With 30 years of healing behind him, McLintock admits, 'I still love Arsenal and when I did become a manager, maybe I should have had a bit more of Bertie in me. When you have been a player, you still have some of the player in you. You have to keep your distance as a manager, like Bertie did, so that if somebody lets you down you can make sure it is not too pally-pally. You have to be thick-skinned as a manager, like Bertie. I admire him a lot, despite the way we finished.'

The break-up of the Double team had already started by the time McLintock moved across London. Early in December, Mee, to the surprise of Arsenal fans, accepted an offer of £120,000 for George Graham by Manchester United manager Tommy Docherty. That two such influential figures should be gone so soon after the triumphs of 1970–71 seems even more of a surprise with the benefit of hindsight, although former full-back Sammy Nelson points out, 'There was a thinking in those days that once you turned 30, that was it. It was not like today when you have guys playing Premiership football at 37. There were different ideas back then. Bertie's job as manager was to make those tough decisions and he certainly never backed away from making them.'

However, the sale of Graham, one of the more graceful and gifted Arsenal midfielders, did seem to confirm Mee's acceptance that his team would never be another Holland. Graham himself remembers the 'absolute class' with which Mee handled the transfer. 'I was always the one in and out of the team, so I realised that when things were slipping I would be one of those on the move. Bertie handled it brilliantly. He said, "George, we are accepting bids for you and we have set a price of £120,000. Three clubs have matched our offer: West Ham, Everton and Manchester United. I have organised a room at the White House Hotel in Euston Road so you can meet the three managers at your convenience."'

Despite the uncertainty over the team's playing style, the disputes with the younger players and the doubts surrounding some of the older generation, Arsenal again found themselves in a position to win the Double until a run of poor results in April. Hopes had been at their highest after a 2–0 victory at Anfield a couple of months earlier, but four League games without a win allowed Liverpool to establish what would end up as a three-point winning margin in the Championship race. The FA Cup campaign, meanwhile, came to the most unlikely of endings at Hillsborough.

A third successive semi-final place had been earned in an epic two-game sixth-round tie against Chelsea. After beating Leicester,

Bradford City and Carlisle in the early rounds, Arsenal travelled to Stamford Bridge in the midst of a crop of injuries and illness, and drew an exciting game 2–2. All four goals were scored in the first half, with a rare Ball header and an opportunist effort by George giving Arsenal the lead after the home team had scored first. Chelsea opened the scoring again in the Highbury replay, but Arsenal were level before half-time thanks to a controversial penalty. When Armstrong was brought down by Chelsea midfielder Steve Kember, referee Norman Burtenshaw indicated a free-kick outside the penalty area until an angry mob of red shirts persuaded him to consult his linesman. The conference produced a penalty, gratefully converted by Ball. Thirteen minutes into the second half, Kennedy headed the winning goal.

Arsenal, with Ball playing at the top of his game, approached the semi-final against Second Division Sunderland high on confidence. A return Wembley date with Leeds, drawn to play Wolves in the other tie, beckoned. Even when McLintock, enjoying an extended run in place of the injured Blockley, was himself injured a week before the big game, few experts predicted anything other than an Arsenal win. George retained his place in the forward line after scoring four goals in five games in place of Radford, who was left on the substitute's bench in spite of his restored fitness.

Despite having played only one reserve game in six weeks, Blockley was back in the team, although Steve Burtenshaw recalls, 'He wouldn't have played if Frank had been fit. Jeff wasn't at his fittest.' It took only 19 minutes for Blockley's lack of sharpness to be exposed as he left a back pass to Wilson horribly short and the Sunderland centre-forward, Vic Halom, took advantage to score. After 56 minutes, Blockley made way for Radford, but a header from Billy Hughes increased Sunderland's lead. George swept the ball in with six minutes left but there was too little time left for another great FA Cup escape. 'It was my fault,' said a distressed Blockley. 'I wasn't fully fit and I was probably wrong in offering to play.'

19

FAMILY AT WAR

A family is a little kingdom, torn with factions and exposed to revolution.

– Samuel Johnson

BERTIE MEE'S REIGN AS ARSENAL MANAGER COMPRISED THREE distinct periods. First was the rebuilding phase of 1966–69, when young players were phased in, old lags and disruptive influences weeded out, and character-building lessons were learned in two Wembley defeats. Then came a four-season stretch when, by winning or contending for major trophies, Mee could claim to have one of English football's elite teams in his charge. Arsenal's final three seasons under his leadership, however, make for less comfortable recollections.

It was a period when the sands of English football were shifting noticeably. Don Revie's Leeds United were about to enjoy one last glorious fling, winning an overdue second League Championship before making way for Liverpool's decade of dominance. Poland's escape act at Wembley produced the unthinkable consequence of a World Cup without England, leading to Sir Alf Ramsey's dismissal and the advent of a new, commercially driven era under Revie. Two of the biggest and most romantic names in football – Manchester United and Chelsea, the swaggering stylists of the '60s and early '70s – ended up in the Second Division. Attendances at stadiums were down alarmingly, with the game's increasing dependence on defensive tactics cited as a major cause. Meanwhile, hooliganism threatened to drag the game into the deepest of gutters. It forced even more fans to stay away, terrorised many of those who did attend and precipitated deterrent measures that would achieve their catastrophic consequence at Hillsborough more than a decade later.

Asked to offer a solution to the game's problems early in 1974, Mee suggested it was time for football to be run by an American-style commissioner. 'With so many clubs acting out of self-interest, we have to have more positive leadership,' he said. He also suggested shrinking the size of the First and Second divisions and supported the idea of a European Super League, in which national champions would compete for a season before returning to domestic competition.

The environment of negativity and unrest in which English football was operating was reflected at Highbury. Early in September 1973, with a 3–0 opening-day win against Manchester United having been more indicative of the chaos at Old Trafford than the promise at Highbury, Mee faced his first demonstration of unified player power. Groups of two or three players had previously taken on the club over salaries or absence from the first team, but now there was a direct challenge to his judgement and authority.

Feeling that the team was losing its way, members of the senior squad proposed that new club captain Bob McNab tell the manager that, in their opinion, Steve Burtenshaw should be replaced as coach. It was an awkward predicament for McNab. Not only was he Burtenshaw's neighbour and close friend, but he did not feel it was the players' job to dictate coaching appointments to the manager. However, he, Bob Wilson, George Armstrong and Alan Ball agreed to discuss the situation with Mee after the players voted overwhelmingly in favour of pushing for a change.

On hearing the players' demands, Mee, assessing the situation with the speed he had been taught in the army, said, 'Absolutely, I agree.' Burtenshaw's resignation quickly followed, coming the day after Arsenal achieved only their second win in their first six games. Whether Mee genuinely agreed that Burtenshaw was not the man for the job may never be known, but he was realistic enough to know that if the players believed they could no longer work with a particular coach, the only sensible thing to do was to bring in someone else. No football season was long enough to risk months of poor results because you wished to make a stand. Fred Street, whose role as team physiotherapist gave him the perfect vantage point on Mee's relationship with his coaches, says, 'Bertie knew that if you lost the players, you could be making all the right noises but would be wasting your time.'

John Radford admits to feeling that a new coach was needed, but believes the players should not have been required to make their feelings known in order to effect change. 'It was a big blow to the players when Don Howe went,' he says. 'The momentum of winning things was there, but Steve hadn't got a strong personality like Don. Nothing was going to crack up inside a year, but little things started to creep in. To be honest, it should never come to the situation where the manager is going to listen to a vote by the players. He should stand by the guy, or he should already have said, "I am going to get another coach."'

Inevitably, when discussing events of three decades previously, participants will take different historical paths. Burtenshaw plays down the role of the players in his departure. 'That's a load of crap,' he says, putting his decision to leave the club down to the general philosophical rift that had developed between him and Mee. 'Bertie wanted to change things around. I was not 100 per cent with him on all the players he brought to the club or the way he wanted to change things.'

But Bob Wilson says, 'There was growing discontent in the dressing-room. Steve was unfortunate because following Don Howe was like following the Messiah. He did a brilliant job with the reserve team and he had a great eye for a player, but if you don't win anything after the Double, it is seen as having underachieved. Steve was more mild-mannered than Don; it wasn't his way to be confrontational.'

Sammy Nelson believes that Burtenshaw's lack of top-level experience as a player may have eventually worked against him. 'Steve had good coaching qualities and was knowledgeable about the game, but when he started having to deal with senior players maybe he felt inhibited. You wonder if people are saying, "How do you know? You never played at this level."'

Bob McNab says there was an unavoidable reaction to winning the Double. 'I'm not sure any player intends to let things slip, but they do.

Then there were strong feelings against the club again for allowing Don to leave and Steve probably bore the brunt of that. Some players started taking advantage and he had little chance.'

Mee, it appears, had adopted the same approach towards Burtenshaw as he had earlier to Howe, when he had allowed Don to fight his own battle to win the approval of the players when he succeeded the popular Dave Sexton. Perhaps this time he needed to intervene to a greater extent in support of Burtenshaw to ensure that the support he required was forthcoming. After all, team discipline was at stake and Mee had rarely been slow to be an enforcer in that area.

Street recollects Burtenshaw sensing that his time at Arsenal was almost up. 'I remember Steve coming to me one morning in front of the hotel in Sheffield, where we were playing that night. He said, "I think this is going to be my last game." Steve inherited a team that had won the Double and now they knew it all and wouldn't listen to anyone. There was nothing nasty about it, but it was a difficult situation.'

Ball remembers Mee being 'upset that it had to happen', while Mee himself described the decision to release Burtenshaw as 'the most difficult I have had to make'. But Bertie explained, 'He had reached the point where the players would not respond to him.'

The man to whom Mee turned was Bobby Campbell, a former Liverpool wing-half who had moved down the divisions before seeing his playing career cut short by injury. Since turning to coaching, he had helped Queens Park Rangers manager Gordon Jago to guide an exciting young team back into the First Division. His outgoing, abrasive personality was only emphasised by succeeding the more subdued Burtenshaw. Mee told reporters, 'Bobby is the extrovert. He's vocally aggressive. We complement each other.'

The Arsenal players quickly discovered the extent of that aggression. Many still wince at the memory of Campbell's opening speech to the squad at the London Colney training ground, where he ripped into every one of them. The gist of the message was that success had spoiled them, made them soft. As Campbell turned to McNab, the former England left-back made it clear that he disagreed with everything the new coach was saying and left an expletive hanging in the air as he stormed off. They clashed again later in the day when McNab felt Campbell failed to appreciate a defensive manoeuvre to foil Charlie

George and David Price in a two-on-one attack. 'Bobby got within two inches of my face, screaming about something,' says McNab. 'I recall thinking, "This man has no idea what I just did." Bobby came in with a bang, wishing to establish a strong position. I could see what he was trying to do with all the shouting and ranting.'

Wilson continues, 'We saw the writing on the wall because of what happened on that first day. It was a bravado thing by Bobby. Within two days, the headlines were about him buying new players.'

Those headlines landed Arsenal in trouble after QPR manager Jago accused them of, in effect, making an illegal approach for goalkeeper Phil Parkes and midfielder Gerry Francis by leaking their interest to the press. Wilson and McNab were mentioned as candidates to journey in the opposite direction. A subsequent Football League hearing fined Arsenal £2,000, with secretary Bob Wall confessing that Campbell had 'extended his brief' during a visit to see Jago. Again, Mee seemed uncharacteristically divorced from affairs that were having such an effect on his club.

On the field, things could not have started any worse for Campbell. Early in October, Arsenal were knocked out of the League Cup at Highbury by Third Division Tranmere. The FA Cup brought defeat in the fourth round at the hands of Aston Villa of Division Two. Meanwhile, the First Division produced stuttering performances. Only twice did Arsenal win consecutive games as they stumbled to tenth place. The season was notable mostly for the decision of Bob Wilson to retire at its conclusion to become a full-time broadcaster with the BBC and the 13 League games played by Liam Brady, a young Irish midfielder with a killer left foot. Brady's first goal came in the final game against QPR, a match that saw Alan Ball break his leg while tackling Terry Venables.

Other former youth-team players – defenders Brendan Batson and Richie Powling, midfielder David Price and forward Brian Hornsby – featured in several games, but it was only Brady whose talent was risked in the latter part of the season. Going into March, Arsenal were still mathematical candidates for one of the relegation places, which had been increased to three. 'I refuse to introduce young players to this sort of atmosphere,' said Mee, whose reliance on the older players resulted in only one loss in the final eleven games.

Ray Kennedy scored a winner at Liverpool to confirm Leeds,

unbeaten for 29 games at the start of the season, as League champions. But despite playing all 46 competitive games, he totalled only 13 goals and fought a season-long battle with his weight. Few, however, were expecting the bombshell Mee dropped on 12 July, five days after West Germany had beaten Holland in the World Cup final. As thoughts turned to the new English season, Kennedy, still only 22, was sold to Liverpool for £200,000, apparently the long-term replacement for John Toshack. For Liverpool supporters, the shock was nothing compared with the same day's news that Bill Shankly was to retire as manager.

Little more than three years on from the triumphs of 1971, Double stalwarts Wilson, McLintock, Sammels, Graham and Kennedy were gone, along with squad members Roberts and Marinello. Jimmy Rimmer, the former Manchester United keeper who had been bought for £40,000, was joined by another ex-Old Trafford star, Brian Kidd, the scorer of one of United's goals in the 1968 European Cup final victory on his 19th birthday. Kidd was sold for £110,000 as part of Tommy Docherty's clear-out in the wake of the club's relegation. Mee's first selection of the new campaign included only five of the eleven who had started at Wembley three years earlier. For the home game against Leicester, won by a single goal by Kidd, Arsenal fielded: Rimmer, Matthews, Nelson, Storey, Simpson, Kelly, Armstrong, Brady, Radford, George, Kidd. Sub: Price.

One of the most frequent criticisms of Mee's Arsenal career is that the turnover of talent in the post-Double years was simply too quick. Within another 12 months, McNab and George would also be gone and, of the first-choice players of 1970–71, only Armstrong and Rice would retain that status. In *Arsenal in the Blood*, Mee confessed to the belief that 'the side broke up too soon'. However, he explains, 'There were offers to players to further their careers.'

That comment begs the question of why Mee felt that players had to leave Highbury to achieve personal progress at that time. Did he really expect only decline in Kennedy, and not development, had he remained at Arsenal?

McNab, who says he would have 'sold the North Bank before I sold Ray Kennedy', claims, 'I and a few others had become extremely concerned about the sale of players who had achieved so much. Ray had put on weight and was causing discipline problems, but I would not have sold him. He was young and immature, but what a talent. I felt the same when they sold Charlie. You just do not get players of that quality.'

Interestingly, Graham, the one member of the Double team to go on to managerial success and the first of that side to depart Highbury, is philosophical about Mee's dismantling of a successful side. 'That is the football life. Sometimes you need new blood and you think you see it early. Sometimes you can keep people for too long. You can't always get it right, but if you can be correct 75 per cent of the time you are going to have success. As a manager you should never sit on the fence and Bertie didn't. All the great managers are tough; they make hard decisions about letting players go and leaving people out of the team.'

After winning two of their first three games of 1974–75, Arsenal went ten matches without victory and hit the bottom of the First Division for the first time under Mee. New captain Alan Ball, who missed the first eight games after fracturing his leg again in a friendly in Holland, commented, 'I doubt the Manchester United players thought they'd go down, but if United can be relegated anybody can.'

Blockley was a casualty of the bad run, responding to his exclusion by asking for a transfer and ending his unhappy two years at Highbury by joining Leicester for a cut-price £80,000. Inevitably, the situation was not quite as straightforward when it came to Charlie George. Dropped in September, he once again asked to leave the club. The rift between player and manager grew even wider in November after Mee left George on the bench at Coventry, claiming he was not match fit and adding that he had still not received George's written transfer application. Mee said, 'If he hands in a request, he can go as soon as we sign a replacement. He knows that.'

George shot back, 'The manager is making a fool out of me. It seems he will pick anyone before giving me a chance. I must get away because I am deeply worried about my future.'

Mee might have fretted about his own future if he'd paid attention to tabloid tittle-tattle. Eight years after first being linked with Arsenal, Sir Alf Ramsey, fired by England in the spring, was once again touted in the press as the club's potential new manager. Club chairman Denis Hill-Wood insisted, 'We have no intention of changing our manager. Obviously we don't feel very comfortable at the bottom of the table, but I can assure you we are not alarmed.'

Amid the mayhem, Rimmer was proving one of Mee's more successful recent signings. Surplus to requirements at Old Trafford, he had been loaned to Swansea, where he had come under the reviving influence of former United keeper Harry Gregg. Such was the reborn Rimmer's instant rapport with the North Bank that fans dismissed paper talk that Arsenal might be considering a bid for Leicester and England's Peter Shilton. Meanwhile, fellow United exile Kidd was scoring important goals, but remained a committed Mancunian, often asking for United's result as soon as he returned to the dressing-room.

Mee obviously needed to move again in the transfer market if the spectre of relegation was not to become a walking, talking reality. Perhaps the thought of the Blockley and Marinello failures weighed heavily, or maybe it was Campbell's influence, but when Mee announced his new signing, it was not a big-money international or a player offering youthful potential. It was the £20,000 purchase of the bald QPR and former Orient centre-back Terry Mancini, a 31-year-old journeyman noted mostly for his love of a laugh and his antics in comedy clips shown on *The Big Match*. No longer a regular at Loftus Road, he had marked his final Rangers appearance by dropping his shorts in front of the directors' box, earning a two-game suspension. Not exactly behaviour of which his new manager would approve.

There are two ways of looking at the Mancini transfer. Maybe it was an example of how low Arsenal's ambition had been allowed to fall in the latter years of Mee's reign. Alternatively, one can applaud Mee for inspired pragmatism, his recognition that here was a man who possessed the personality that would make up for any technical shortcomings, whose injection of honesty and desire would be more therapeutic than any silky skills. By the start of the following season, Mancini had even been appointed club captain, in parallel with team skipper Eddie Kelly.

McNab, however, recalls, 'I was told Terry would be great for the dressing-room. I just remember thinking, "Why didn't we get Freddie Starr? He is far more funny."' In his autobiography, *So Far So Good*, published in 1980, Liam Brady wrote, 'Most of the players did not find him funny at the time. They had too much on their minds – and it left no room for being light-hearted.'

As a young player coming into the dressing-room, Brady was disturbed by the 'disputes and personality clashes which were evident from the start of the season and got worse as the months went by'. He spoke of the 'cold and clammy hand of disenchantment tightening its grip on Arsenal' and spent months avoiding eye contact that might be misinterpreted as either support or disapproval. It was here, as much as in the heart of the defence, that Mee became a victim of his decision to offload Frank McLintock. Such was the strength of the Scot's personality, the grip he held on the mood of the dressing-room, that it is hard to imagine such factions and friction manifesting themselves under his continued captaincy. McLintock would have given everyone a bollocking and told them to get on with it.

Early in December, undeterred by his previous unhappy experience with Hibernian wingers, Mee spent £150,000 on Scotland international Alex Cropley, another skilful yet slight specimen. Born in Aldershot and considered one of the hottest properties in Scottish football, despite a slow recovery from a cartilage operation, Cropley had been under Mee's scrutiny for 18 months. It meant more unhappiness for Brady, who, despite assurances from Mee and Campbell, was the player to make way for the new signing. He was soon back, though, after Cropley broke his leg in his seventh League game and was lost for the season.

Some drawn-out battles in the FA Cup offered the only respite from the club's ongoing struggle to pull away from the bottom reaches of the First Division. Kidd's hat-trick took care of York City in a third-round replay, before two games, and George Armstrong's first two goals in nearly two years, were needed to get past Coventry. It was not until five minutes before the end of extra time in a third game against Leicester that Radford secured the Gunners' place in the quarter-finals.

The participation of Ball and McNab in the home tie against West Ham was in doubt following their sending off for dissent in a defeat at Derby, only the second time since the Second World War that a team had seen two players sent off in the same League game. Frank McLintock and Peter Storey had earned Arsenal that dubious distinction seven seasons earlier. Not for the first time – Charlie George at Glentoran, for example – Mee and the club decided they would not back an appeal by the players, even though its timing would have guaranteed their availability against West Ham. Mee was perhaps remembering the criticism he had received from Sunderland manager Bob Stokoe when appeals against a pair of bookings had enabled George and Pat Rice to play in the previous year's semi-final.

The ever-volatile Ball described the club's stance as 'a kick in the guts' and spat out, 'Arsenal and I can never be the same again.' But there was little that irked Mee more than seeing players talk themselves into trouble and, five months later, he would go as far as announcing fines for players booked for dissent. Ball and McNab decided to go ahead with their own appeals – subsequently lost – allowing Mee to take advantage by picking them both to face West Ham. But Brady recalled that 'Arsenal's decision angered the whole team.'

On a dirty, muddy day at Highbury, one reporter described Arsenal as 'tired old dinosaurs' as they went down 2–0, with a spindly 21 year old called Alan Taylor scoring both goals in his first game for West Ham following a transfer from Rochdale. As Mancini struggled, it was down to Rimmer and Simpson to keep Arsenal in the game and, despite Radford's claims for a penalty, few could argue with the result.

Two days later, Ball at least had the consolation of being named captain of the England side that would beat World Cup holders West Germany 2–0 at Wembley, a move that prompted questions in the House of Commons by MPs indignant that such an honour should go to a man whose disciplinary file was so thick, including a dismissal on his most recent England appearance almost two years earlier. Don Revie was more interested in rewarding Ball's consistent performances in a troubled Gunners team. 'I don't think Arsenal got the best out of me in my first couple of seasons there,' Ball admits. 'But then along came young players like Liam Brady and we turned our style around slightly. Bobby Campbell wanted the ball to be played through midfield and consequently that suited me a little more. I liked Bobby's style of coaching and my play benefited from it.'

The same could clearly not be said for the fortunes of the team as a whole. For the rest of them, FA Cup defeat meant that the only thing left to anticipate was a fight for First Division survival. And fight they did, prompting Sheffield United manager Ken Furphy to comment after his team's 1–0 loss at Highbury, 'I never thought I would live to see the day when Arsenal players fought among themselves, pulled shirts, wasted time and so freely indulged in foul tactics.' Kidd's two goals against Coventry just about made Arsenal safe, even though victory over struggling Tottenham on the final Saturday of the season was their only win in the final five games. Kidd's 19th League goal of the season lifted his team to a finishing position of 16th and left their rivals, now managed by former Arsenal captain Terry Neill, needing to beat European Cup finalists Leeds in a final midweek game to avoid relegation, a feat they duly achieved.

The summer of 1975, Bertie Mee's last at Highbury, was long and hot, with the West Indies winning cricket's first World Cup and the bespectacled David Steele becoming a national hero for standing up to Dennis Lillee and Jeff Thomson. Of greater import to the North Bank fans, however, was the news breaking early in July that Charlie George, one of their own, was to join Tottenham. George went through his White Hart Lane medical and a press conference was even called before one of his own football heroes, Derby manager Dave Mackay, stated that the new champions were interested in his services. Mee agreed a fee of £90,000 and the player who had sealed his greatest managerial achievement and caused his most extreme anxieties was on his way to the Baseball Ground. Potential outcry among the Arsenal fans had turned, somewhat at least, to relief that the white shirt George would be wearing was not that of the hated enemy.

Meanwhile, Alan Ball requested a transfer, which cost him the club captaincy. In his 1978 book *It's All About a Ball*, he wrote, 'I was becoming more restless and disillusioned. I could see things needed to be done to improve the team but nothing was happening. I didn't want to take over but I thought my ideas were worth listening to. I thought my request would shake Mee into action.' Instead, Ball found himself out of the team as the season kicked off.

Some Arsenal players worried that the relationship between Ball and Campbell was becoming the dominant force in the club and that Mee was, either willingly or unwittingly, being forced into the background. John Radford says, 'I didn't like Bobby Campbell as a coach and, as much as I liked Alan Ball, the two were running the place. The feeling about the camp was that Bobby was angling for Bertie's job.'

Brady claimed that the players were unhappy with 'what they considered to be Mee's lack of interest in the team'. He felt that Bertie was becoming distant and explained 'we saw less and less of him'.

Recalling frequent meetings between groups of players to discuss the problems, Brady concluded, 'It was a terrible time to be at Highbury. Senior players were soured by events, the backbone of the team wanted to go, the directors were unhappy with the players, the fans were unhappy with the board and players, and all around me I saw one of the game's institutions being reduced to the level of a troubled giant.'

Such issues had been McNab's motivations for wanting to leave Highbury. 'Bertie did not seem quite as strong or sure of himself,' he says. 'The dressing-room had gone from a very positive atmosphere to one of backbiting. Before I left, there were rumours that Bobby Campbell wanted the manager's job, with Ballie as first-team coach and Terry Mancini as youth coach. By then, Bobby, Ballie and Terry were very close. There seemed to be lots of whispering. By the end of the 1974–75 season, I could not stand another minute at the club. In my mind, Rome was burning and Bertie seemed to me to be playing the fiddle.'

Ball, who had to counter whispers that his elevated status as England captain had given him ideas above his Highbury station, offers a different perspective. 'I don't agree that Bobby and I started to run the place. There were still a lot of good players and strong characters there. And I don't think Bertie was losing interest; he was still as passionate about the club up until the day he left. I think he was just getting older and a little more blasé about things. Even though he had been disappointed that Steve Burtenshaw had to leave, he gave Bobby Campbell all the support he needed.'

Sammy Nelson also downplays the influence of the Campbell–Ball relationship on Mee's control of the club. 'Bobby was the coach, so he was obviously going to have a lot of input. Ballie was the senior player and he always wants to voice his opinion. But they didn't make any decisions – that was down to the board.'

Ball later dismissed suggestions that he had been plotting to increase his own influence at Arsenal as 'nonsense' and explained his subsequent decision to withdraw his transfer request. 'Bobby Campbell was perhaps the only one at the time who knew how I felt and it was he who finally persuaded me to stay at Highbury. I knew I could work well with Bobby.'

Alan Ball's was probably the signing about which Mee was questioned most often in later years. Quite simply, he never managed to harness Ball's ability to the collective benefit of the team. Even Ball himself concedes that he was discontented with his personal play during the earlier seasons of his Arsenal career, when the club was still challenging for honours. Yet, as the team's fortunes waned, so Ball's own game flourished. How much more rewarding might Mee's final seasons at Highbury have been had he and his coaches been able to solve the conundrum of why the form of the team and that of its most renowned player appeared to be mutually exclusive.

Mee remained steadfast about the wisdom of the move, despite all the issues that accompanied Ball's supreme talent to Highbury. As well as his union with Campbell, which some colleagues saw as unhealthy, Ball was famously close to his father, Alan Ball senior, a football manager himself, whose guidance was evident throughout his son's career. Mee, intriguingly but without further illumination, alluded to that relationship when discussing Ball in the book *Arsenal in the Blood*:

> I don't regret signing Alan Ball, I think. We wanted players of his calibre. He was an absolute one hundred per center. He had a lot of ability as well so that I had no regrets on that basis, but then, later on, his father started coming into the picture and influencing him.

As for Ball, he reflects, 'I loved my time at Arsenal and the one thing that galls me to this day is that we did not win a trophy, even though we were often knocking on the door. It wasn't an easy time to join them because they were trying to live up to the Double success, but I was desperate to help them to win something, not just for me but for Bertie Mee, who had spent so much money on me. We had a good crop of kids coming through who went on to great success and, at times, we played great football. Overall, the club was in a healthy state but on the field it was frustrating that we couldn't quite win anything.'

Meanwhile, McNab departed for Wolverhampton on a free transfer before the 1975–76 season kicked off. Having originally heard of the club's intention to demand a £30,000 transfer fee, McNab had taken Frank McLintock's advice of giving the manager 'a good slagging off' in the hope of securing his unconditional release. 'I remember telling Bertie that I thought the decisions regarding players and the staff in the last couple of years had been a disaster,' says McNab. 'I knew Bertie was very angry at me and to this day I really don't know if he ever forgave me.'

A week later, McNab was given the choice of a free transfer or a position on the coaching staff. 'My frustration would not even allow me to consider the offer. Before I left Bertie's office, I informed him of the rumours regarding Bobby Campbell and Ballie. Bertie just looked at me for a long time and then sort of shook his head. I was telling him to watch his back. I never did feel happy saying those unkind words to Bertie, since I still had a strong feeling of respect and gratitude. To this day, I still love Arsenal and owe Bertie and the club a great debt for the wonderful times I had at Highbury.'

With Ball on the sidelines, fit-again Alex Cropley was back in the team for the start of the new campaign, while Mancini's partner at the centre of defence was Dubliner David O'Leary, whose gangly limbs created an ungainly first impression that was quickly replaced by respect for his awareness and composure on the ball. Up front, another youngster from Ireland's capital, Frank Stapleton, was given the chance to establish himself alongside Brian Kidd. Although not prolific in his first season, his potential made John Radford an increasingly peripheral figure.

The Brady, O'Leary, Stapleton triumvirate stands comparison with, and possibly surpasses, the previous crop of young players Mee had helped to usher through the Arsenal system. But whereas the likes of Kennedy, Kelly and George lined up alongside experienced players at their peak in a team that was making clear progress, the Irish trio found themselves pitched into a side evidently going nowhere – unless it was to the Second Division. Alongside them was a mixture of disgruntled and cynical veterans, new signings who were little more than journeymen and youngsters like Powling, Trevor Ross, Wilf Rostron, John Matthews and Brian Hornsby, who would be only footnotes to the latter years of Mee's reign.

Another season scuffling around in the lower half of the table lay in store, struggles made even more poignant by the ageless McLintock leading Queens Park Rangers to within two points of denying Liverpool the first League Championship of their post-Shankly era. Arsenal spent anxious months only one or two places clear of danger after winning only five games in the first half of the season. The two knockout competitions brought the earliest possible exits, including a 3–0 loss at relegation-bound Wolves in the FA Cup.

Turmoil continued to swirl around the team like a bad dream. In February, Peter Storey was dropped and was suspended by Mee the following month after disappearing from the club for ten days. Storey responded by announcing he would never play for the club again and, although he would be back briefly the following season, Mee would never again select the player who had served him so well in times of triumph.

Even Ball's restoration to the line-up and the withdrawal of his transfer request had caused problems for team captain Eddie Kelly. Already sensing his authority was undermined by young players looking to Ball for leadership, Kelly then had to miss five games because of pneumonia. Ball was restored to the captaincy, apparently temporarily. But when Kelly returned for the home game against Burnley a week before Christmas, Ball continued to lead out the team.

'The biggest thing for me was being captain of Arsenal,' Kelly says. 'The only thing I was ever upset about at Arsenal was the way they took the captaincy away from me. I still don't know why they did it. No one ever told me. Bert told me at about quarter to three. I felt so deflated and from that day on I went downhill quick. I wasn't so much bothered about them giving the captaincy back to Ballie, it was the fact they didn't tell me. I said to Bobby Campbell, "Couldn't you have told me two or three days beforehand? Didn't you think of my emotions?"'

As the relegation battle approached its fiercest, Arsenal's players chose to confront Mee over the apparent lack of interest and involvement being shown at managerial level. Mee had shown his oratorial powers before – to the angry shareholders in 1969 and in front of his team as the Double season hung in the balance; now, he turned it on again. According to Brady, 'Just when things were at their lowest ebb, Mee took us aback with a speech of Churchillian proportions.' Speaking thoughtfully, yet with passion, Mee told his men that Arsenal and its players were his life and that his ideal parting from this world would be to walk across the Highbury pitch one day and drop down dead. Brady recalls, 'By the time he finished countering our accusation of neglect, he had earned genuine applause from the players, who, for the first time in many months, felt they had support and someone on their side.' The response was a 6–1 thrashing of West Ham, with Kidd scoring a hat-trick.

But, in truth, the battles were all becoming too much for Mee, who explained to author David Lemmon in *Arsenal in the Blood*, 'It was getting too difficult to drive myself. Motivation goes. I'd done it, achieved most of what I'd hoped. You need a change of environment.'

When Mee's third-round FA Cup exit had left him with a couple of free Saturdays in late winter, he found that he actually enjoyed the inactivity. Meanwhile, the words of close friend Bill Nicholson when he resigned from his position at Tottenham the previous season resonated with Mee. Nicholson said of his players, 'They don't seem to be taking any blasted notice of me. I am not getting through to them and not getting the respect from some of the players that I am entitled to. This may be a sign of the changing of the times but I feel if you don't get that you can't do your job as a manager.'

Mee informed the directors and his players of his intentions and on 22 March made a public announcement that he would resign at the end of the season. Three days later, he sat in front of the media in one of Highbury's banqueting rooms and showed a side of his personality few had ever witnessed. He calmly explained that the pressures of the job had become intolerable. He could not, he said, remember the last time he had enjoyed eight hours' unbroken sleep. He also admitted that, like Nicholson, he was finding it increasingly difficult to motivate a generation of young players whose attitudes and psychological make-up were so different to their predecessors'.

'It started five or six weeks ago,' he responded when asked how long he had been considering his decision. 'We had a Saturday with no match and I woke up in the morning and suddenly realised that this Saturday was completely different. Golly, I thought, what have I been doing with myself these last ten years? I looked at the situation and analysed it. I knew I could live comfortably for the rest of my days. The board were thinking along similar lines to me. Bill Nicholson influenced me slightly. His wife, Darkie, is always saying how much happier he is now he is out of team management.'

It was when a reporter asked Mee for his favourite memory as Arsenal manager that his famous self-control deserted him. He answered, 'Travelling on a bus between Nicosia and Famagusta of all places. Everyone did their party piece, a sing-song. Great.' With that, he slumped forward, put his head in his hands and, for a full minute, allowed the tears to take over before uttering, 'Sorry, gentlemen.' After ten years of coming up against considered responses and occasional frostiness, the last thing the hacks needed was an apology. Mee had at last laid bare, even if only for a minute, a part of his make-up they had waited a decade to glimpse.

Bob Wilson, who covered the press conference for the BBC, says, 'When you saw how upset he was at that press conference, you realised what Arsenal meant to him. He was the one who, after a game, would say, "Don't talk to me now; ring me at ten o'clock tomorrow when I will be rational." It was only when he was about to leave that you saw that other side of him. But everything was done in a dignified way and he somehow tried to say what it meant to him to have been the manager and to have achieved what he did.'

Significantly, Mee said that it was his 'dearest wish' to be allowed to remain at Arsenal in some capacity and to help his successor. It was a wish that would never be granted.

As the club began casting around for a new manager, Real Madrid's Yugoslavian coach Miljan Miljanic was the journalists' early favourite, while Terry Venables would also be approached before pledging his immediate future to Crystal Palace. Bobby Campbell, whether with or without Ball as right-hand man, clearly wanted the position, but physiotherapist Fred Street recalls telling him, 'Bob, if they haven't appointed you already, they are not going to. It is screaming out loud to me that you are not going to get it and whoever comes in will probably clear you out anyway.'

Street was proved correct in the summer as Arsenal continued their tradition of selecting managers with ties to the club by appointing Terry Neill, who thereby achieved the distinction of being successor to both Mee and Bill Nicholson. The move prompted Ball, two years later, to write in his autobiography, 'I, and many other players at the club, were convinced that Bobby Campbell would get Mee's job. We even had a meeting at which we voted unanimously to let the board know the way we felt about him.'

Brady's version of the same meeting has it being a closer vote, with the younger players expressing their preference for a new man to be brought in. But while Highbury was rife with speculation and canvassing, there were still seven games to be contested. Only one was won, but it was an important victory against fellow strugglers Wolves, with Mancini scoring his one and only Arsenal goal to clinch victory. The season concluded with three defeats, including 3–1 at Manchester

City in the last game under Mee's management. In a nice piece of symmetry, the final goal of Mee's reign fell to George Armstrong, who had scored in Bertie's first game in charge and was the only player to feature in both his first and last team selections.

As soon as the last pieces of the season's mud had been scraped off the players' boots, Arsenal announced that Mee's desire to help his successor was to be ignored. Perhaps mindful of the effect of Sir Matt Busby's overwhelming presence in the boardroom on Manchester United managers, it was announced that Mee would be leaving the club.

Mee did not attempt to hide his feelings. 'I wanted so desperately to help somebody else to write another page of history of this great club and I'm disappointed not to have that opportunity,' he said.

Club chairman Denis Hill-Wood responded, 'I am surprised to hear Bertie say that. We agreed when he resigned what would happen.'

Although Mee was too diplomatic to say it, the conviction among friends and colleagues – which persists to this day – is that he was led to believe he would be given a role as a director. Hill-Wood's explanation at the time goes against that theory. 'We didn't offer him a seat on the board in fairness to the man who takes over. We felt there was a chance any unhappy player could go behind the new manager's back and ask Bertie for help.'

Arsenal director Ken Friar adds, 'I don't recall the exact conversations at that time but you have to be a little bit cautious in those situations. You don't want the new man to feel he has the man who used to do the job sitting on his shoulder.'

It is interesting to contrast those remarks with the situation at neighbours Tottenham, where Bill Nicholson went on to become chief scout after retiring as manager and was still attending games at White Hart Lane as club president only weeks before he died in October 2004. And a few days before Nicholson's death, Arsenal chairman Peter Hill-Wood had discussed publicly Arsène Wenger's continued involvement in the club beyond his managerial reign. 'It would be a shame to lose his expertise and maybe [his role] could be as a director,' he said. 'I'm certain he wouldn't interfere in any way with his eventual successor.'

Bob Wilson contends, 'I think Bertie was tremendously hurt when he left. Apart from within his inner sanctum and his close family, he never really said how hurt he was. He was a dignified guy, so he didn't come out with what he felt. But I think he felt he had truly been stabbed in the back. That was our belief.'

Mee's friend Ron Goodman adds, 'My impression was that he had been virtually promised to be on the board and to have a say in certain things. But never would he speak about it. Doris used to speak about it — she was not very happy at all. She was always fighting for him in that way.'

Wilson still ponders why English football is so 'quick to dispose of people whose ability and knowledge are fantastic', while others believe Mee paid the price for not getting closer to the directors during his decade as manager. To the players, Mee sometimes may have seemed as though he belonged more in the boardroom than the changing-room, but the distance he placed between himself and his team also applied, according to Fred Street, to his bosses.

'If he had been more matey, and got on better with the board, he might have been offered a place,' says Street. 'He already had a certain arrogance and winning the Double didn't help that. It made him famous and lionised. He did cross a few swords with some of the people at director level. He didn't suffer fools and he didn't nurture or cultivate friendship with some people when it might have paid him to do that. In some ways, it is admirable that he was his own man and, in effect, said, "Sod you." But there comes a day when you are no longer flavour of the month, and you might rely on those people. He didn't exactly make enemies but he could have made more friends.'

Goodman has similar memories. 'Bertie just wanted to come to matches and board meetings and didn't want to be involved any further than that. But there were certain people he was not prepared to be too friendly with because they were too friendly with directors — you might say something that could be passed on. He never courted the directors. He pushed them away and some of them didn't like it. The only one he really respected was Denis Hill-Wood.'

Whatever the whole truth, the fact is that a combination of issues — his disappointment at not being offered a place on the board, the unseemly preoccupation of the players to dictate the identity of the new manager and the struggles of a team fighting against relegation — resulted in Mee's departure from Highbury being less dignified than his achievements and his commitment to the club deserved. And what is often overlooked in the disappointing results of Mee's final couple of seasons – as it was in Billy Wright's case – was the introduction of several youngsters who would form the foundation of future success. As one of those players, Liam Brady, would write, 'Bertie was always a fair man and deserved a better farewell.'

20

YELLOW BRICK ROAD

The greatest thing that happened to Bertie after he
left Arsenal was that a very wise Graham Taylor and
Elton John realised what he could give to Watford.

               – Bob Wilson

IF BERTIE MEE GLANCED AT THE FRONT PAGES OF THE TABLOIDS
or checked out the various current-affairs programmes aired during the
1976–77 football season, he must have wondered what had happened
to the world he knew. The faces that snarled out at him were certainly
not those of the young men with whom he had served his country.
Punk rock was moving from the streets and clubs of London and
Manchester into the mainstream media and, if Mee had struggled to
understand the long-haired youth of the '60s, heaven knows what he
made of the sneering and swearing of the Sex Pistols. He remained
convinced, however, that there was still a place for someone who
believed in the 'old-fashioned' virtues of discipline, manners and pride
in oneself – although when he considered resuming his health service
career, Fred Street had a warning for him. 'Bert, they might have you,
but it would drive you barmy. You have been Arsenal manager, a big
name. If you go back, the staff are not like they were when you were
there and you treated us like corporals. They will wear scruffy trainers;

they won't have their hands inspected every morning like you did. And you can't pick and choose who you have working for you. They are short-staffed.'

At the age of 58, Mee intended to continue working. He had deliberately not cultivated a media profile that could have afforded him a steady income, nor had he undertaken the kind of work while at Arsenal that could have established a tidy nest egg. And, having left Highbury, he had no desire to rush out an autobiography or sell lurid tales to the tabloids.

There was an offer from Fulham chairman Ernie Clay to work as an adviser, ultimately declined, before Mee's organisational skills were put to good use in the running of a tournament in the Far East, featuring Celtic and Arsenal. He was also involved in setting up a 1978 World Cup trip to Argentina for a group of English football representatives. In addition, he was to play a key role in the first visit of a professional English club to play football in China when West Bromwich Albion ventured behind the 'Bamboo Curtain' in 1978. His part in that venture came about through Graham Perry, who had first met Mee when he invited him to speak to the North Middlesex Referees Society. They were to become friends for the rest of Bertie's life. Perry's company was involved in general trading with China at a time when such activity was uncommon and he had helped to organise visits for table-tennis players to and from the country.

'The Bamboo Curtain was being pulled back and sport was a great diplomatic tool,' Perry explains. 'It occurred to us to do something similar in soccer. We asked Bertie to become involved because he was a soccer notable, a respected figure who moved nicely in the corridors of power. He was synonymous with stability and good intention; there was nothing murky or manipulative about him. We needed to be guided by him in the politics of the sport and how to deal with the Football Association, who needed to sanction the trip and make a team available.'

By the time Mee travelled to China as part of the initiative he had worked hard to bring to fruition, he was back in football full time – although not exactly at the glamorous end. Watford had seen little of the limelight since their unlikely FA Cup heroics of 1970 when, as a newly promoted Second Division team under the leadership of Ken Furphy, they had knocked out Bill Shankly's Liverpool in the last eight. A semi-final tie against Chelsea, lost 5–1 on a White Hart Lane sandpit, had proved a dream too far. By the summer of 1977, the club was down in Division Four, having been through two more managers and witnessed endless boardroom bickering. There had been a significant development, however, in 1976 when the club's most famous fan, Elton John, one of the country's most successful and colourful pop stars, became chairman. He had bought the club's majority shareholding from the seemingly immovable Jim Bonser, against whom several fan protests had been waged over the years, and was intent on doing more than signing cheques from afar. A year into his boardroom reign, he went in search of a new manager. Despite lengthy speculation that former England captain Bobby Moore, one of John's acquaintances, would be offered the job, it was 32-year-old Graham Taylor, who had led Lincoln City to promotion from Division Four, who was placed in charge at Vicarage Road.

Taylor recalls, 'Elton changed his mind about signing Bobby after two directors had said there was a young fellow at Lincoln he ought to be interested in. Elton followed England quite a lot and asked Don Revie what he thought. He recommended me as well, so the offer Elton had been going to give to Bobby never materialised.'

Taylor was reported to be earning £20,000 per year, which, for Watford, was an astronomical amount, but his chairman clearly had ambition to match his generosity. 'This was a club that had only ever been in the old Second Division and had a history of being in the lower divisions,' Taylor continues. 'I thought Elton might have said he'd like to get back in the Second Division but he said he wanted to get into Europe. That was our target.'

When a letter of good luck from Bertie Mee dropped on his desk in his new office, Taylor wondered if he was looking at a veiled job application. Mee's family and friends explain that pride would have prevented him from seeking out work in such a way and the informal offer of assistance was no more than that. But whatever the motive for the letter, Taylor's interpretation of it encouraged him to telephone Mee, even though his only previous contact with him had been an unnerving experience.

'When I was just starting out at Lincoln, I'd wanted to get a couple of players on loan. One of them was Brian Chambers at Arsenal. I had only been a manager six weeks and I had the job of phoning Bertie

Mee at a time when Arsenal weren't doing that well. I was very nervous. There was sweat pouring off me when he picked up the phone. I could hardly make a sentence. "Mr Mee, could I? . . . Brian Chambers . . . loan?" I was hammering away very nervously. He said to me in a very sharp voice, "Arsenal Football Club has 36 players. At the present time we have seven of them injured. Why should I help you?" So there I was, four years after having a very sharp conversation with him, with this letter. I said to Elton that we should meet him.'

The three men spent an evening in deep discussion at the Clarendon Hotel in Watford. 'We got on very well,' Taylor continues. 'We even got to the stage of asking about money. He explained that he had a pension and that the money we were offering would suffice, so he became assistant manager.'

As well as the knowledge and contacts that Mee could take to Watford, the name of a former Double-winning manager added a certain *gravitas* to the club's hierarchy. 'Who really knew me?' asks Taylor. 'I had played for Grimsby and Lincoln, and managed Lincoln. I was coming to a place where they didn't even know where Lincoln was. We had a pop star as chairman. The media couldn't quite understand what was going on at Watford, but signing Bertie showed that we should be taken seriously.'

Mee's initial comments on being appointed served exactly that purpose. 'Elton John is young and surprisingly sincere about football,' he said. 'People may find it hard to reconcile a pop image with a serious soccer ambition but the Watford chairman has it. I believe he showed it when he appointed Graham Taylor as manager. And I believe, immodest as this may sound, that he confirmed his intentions when he appointed me as Graham's managerial assistant.' Mee concluded, 'Watford are going to give me the chance to do what I thought I might have been able to do at Arsenal.'

Even though it had not been determined at the initial meeting, Mee's role was quickly defined. Working with former Watford player Tom Walley, he took charge of the club's youth-development programme, establishing an efficient scouting system and overseeing the welfare of young players coming into the club.

'It gave him a day-to-day role,' says Taylor. 'Bertie was a magnificent organiser, so it meant I could concentrate solely on the first team. He would know all the young players and there was great respect for him.

They were in awe of him. They knew what he had won. There was no point him coming to watch first-team training sessions every day, but he was part of the first-team management. If I had a selection problem, I would discuss it with Bertie. I think he was very happy doing what he did. He had the immediate ear of the manager of the first team, socialised with us all and oversaw all the youth development.'

As much as he admired Mee, Taylor was not so starry-eyed as to be unaware of the potential problems of having a strong-willed former manager as his assistant. 'I could see that Bertie could have taken over. He could be very intimidating. Boy, if you were a minute late for something, you were in trouble. We used to have meetings at nine o'clock each day before training and – it sounds somewhat egotistical of me and probably wrong – I started arriving at those meetings deliberately late. He would look at me when I came in, but I was making a point. I was saying that I was the manager and if anyone could be late for those meetings, it was me. Bertie was a little annoyed but I did it deliberately. Not all the time, but it didn't take long for Bertie to realise I was the manager.'

With the chairman promising to make available whatever funds Taylor felt were necessary, a couple of astute signings strengthened the playing squad. Taylor, much in the manner of Mee taking charge of Arsenal more than a decade earlier, also laid down a new set of laws. Fitness, discipline and dedication were all stressed to the players, who responded by winning the Fourth Division title with six games to spare.

Taylor's success, close to the London media hub and at a club with a certain novelty value, carried his name into a wider consciousness. Yet he had initially struggled to devote himself fully to the Watford cause because of his ties to his former team and former home. It needed a stern talking to from Mee at one of their regular Friday meetings to shake him out of his homesickness.

'I wear my heart on my sleeve and I had been at Lincoln City for a long time. I was moving into a completely different world. I couldn't believe the price of houses compared to where I had been and there seemed to be 50 times the traffic. I would talk about Lincoln a lot and Bertie said to me one day, "You are manager of Watford now. Put Lincoln out of your mind."'

Mee played an important role in the club's search for a chief executive in 1978, a position that eventually went to Eddie Plumley, who had held that position at Coventry City. Having got to know Plumley while he was at Highfield Road, and previously at Leicester, Mee sought his advice on potential candidates before, typically, taking matters into his own hands. 'Bertie came to see me a few times and asked if I knew anyone who'd be interested in taking over the administration of Watford. I rattled off a few names and he looked unimpressed. I wasn't top of their list but during conversations I went through what I thought they needed and Bertie said, "Right, then. When do you want to start?"'

Watford's 1978–79 campaign saw the establishment of a successful striking partnership between Luther Blissett and the lanky Ross Jenkins, and featured some memorable nights during a run to the League Cup semi-finals. There were victories over Newcastle and Manchester United, where Blissett contributed two spectacular headed goals after Watford had fallen behind. Ultimately, the season brought another promotion when a 4–0 thrashing of Hull City in the last game, before 26,397 at Vicarage Road, sealed second place in the Third Division table.

The curve of Watford's progress levelled out in their first season back in Division Two. Relegation was a possibility for a while but signings such as Brighton striker Malcolm Poskett and Sunderland's Wilf Rostron, a winger who had made his League debut under Mee at Arsenal and would later be converted into an effective full-back, relieved that threat. The season's excitement was provided by a run to the quarter-finals of the FA Cup, where Mee came into opposition with his former team for the first time. Frank Stapleton scored twice for an Arsenal team intent on retaining the trophy they had won a year earlier, their first major success since Mee's men had achieved the Double.

In 1980–81, Watford achieved the highest League position in the club's history to that point, ninth in Division Two, and made more national headlines in the League Cup. First, they overturned a 4–0 first-leg deficit against high-flying Southampton with an astonishing 7–1 win at Vicarage Road. In a later round, they beat European Cup holders Nottingham Forest 4–1, revenge for their semi-final defeat of two seasons earlier. The additional revenue being generated by such games enabled Taylor to make more signings, including Tottenham striker Gerry Armstrong and – on Mee's advice – Pat Rice, who arrived from Highbury for £20,000 and was given the club captaincy.

The summer of 1981 famously saw the birth of a British sporting legend as Ian Botham saw off Australia's cricketers almost single-handedly. It also marked the first significant step towards stardom for a figure who would become another of the country's most debated sportsmen of the next 15 years. And the fact that 17-year-old John Barnes signed to play for Watford owed a great deal to the influence of Bertie Mee.

A Watford fan, whom Barnes recalls as being a taxi driver, had seen the youngster play in a game in Sudbury, Middlesex, and excitedly alerted his favourite club. Watford would act on such a tip only once every couple of years but, after receiving an encouraging follow-up report from the club's local scout, Mee went along to see what all the fuss was about. The story goes that he watched for only ten minutes before securing the youngster's address and telephone number, setting in motion the wheels that would lead to 79 England caps, including one of his country's most famous goals of all time in Rio's Maracana Stadium, and two League Championship medals with Liverpool.

Barnes takes up the tale. 'Watford said they would like me to join them. But my dad was a military attaché in the Jamaican Army. He was in England on a four-year posting and was due to be going back to Jamaica in six months' time, but I wanted to stay and play football.'

It was left to Mee to convince the Barnes family that young John would be safe in the care of Watford. 'Bertie arranged to come home and meet my mum and dad,' Barnes continues. 'He wanted to assure them that I would be well looked after and to convince them to let me stay. My dad found out a couple of days before the meeting that it would be Bertie who was coming. He recalled Bertie from when Arsenal had played in Jamaica in the early '70s. He had previously played for Jamaica and was president of the Jamaican FA and had arranged all the security for the match. He remembered Bertie, although he wasn't sure if Bertie would remember him.'

Over a gin and tonic, Colonel Barnes and Sergeant Mee got on famously. The family environment that surrounded young John merely added to Mee's infatuation with the boy's talent. Meanwhile, the reputation and stature of the former Arsenal manager and his ability to sell the values and virtues of Watford soothed any parental anxieties. Barnes goes on, 'Bertie and my dad sat down and spoke for about half an hour. I wasn't in the meeting, but I did sneak into the room once or twice. Once my dad had spent some time with Bertie, he knew that it was going to be all right if I stayed. He knew Bertie was a great disciplinarian and Graham Taylor mirrored that in the way the club was organised. My dad knew that the club would offer the right environment for young players.'

Taylor adds, 'Bertie was the older man, the successful man, the man who could talk about other things than football. John's father was very intelligent and the way Bertie conducted himself played a major part in him allowing John to stay. They trusted Bertie. We knew John had a special talent and we were determined to get him. When we saw him we wondered why nobody else had seen his ability.'

Taylor's own first glimpse of Barnes was in a reserve game against Leeds. 'At one point, he pulled the ball down, saw the keeper off his line, did a Pelé shot and hit the crossbar. You didn't have to be an expert to see he was something special.'

Barnes, after an early-season debut as substitute against Oldham, became a first-team regular more or less instantly. 'I was lucky in that I got into the first team a couple of months after joining them, so my contact with Bertie after that was limited,' he says. 'But he went out of his way to look after me and I saw the way he was with the other young players. He knew they needed more than just football; he made sure they went to college and developed off the field.'

Barnes scored 14 goals in his first season as Taylor's team marched towards the fulfilment of their chairman's ambition of First Division football. Promotion, in second place behind division champions Luton, was achieved with a home win against Wrexham. It had taken only five years. Even the growing criticism of the team's long-ball tactics did nothing to take the gloss off the achievement. Bertie Mee, for one, was used to such sniping. And the crowning moment of the season for him was still to come, when Watford's youngsters beat Manchester United 7–6 over two legs to win the final of the FA Youth Cup.

Mee's career had taken another turn during the season and, ironically, it ensured that when Watford visited Arsenal the next season, he would at last be able to sit in the Highbury directors' box as a board member. In February 1982, Watford had made Mee their first paid director, adding the brief of overseeing the development of the Vicarage Road stadium to his responsibility for youth football. Announcing the move, Elton John commented, 'Bertie is one of the most prestigious men in football and I'm absolutely delighted to get him on our board. We will be looking to him to give me and my directors a kick up the pants.'

Eddie Plumley recalls Mee doing exactly that. 'He didn't suffer fools lightly and he was the kind of man who wanted to talk about it if there was a problem. He wouldn't do anything underhand or behind anyone's back. The strength of him was his personality and if one of the directors said anything out of line, they knew they had to face Bertie. I can only remember one real problem, which was when we had to take a director to task about something he said publicly about a player, which we did not agree with.'

The records show Mee listed as executive director or general manager, but Taylor recalls that he played an important personal role for the club chairman. 'Elton loved Bertie and he adored Doris. Elton effectively appointed him as his football adviser and I think he may even have paid his wages himself, through the club, because that was how much he thought of him.'

The next two years at Watford were the stuff of dreams. They led the league in September of their first season in the top flight, smashing Sunderland 8–0 in the same month. Although unable to keep pace with Liverpool, they did beat the Anfield side on the final day of the season to clinch second place. They lost only six games all season, the same number as Mee's team in 1970–71, and they beat Arsenal home and away for good measure. The Gunners, meanwhile, would soon be ending Terry Neill's reign as manager and finally giving Don Howe the opportunity to manage the club.

The summer of 1983 saw Watford sell Luther Blissett to AC Milan for £1 million, but the prospect of European football made up for the fans' disappointment. After a win against German side Kaiserslautern in the first round of the UEFA Cup, victory at Levski Spartak in Bulgaria after a drawn home leg was particularly satisfying for Mee as injuries had forced Taylor to field six members of the FA Youth Cup-winning team. The adventure ended in the next round against Czech side Sparta Prague, but there was even more excitement to come in the FA Cup.

After beating local rivals Luton 4–3 in a thrilling replay, Watford took care of Charlton and Brighton to earn a quarter-final tie against Birmingham, where Barnes scored twice in a 3–1 win. For the second time in their history, Watford were in the semi-finals. But whereas in 1970 they had been overwhelming underdogs against Chelsea, a tie against Plymouth Argyle made them clear favourites to reach Wembley. It was no walkover, however, with Barnes setting up striker George Reilly for the only goal of a tense game at Villa Park.

The final against Everton remains most memorable to the neutral fans for the sight of Elton John in tears in the Royal box during the pre-game ceremonies. With only three players above the age of 22 in their team, Watford went down to goals by Graeme Sharp and Andy Gray, having given a performance that never lived up to the expectations created by their previous two seasons. For Mee, it was a fourth defeat in five Wembley finals.

The glory days at Vicarage Road were effectively over, although the FA Cup semi-finals were reached again in 1987. Arsenal were Watford's quarter-final victims before Tottenham ended Taylor's hopes of a second final appearance. The semi-final was the last big Watford game played by Barnes, sold that summer to Liverpool for £900,000. Taylor, meanwhile, was given permission to apply for the vacant manager's position at Aston Villa, a job he was offered and he accepted.

Dave Bassett, who had performed the kind of miracles at Wimbledon that Taylor had achieved at Vicarage Road, was Elton John's choice as the new manager, a decision made without consulting his adviser. Taylor recalls, 'Bertie was upset that he and the board had not been consulted. It was totally Elton's appointment. He just announced it and I know people like Bertie, who had more experience than all of them put together, were upset.'

The reign of Bassett lasted for only half of a season that ended in Watford's relegation. Former coach Steve Harrison was chosen to replace Bassett, with Mee's role in that appointment playing an important, if unintentional, part in the development of Taylor's Villa Park career. Harrison had declined to sign a new contract as Watford coach because, believing that Taylor would soon be moving to bigger and better things, he wanted the freedom to accompany him if offered the chance. When Bassett made wholesale changes on arriving at Watford, Harrison took that opportunity.

Taylor explains, 'Things didn't work out with Dave and, around Christmas, Watford tapped up Steve Harrison. A friend of Steve's told me and I was less than happy. Then our chairman, Doug Ellis, phoned and said that Elton had asked for permission to talk to Steve and that he had given it. I said, "What if I told you they had been tapping him up for a fortnight?" He asked why I hadn't told him and I said that I didn't think I needed to. If he'd made Watford talk to me before giving them permission to approach Steve, I could have told him then. I said we had better ask for compensation, so we asked for £25,000. Watford went mad because they had more or less let me go to Villa for nothing.'

Harrison duly returned to Watford and, a short time later, Taylor ran into Mee at a social event. 'I took Bertie to one side and said to him, "Look, I don't want to fall out with you, but I know what you have done and I think it was out of order. But you did me a favour because now I couldn't give a shit about Watford." I'd had exactly the same feelings about Watford in the first six months after I left that I'd experienced after leaving Lincoln. Watford had been such a part of me that sometimes I drove down from Birmingham, drove around Vicarage Road and drove back again. That was how committed I was to the club. I couldn't believe I had left it. But when Bertie and Tom Walley tapped up Steve it helped to get Watford out of my system. That was the other side of Bertie. He was not all goody two shoes, none of us are. He could be determined and ruthless.'

By that time, Mee's standing in the game had been underlined by other honours and appointments. As well as serving as chairman of the Football League Executive Staffs Association, he was co-opted late in 1986, along with Ron Greenwood and Jimmy Hill, by the Football League Management Committee to represent the south of England on a panel of experts charged with examining and suggesting improvements to the sport. Among other entries on his résumé were the chairmanship of the Milas Group of healthcare companies, leading roles on FA medical committees, membership of the Institute of Sports Medicine, and being made a Freeman of the City of London by the Worshipful Company of Fan Makers.

Of greatest pride to him and his family, however, was being made an OBE, an Officer of the Order of the British Empire, in the Queen's New Year's Honours List at the end of 1983, an award made for services to football.

As the '80s drew to a close, Mee's time at Watford was nearing its conclusion. Personal and professional issues began to weigh increasingly on Elton John, who began moves to sell his majority shareholding of the club. In 1992, after Jack Petchey had bought out John and assumed leadership of the club, Mee departed Vicarage Road.

Graham Taylor explains, 'Jack couldn't see the role Bertie was playing and to a degree that was right because he had been very much working for Elton.'

Eddie Plumley adds, 'I can't say enough about how highly Bertie was appreciated at the club. But the feeling was different under Jack. He had a different way of approaching the job of chairman; he wanted all the 'i's dotted and 't's crossed, and Bertie maybe thought, "I don't want this at my time of life." Bertie's role had been as an adviser and, as new managers came and went, and Jack took over as chairman, he was not as happy. I can't remember any great animosity. I think he and Jack just agreed to disagree over certain things. It seemed the perfect time to retire.'

So, the final chapter of Mee's professional life came to a close, one that had brought him much happiness and healed the scars that endured from his departure from Arsenal. His friend Elli Baram says, 'After he left Arsenal, he was not feeling too good. He'd wanted to connect his life with the club and for some reason they didn't want him. But I think the years he spent with Watford were very happy ones. Elton John and Graham Taylor treated him very respectfully and that meant a lot to him.'

21

A PLACE IN HISTORY

> While so modest in life, we feel it would be a
> wonderful tribute if there were some kind of
> memorial in Arsenal's new stadium in recognition of
> his achievements with the club.
>
> – Bertie Mee's daughters, Beverley and Allyson

BERTIE MEE MIGHT HAVE OFFICIALLY RETIRED AFTER DEPARTING
Vicarage Road, but the place he'd established for himself in football
ensured he still had a role to play. As well as being sought out for advice
from contacts within the game and the business world, he was
frequently called upon as an independent adviser and consultant in
cases of sports injury claims, such as Chelsea defender Paul Elliott's
action against Liverpool's Dean Saunders in 1994. A year into his
retirement, he told an interviewer, 'I enjoy my work as an adviser on
several fronts, and being able to pick and choose what I do. It fits in
perfectly because I can stay involved in football and keep up my family
obligations, which I neglected during my time at Arsenal.'

In the same interview, Mee discussed his relationship with Arsenal
manager George Graham, his former player, and spoke of the
increasing pressures of the modern game. 'I still speak to George and I
would like to think he may have learned something from me. I have a

great deal of sympathy for him in the job because I know that I would not be able to handle some of the pressure put upon him. One of the hardest forms of pressure is from the media, who no longer request interviews and so on – they demand them.'

Graham had been instrumental in re-establishing Mee's connection with his old club. While still at Watford, Mee found Graham turning up on his doorstep for friendly advice. 'I used to pop up and have a cup of tea with Bertie and Doris at their house in Southgate,' says Graham, recalling the pleasure Mee took in being involved again, however peripherally, with his beloved Arsenal. 'I would have little chats with him about certain aspects of management, the different things that come up. We would talk about football and life, and he was a great help to me. There were certain things I agreed with, where it was advantageous to take Bertie's advice, and some occasions where I may have done things a little differently. I think he took great pride from the fact that one of his ex-players was now Arsenal manager and took a bit of satisfaction from being my mentor.'

After he returned to Watford as manager early in 1996, Graham Taylor, another former colleague, urged Mee to become a regular once more at Vicarage Road. 'I would have loved Bertie to have been there for my second spell at Watford and to come to some games. But he wouldn't come because of the way things had ended there. He had this immense pride. It is a shame because he would have been welcomed once Elton came back on the board. Also, Doris had become ill and he cut himself off. Bertie really wanted to look after Doris and I can understand that.'

Mee's world had been turned upside down early in May 1994 when Doris, in her 72nd year, suffered a stroke. Four months later, following a partial recovery, she was struck down again, leaving her with minimal use of her left side and in need of constant care. For Bertie, it was a simple decision. He would give up any activity that took him out of the home and attend to her himself. He told his daughters, 'Your mother spent so much of her life caring and looking after me. It is time for me to look after her.'

Allyson adds, 'Daddy was a devoted husband and father. When he was determined to do something, there was no changing his mind. He became very domesticated and was our mother's main carer, a job he did so beautifully.'

Family friend Graham Perry says, 'However much Bertie tried to protect some time for family, he still felt that Doris had sacrificed everything for his career and, now that he was out of football, he felt that his first duty was to her. It was part of the modesty and quality of the man. Duty and devotion, exemplified in a positive sense – he didn't use it to bully or impose prejudices. He had always enjoyed coming over to us for dinner, or being a guest of mine at Lord's, where we would sit and talk all day. But in the latter years, it was hard to get him out because he wanted to make sure there was cover for Doris and he didn't want to impose on his daughters. The selflessness of the man was apparent. I think he knew that once you were a manager, it was hard to enjoy the routine of family life. He could rationalise the demands of football, but now he was determined to rectify the balance.'

Bertie and Doris moved from their house in Southgate into a retirement home in nearby Winchmore Hill in 1997, by which time Bertie was rarely, if ever, seen outside the family circle. The photograph of the 1971 Arsenal squad, reunited on the 25th anniversary of their historic achievement, has one obvious absentee. And as the Gunners positioned themselves to emulate the feat of that team in 1998, Mee's thoughts on new manager Arsène Wenger remained a mystery to most people.

By the autumn of 2001, Mee had disappeared so far from public view that even Arsenal fans wondered what had become of one of their club's greatest managers. On 21 October came the news that answered that question. Bertie Mee, aged 82, had died after a short illness.

Mee and his family had heard the diagnosis of cancer, and the severity of the prognosis, only a week earlier. Typically of a man who spent much of his life trying to avoid being the centre of attention, his instructions to his daughters were once again emphatic. Only the immediate family were to be told of his illness and allowed to visit him at the North London Hospice in Finchley. Upon his death, no extensive details were to be issued. The announcement of Mee's passing left his daughters fielding numerous calls from shocked friends and colleagues, who'd had no idea that Bertie had even been ill.

Five days after his death, Bertie Mee's funeral service was held at Trent Park Crematorium in Cockfosters, where family and friends were joined by former players, colleagues and other dignitaries from the world of football. The order of service, a 'celebration of life', included a poem read by his granddaughters, eulogies by Harry Hopker and Graham Taylor, the playing of Bertie and Doris's favourite piece of music, 'Feelings', and, appropriately, the traditional FA Cup final hymn, 'Abide With Me'.

The tributes that appeared in the days after Mee's death were a timely reminder to Arsenal fans, revelling in the construction of another Double-wining campaign, of the debt the club owed to Mee, the hard times that older followers of the club had endured and the unique achievement of a medical man-turned-manager in the most competitive of football eras.

No one could ever promote the notion that Mee's success at Arsenal was simply down to being in the right place at the right time. As powerful as the club may be in the twenty-first century, there was no guarantee that Arsenal would have freed themselves from the treadmill of mediocrity and chaos to which they were tethered in the 1960s. Four previous managers had failed to achieve that feat. And, had Mee not lifted Arsenal out of their rut, mediocrity could easily have led to worse. These days it is impossible to imagine the likes of Arsenal, Manchester United or Chelsea ever losing their place on the game's gravy train, but the mid-'70s saw both United and Chelsea, as well as another of the previous decade's giants, Tottenham, all suffer relegation.

'It's no exaggeration,' says Don Howe, 'that Arsenal's future as a Division One club was in the balance when Bertie became manager. He turned things around.'

The fact that Mee revived Arsenal's fortunes on the field in concert with accomplished coaches should not diminish his own contribution. After all, he didn't simply inherit the men upon whom he relied so heavily. Someone had to identify Dave Sexton as the man who could inject the enthusiasm and direction that had been lacking during the haphazard days of the Billy Wright regime. And it was surely more than good fortune that Mee recognised the potential of the crocked full-back Don Howe, who would construct some of Arsenal's greatest achievements and develop into one of English football's most accomplished coaches.

As this is being written, Brian Clough is being mourned by the football world. Quite rightly, none of the tributes to one of football's most remarkable managers has sought to downgrade his achievements by pointing out that he never won anything worth a damn without Peter Taylor at his side.

Some of Mee's biggest supporters suggest that the input of Sexton and Howe, aligned with his own modesty, may even have masked the depth of his own football knowledge. Graham Perry ventures, 'The way Bertie talked about management and administration conveyed to the public that he was aware of his limitations, but I think the story got a little out of balance. I don't think he ever got the true praise and respect for what he did on the footballing side, as well as sharpening up the administration. He was a bit hard done by because of his reputation. I remember talking to him after a game in which John Matthews had given away a penalty. Bertie explained that under pressure you revert to type. There are things you can do to educate and instil things in the minds of footballers, but you don't know if you have succeeded until they are put under pressure and they manage not to revert to their former ways. Things like that were part of the great man-management skills that played such a big part in Arsenal's success.'

Working with his coaches and supported by an efficiency of organisation that provided the club with much-needed stability, Mee's era, certainly the earlier years, saw the nurturing of considerable home-grown talent. Much of it had been brought to the club by Billy Wright, but the likes of Peter Simpson and John Radford were helped to maturity by the more settled environment under Mee. Meanwhile, teenagers Charlie George, Ray Kennedy, Pat Rice, Eddie Kelly and Sammy Nelson were thoughtfully and successfully introduced to the team to play pivotal roles. There are not too many instances between 1966 and 1972 of youngsters failing to measure up to the task after being given a senior opportunity.

No manager in history has been without his faults, and Bertie Mee would certainly never have made that claim for himself. The longevity, or lack of it, of the period of Arsenal success under Mee is often cited against him, and in only two seasons did Mee's team actually win silverware. But they did finish in the top two in major competitions in six successive seasons. Even in the two years after the Double, as the team was being broken up prematurely, they were runners-up in the FA Cup and Division One. And this was an age when few teams remained at the top year after year. In the first seven years of Mee's reign, seven different teams won the Football League Championship. A total of thirteen clubs shared the twenty Championships and FA Cups available while Mee was Arsenal manager. By comparison, only four teams won the eighteen major domestic prizes on offer during the nine seasons leading up to the summer of 2004, with Arsenal and Manchester United sharing fifteen of them. As Howe points out, 'Football's a harsh world. If you'd done the equivalent of winning the Double in the business world, you'd be made for life. In football, people want you to do it again and again.'

If Mee had never won another meaningful game, accomplishing the Double with a team that was not overblessed with natural talent puts him into an exalted place in football history. Success was gained with a group of closely bonded professionals who proved that their total achievement could indeed exceed the sum of their individual parts. Mee's discipline, his understanding of the mental and physical capabilities of his men, and his careful assembling of players with the required character all played a part in the nurturing of that often elusive team spirit.

None of which is intended to ignore the fact that Arsenal could, and probably should, have won more major prizes under Mee. Perhaps a style of management that was based so heavily on law and order can only ever work for a limited period. He did, after all, inherit a group of players who had never known success. Of the Double team, only George Graham had ever won a major winner's medal. That made them impressionable and pliable, willing to knuckle under in the hope of altering the course of their careers. Once those players had matured, tasted success, become more confident and formed their own opinions about the game, Mee's somewhat pedantic methods began to lose their effectiveness. It certainly seems to be more than coincidence that so many players – George, Ball, McLintock, McNab, Kelly, Storey, to name a few – ended up falling out with their manager. In Mee's favour, however, is the fact that most of those same players now recall him with admiration and affection.

The magic touch Mee had in his early years when it came to appointing coaches and buying players also eventually deserted him. Few would claim, for example, that Bobby Campbell's selection as coach was a success, although Steve Burtenshaw's reign does suffer more than is deserved because of the nature of its conclusion and through comparison with the Don Howe era that preceded it.

It is hard, however, to make great claims for Mee's transfer record after the Double. While many of the stars of 1970–71 were departing, Mee brought in Alan Ball, Jeff Blockley, Brian Chambers, Alex Cropley, Terry Mancini, Jimmy Rimmer and Brian Kidd. Not too many of those went on to earn a place in the pantheon of Arsenal history, and only Ball played a major role at the club for more than three seasons. Perhaps more significant than the players he brought to Highbury, however, was one player who was allowed to leave. Frank McLintock was a captain who, however often he fell out with his manager, would have shed blood for his boss and the club they represented. And the rest of the team were united in their love and respect for their leader. Much of the infighting that undermined the team's efforts in Mee's final years in charge would have dissipated in the heat of a rollicking from McLintock. Fewer players would have been left casting their eyes around for a dominant force in the dressing-room with whom to align themselves. That, more than any debatable signing or insistence on tactics alien to his players, could be argued to be the costliest mistake of Mee's Arsenal reign.

On the balance sheet of Mee's working life as whole, due credit must be given to his work in the Royal Army Medical Corps and National Health Service, which brought comfort and benefit to so many; to the new standards he introduced to the profession of the football club physiotherapist; and to the contribution he made to the rise of Graham Taylor's Watford. Yet it is his ten years in charge of the Arsenal team that determines his professional legacy. And despite the undeniable entries in the debit column, the only just conclusion is that Mee emerges from the final accounting of his career as Arsenal manager as a rich man indeed.

As Arsenal's shiny new stadium takes shape and the memories of Highbury are aired and analysed for a final time before being packed off down the road to Ashburton Grove, Mee's achievements are sure to be debated. Where should he be placed in the history of the game? Should he have a memorial at Arsenal's new home? Could he have achieved success in the modern game? Those who worked most closely with him are best placed to offer valid opinion and even those whose relationships with Mee were not always sweetness and light argue his case passionately.

Bob McNab says, 'I think it's fair to say that, in his last couple of years at Arsenal, Bertie lost the plot a little. Maybe he trusted the advice he was getting from his staff and not appreciating that it might not have been in his or the club's best interests. But should Bertie be given a bust in the new stadium, like Herbert Chapman? My answer is yes. George Graham and Arsène Wenger should also be honoured, although neither of them inherited the mess Bertie Mee inherited. Bertie was the right man for that assignment at that time. You can only be the best in your era and in my view Bertie was.'

George Graham, the next manager to take the Championship back to Highbury, 18 years after Mee, believes his mentor's methods would have transferred successfully to the modern football era. 'The same strengths that he had are as important now. Bertie's biggest assets were his organisational skill and his ability to delegate because he didn't have a background in football. The same things people say about Sir Clive Woodward and whether he could be successful in football after a career in rugby apply to Bertie. He showed his cleverness by taking on good people who could do the things he couldn't. There was professionalism in everything he did and he would still identify and employ good coaches today. These days, you hear about the foreign coaches bringing in specialist staffs and certain diets. Bertie did all that in the '60s. When I was a youngster at Aston Villa, we used to have steak and chips before games, but Bertie started the trend of eating carbohydrates.'

An avid historian of the club he played for and managed, Graham concludes, 'Bertie set new standards for Arsenal after winning the Fairs Cup and the Double. It is very hard to keep that up year in and year out, and as soon as he fell below those standards there was a small criticism. But he deserves to be up there with the greatest managers in Arsenal history. For me, Herbert Chapman is still number one because of the revolutionary changes he made and Arsène Wenger's achievements are unsurpassed. But nobody apart from Bertie in English football at that time did the Double and he was the first Arsenal manager to win in Europe. He brought professional standards back to the club at a time when they were struggling.'

Bob Wilson takes the same view. 'If you study the history of the club, the person who made Arsenal is Herbert Chapman. People following in his wake like George Allison and Tom Whittaker did fine and deserve their little place, but then there were 17 long years when the club who set all the standards, with things like dress and travel and tradition, did not win a trophy. Bertie was the guy who knew the history of the club and had this military bearing about him. He brought us back. He should get a bust at the club like Herbert Chapman. Arsène Wenger will get one – actually, he will probably get a bloody great statue – but Bertie deserves his place in history. Little Bertie Mee brought Arsenal back from the dead.'

At the time of writing, Arsenal remain uncertain about whether Mee's achievements will be honoured at the Emirates Stadium. Director Ken Friar, who describes Mee's greatest qualities as 'man-management, loyalty and clarity of thought' and has played a major role in the development of the club's new home, says, 'We really don't know whether there will be any kind of memorial for Bertie and others. We have lots of ideas and we are constantly thinking about things. There has been talk of building statues for certain people, but finances will play into it as well.'

The stadium to which Mee returned pride and glory on a memorable spring night in 1970 will soon be history. But, just as Highbury's famous stands will be safe from the bulldozer, thanks to the conservationists, so the esteem with which Arsenal fans recall their former manager seems certain to endure. While every Arsenal team in the Mee era had to stand comparison with those of Herbert Chapman, it is the 1970–71 squad against whom current triumphs have been measured. Mee has long since been forgiven for any shortcomings during the latter years of his reign, possibly because he was smart enough to get out before subjecting his reputation to the ignominy of being fired. When his death was announced in 2001, BBC Sport's Internet site had little problem rapidly filling its pages with tributes from Arsenal fans. Similar messages poured into the mailbox of the club's own site. Fans of other teams taken with his modest acceptance of success and perhaps mourning the passing of a symbol of a bygone, less abrasive, age sent their own messages of respect and condolence.

Mee was a man who saw his achievements as the successful execution of duty rather than an opportunity for self-congratulation. And, as someone who had experienced life – and death – beyond football, he treated victory in an important game as no more an accomplishment than the successful rehabilitation of a wounded soldier or the return to work of an injured miner in his care.

It is the humility of a man who never courted publicity that remains most powerfully with those fans lucky enough to meet him. Brian Dawes remembers Mee taking time, only 90 minutes before kick-off, to greet the 1,500 Arsenal supporters who ventured to Belgium for the Fairs Cup final. 'He came outside to shake fans by the hand and personally thank us for our valued support, which he told me was very much appreciated. Here were Arsenal about to play in a major European match and the manager, a dapper little man in a brown suit, was very politely thanking the fans for their efforts. It struck me at the time that this was a very considerate thing for him to have done.'

Upon hearing of Mee's death, Richard Boyes wrote to Arsenal chairman Peter Hill-Wood from his home in Australia to recount the story of when he took his four-year-old son to Highbury for the first time for the Boxing Day game against Manchester United in 1968. Having had no luck at the turnstiles, Boyes and his son, who was decked out in an Arsenal kit made by his mum, went to the main entrance on Avenell Road, where one of Arsenal's uniformed commissionaires confirmed that the game was sold out. 'We turned to leave and bumped into a smiling Bertie Mee. He complimented my son on his Arsenal kit and asked me what the problem was. I told him my story and he said, "Be my guest." He spoke to the commissionaire, who took us through some doors. We heard the clatter of boots and there was the Arsenal first team coming back from their warm-up. John Radford, my son's hero, smiled at him and patted him on the head. We were given seats next to the Arsenal reserve and apprentice players and we won 3–0. It was a perfect day, made so by a perfect gentleman who, in spite of being so busy and under so much pressure, still had time to notice a little boy.'

Joe Marshall, who emigrated to Canada in 1979, recalls running into Mee on one of his return visits to Highbury. 'I have been back almost every year and had the good fortune to meet Bertie and his wife twice within the space of a week back in 1994. I got to drink tea and chat with Bertie in the reception rooms for guests. He seemed taken aback that anybody would be interested in him. I spoke to him at length about how much I admired him and the Arsenal team of '71 and we talked about a few key moments from years gone by. My most intense memory of Bertie is that he was such a delightful and modest person. When I saw him for the second time, he was making jokes about having to arrange another game so we could meet again before I went back to Canada.

'He was a football great, but he made me feel like a friend after our two meetings. He had to toddle off to Cockfosters on the London Underground with his wife. He was clearly a devoted husband. It struck me as poignant that this Highbury legend could just stroll down to Arsenal station and get on a train just like the rest of us, almost anonymous. It seemed to symbolise how humble this man was. No fuss, no muss. A gentleman of the first order.'

More than any statue or memorial, Bertie Mee would have settled for that as a monument to his life.

APPENDIX

Bertie Mee's record as a player

Club	Division	Season	Games	Goals
Mansfield Town	Division Three South	1938–39	13	1

Bertie Mee's record as Arsenal manager

DIVISION ONE

	P	W	D	L	F	A	Pts	Position
1966–67	42	16	14	12	58	47	46	7th
1967–68	42	17	10	15	60	56	44	9th
1968–69	42	22	12	8	56	27	56	4th*
1969–70	42	12	18	12	51	49	42	12th
1970–71	42	29	7	6	71	29	65	1st
1971–72	42	22	8	12	58	40	52	5th
1972–73	42	23	11	8	57	43	57	2nd**
1973–74	42	14	14	14	49	51	42	10th
1974–75	42	13	11	18	47	49	37	16th
1975–76	42	13	10	19	47	53	36	17th
Total	**420**	**181**	**115**	**124**	**554**	**444**	**477**	**Average: 8.3**

*Qualified for Fairs Cup

**Denied entry to UEFA Cup by one-club-per-city rule

FA CUP

	P	W	D	L	F	A	Performance
1966–67	4	2	1	1	6	1	5th round
1967–68	5	2	2	1	6	4	5th round
1968–69	4	2	1	1	4	1	5th round
1969–70	2	0	1	1	3	4	3rd round
1970–71	9	6	3	0	16	7	winners
1971–72	9	5	3	1	11	6	final
1972–73	7	4	2	1	13	9	semi-final
1973–74	3	1	1	1	2	3	4th round
1974–75	8	3	4	1	10	6	6th round
1975–76	1	0	0	1	0	3	3rd round
Total	52	25	18	9	71	44	

LEAGUE CUP

	P	W	D	L	F	A	Performance
1966–67	4	1	2	1	8	5	3rd round
1967–68	8	6	1	1	16	10	final
1968–69	7	5	1	1	17	7	final
1969–70	4	1	2	1	3	2	3rd round
1970–71	5	2	2	1	5	2	4th round
1971–72	4	2	1	1	5	2	4th round
1972–73	4	3	0	1	8	4	5th round
1973–74	1	0	0	1	0	1	2nd round
1974–75	2	0	1	1	2	3	2nd round
1975–76	2	0	1	1	2	3	2nd round
Total	41	20	11	10	66	39	

FAIRS CUP

	P	W	D	L	F	A	Performance
1969–70	12	7	2	3	23	6	winners
1970–71	8	4	2	2	12	5	4th round
Total	20	11	4	5	35	11	

EUROPEAN CUP

	P	W	D	L	F	A	Performance
1971–72	6	4	0	2	13	4	3rd round

ALL GAMES

	P	W	D	L	F	A
Total	539	241	148	150	739	542

Watford's honours with Bertie Mee as assistant manager/director

1977–78: champions, Division Four
1978–79: runners-up, Division Three
1981–82: runners-up, Division Two
1982–83: runners-up, Division One; winners, FA Youth Cup
1983–84: finalists, FA Cup

BIBLIOGRAPHY

Bagchi, Rob and Paul Rogerson *The Unforgiven: The Story of Don Revie's Leeds United* (Aurum Press Ltd, 2002)

Ball, Alan *It's All About a Ball* (W.H. Allen, 1978)

Brady, Liam *So Far So Good* (Stanley Paul, 1980)

Burtenshaw, Norman *Whose Side Are You On, Ref?* (Arthur Baker, 1973)

Clarke, Brian *Docherty* (Kingswood Press, 1991)

Cooper, Henry *An Autobiography* (Cassell & Company, 1972)

Douglas, Peter *The Football Industry* (George Allen & Unwin, 1973)

Eastham, George *Determined to Win: Arsenal FC and England* (Stanley Paul, 1964)

Finney, Tom *My Autobiography* (Headline, 2003)

Giller, Norman *Billy Wright: A Hero for all Seasons* (Robson Books, 2002)

Graham, George *The Glory and the Grief* (Andre Deutsch, 1995)

Gray, Eddie with Jason Thomas *Marching on Together: My Life with Leeds United* (Hodder & Stoughton, 2002)

Greaves, Jimmy with Norman Giller *The Sixties Revisited* (Lennard Queen Anne Press, 1992)

Greenwood, Ron with Bryon Butler *Yours Sincerely* (Collins Willow, 1984)

Hill, Dave *Out of his Skin: The John Barnes Phenomenon* (Faber & Faber, 1989; WSC Books, 2001)

Inglis, Simon *The Football Grounds of England and Wales* (Collins Willow, 1983)

James, Gary *Joe Mercer: Football with a Smile* (ACL & Polar Publishing, 1993)

Keegan, Kevin with Norman Giller *The Seventies Revisited* (Lennard Queen Anne Press, 1994)

King, Jeff and John Kelly *The Cult of the Manager: Do They Really Make a Difference?* (Virgin Books, 1997)

Lees, Dr Andrew and Ray Kennedy *Ray of Hope: The Ray Kennedy Story* (Pelham Books, 1993)

Lemmon, David *Arsenal in the Blood: An Oral History of the Gunners* (Breedon Books, 1998)

Mourant, Andrew *Don Revie: Portrait of a Footballing Enigma* (Mainstream Publishing, 1990)

Neill, Terry *Revelations of a Football Manager* (Sidgwick & Jackson, 1985)

Pardoe, Rex *The Battle of London: Arsenal versus Tottenham Hotspur* (Tom Stacey Ltd, 1972)

Pawson, Tony *The Football Managers* (Eyre Methuen, 1973)

Phillips, Oliver *The Official Centenary History of Watford FC* (Watford Football Club, 1991)

Ponting, Ivan *Arsenal Player by Player* (Hamlyn, 1998)

Russell, Dave *Football and the English* (Carnegie Publishing, 1997)

Sammels, Jon with Robert Oxby *Double Champions: Playing the Arsenal Way* (Arthur Baker, 1971)

Soar, Phil and Martin Tyler *Arsenal: 1886–1986* (Hamlyn, 1996)

Spurling, Jon *Rebels for the Cause: The Alternative History of Arsenal Football Club* (Mainstream Publishing, 2003)

Steen, Rob *The Mavericks: English Football When Flair Wore Flares* (Mainstream Publishing, 1994)

Tossell, David *Seventy-One Guns: The Year of the First Arsenal Double* (Mainstream Publishing, 2002)

Varley, Nick *Golden Boy: A Biography of Wilf Mannion* (Aurum Press, 1997)

Wall, Bob *Arsenal from the Heart* (Souvenir Press, 1971)

Watt, Tom *The End: 80 Years of Life on Arsenal's North Bank* (Mainstream Publishing, 1993)

Whittaker, Tom *Tom Whittaker's Arsenal Story* (Sporting Handbooks Ltd, 1957)

Wilson, Bob *An Autobiography* (Pelham Books, 1971)

Wilson, Bob *My Autobiography: Behind the Network* (Hodder & Stoughton, 2003)

The following annuals have also been of great assistance with my research:

All Stars Football Book (World Distributors, various years)
Arsenal Football Book, nos. 1–6 (Stanley Paul, various years)
Charles Buchan's Soccer Gift Book (IPC, various years)
Goal Football Annual (IPC, various years)
International Football Book (Souvenir Press, various years)
London Soccer Annual (Pelham Books, 1968)
London Soccer Annual 1970 (Pelham Books, 1969)
Rothmans Football Yearbook (Queen Anne Press Ltd, various years)
Shoot! Annual (IPC, various years)
The Sun Soccer Annual, 1972–77 (World Distributors, various years)
The Topical Times Football Book (DC Thomson, various years)